Future Employment and
Technological Change

FUTURE EMPLOYMENT & TECHNOLOGICAL CHANGE

Donald Leach and Howard Wagstaff
with
Anne-Marie Bostyn, Colin Pritchard and Daniel Wight

Kogan
Page

First published in Great Britain in 1986 by
Kogan Page Limited
120 Pentonville Road, London N1 9JN

British Library Cataloguing in Publication Data

Leach, Donald
  Future employment and technological change.
  1. Labor supply – Effect of technological
  innovations on
  I. Title II. Wagstaff, Howard
  331.12′5   HD6331

ISBN 1-85091-017-0

Printed and bound in Great Britain by
Billing & Sons Ltd, Worcester

Contents

Part 2: Rethinking Employment Strategies

Appendices

Acknowledgements

The first debt we must record is to SPHERE — Seminar on Physical, Human and Environmental Resources in the Economy — an informal discussion group which met between 1981 and 1983 in the University of Edinburgh. Although this was not the beginning of our interest in the problem of employment, it was the meeting ground out of which came the idea for this book. In particular, it is necessary to record our debt for argument and encouragement to Ulrich Leoning, Aubrey Manning and Mick Common — they helped even when they disapproved.

We are also indebted to Robert Turner for establishing the link with Anne-Marie Bostyn and Daniel Wight, whose research (funded by the Economic and Social Research Council at the University of Edinburgh) was the basis of Chapter 7, and who offered painstaking criticism of the rest of the book. We are similarly indebted to Colin Pritchard, of the Department of Chemical Engineering, University of Edinburgh, both for his contribution and for criticism from the standpoint of an engineer with experience of management in industry. Thanks are also due to Roy Fawcett for his valuable advice on the structure of the book.

We are indebted to Napier College, Edinburgh, for the provision of support; indeed, the typescript would never have been ready on time without the devoted work of Maureen Cook and we record our grateful thanks for all her efforts. Finally, it is unavoidable that we should record our debt to our families for their tolerance.

Donald Leach
Queen Margaret College, Edinburgh

Howard Wagstaff
University of Edinburgh

Acknowledgements

We are grateful to the following for permission to publish extracts from copyright works:

George Allen and Unwin (Table 1.1, Chapter 1)
Macmillan (Table 4.2, Chapter 4)
Mrs Janette McGinn (Notes and References 23, Chapter 7)
A B Academic Publishers (Appendix 2).

Preface

The concern of this book is the common predicament of Western industrialized nations in their experience of massive unemployment. There have been many books about the supposed 'British disease' of 'industrial failure' but, set in context, the similarities between Britain and other countries in OECD (Organization for Economic Co-operation and Development) are far more important than any differences in the average standard of living or rates of unemployment. Of course, the relatively poor UK economic performance and the monetarist economic policies pursued by the British government has meant higher unemployment than would otherwise have been the case. But such arguments are secondary to the concern of this book, which is the question of how to ensure future employment for the working population of all countries.

This book is not intended as a comprehensive treatise on the causes of unemployment. While the role of technology in relation to long-term investment cycles is an important theme, we touch only briefly on the causal relationships of investment cycles and depressions in capitalist economies, and leave on one side the question of how the level of aggregate investment might be regulated in an industrially advanced socialist economy. Similarly, the problem of the direction of economic activity to the locations where jobs are most needed is not dealt with, and the constraints on implementing such policies within a capitalist economy are therefore not discussed in detail. We are addressing those aspects of the employment problem which not only confront capitalist economies today but which we believe would also arise in a socialist economy at a similar stage of technological development, notwithstanding social ownership of the means of production and overall planning of investment. The problem is how to distribute equitably the benefits of technological change, without destroying the incentive to innovate, when the technologies being adopted no longer require the kinds of task for which large numbers of people are needed.

This book is an interdisciplinary work — it could not have been written by any one of us alone. It has drawn on research by social scientists and on perceptions of the process of innovation deriving from management experience, as well as on economics. As with our disciplinary backgrounds, we represent a spectrum of political, economic and social viewpoints. We do not aim to convince one section of society but to convince people from all sectors — political and social — that they must change their policies and attitudes and that they must do this now.

Our purpose is not to proclaim ready-made solutions, nor is it to detract from the basic political conflicts surrounding such major issues as public expenditure levels, resistance to factory closures and job losses, or control over the use of capital funds within the economy. Our message is simply that the terms within which these political debates are normally conducted have become inadequate, and need to be extended and modified to take full cognizance of the impact of technological change at the stage of development now reached in the industrially advanced countries.

In Part 1 of this book, we argue that faith in economic orthodoxies to solve the problem of a lack of jobs is misplaced and that the idea of a leisure society offers no viable alternative. We start with reviews of the rise in unemployment in industrialized nations since the early 1970s and of the responses of governments to this problem. This sets the scene for the remainder of Part 1: the examination of the adequacy of these responses to create sufficient jobs, the particular role of technological change in economic growth and employment, and the likely outcomes of continuing to rely on these current responses. This leads us to the conclusion that very few nations will be able to secure 'full employment' through current orthodox policies and that new ideas and new policies are essential. In Part 2 we discuss the way in which basic economic ideas require to be modified, especially in relation to the cost of employment and the redistribution of work, and propose policies based on these observations. We conclude with a discussion of the wider implications of our policies for changed attitudes and consequential changes in society.

Part 1:

Where are the Jobs to be Found?

CHAPTER 1

The Rising Trend of Unemployment

According to the economic beliefs that have prevailed in Western Europe and North America since World War II, unemployment can be solved through an appropriate mixture of economic and fiscal policies designed to promote economic growth. It has been assumed that 'growth means jobs'. If the economy fails to generate sufficient employment opportunities for all those seeking work, then it is taken for granted that the remedy must be accelerated economic growth. This view of the world has been held with almost complete unanimity right across the political spectrum. Well-worn phrases such as 'economic recovery', 'stimulating new investment', 'renewed expansion', 'investing the oil revenues at home' and 'regenerating manufacturing industry', all give expression to this consensus. When this consensus is challenged by references to new technology eliminating jobs, it is frequently asserted that new technology will generate as many jobs as it destroys. If this fails to carry conviction, and it is recognized that employment in the production industries is liable to continue to decline, then the service sector is usually seen as coming to the rescue. It is expected that an increase in demand for services will reabsorb the labour no longer required in manufacturing. But how realistic are these hopes? Does the potential for industrial growth really match the demand for jobs, either in numbers or the skills and experience of the work-force? What are the real prospects for service jobs, in the private or public sector? Can we get more jobs by better economic planning? Is the whole concept of 'full employment' to be abandoned, or could there be a new economic boom that would regenerate millions of new employment opportunities? These are the questions addressed in Part 1 of this book.

A long-run trend

Unemployment has shown an upward trend in all the industrially advanced capitalist countries since well before the onset of

15

depression at the end of the 1970s (see Figure 1.1). The rate of increase in the number of jobless was far from uniform, and the absolute levels of unemployment reached by the end of the period also varied widely, but the growing divergence between the number of people seeking work and the number of job opportunities created was evident throughout the OECD countries. In the nine member countries of the European Economic Community (EEC), registered unemployment by the end of the 1970s was more than twice as high as at the end of the 1960s, and in the US and Japan it also doubled. Although the level reached in Japan was far lower than in the other major capitalist countries, the change in labour market conditions since the 1960s was nevertheless evident.

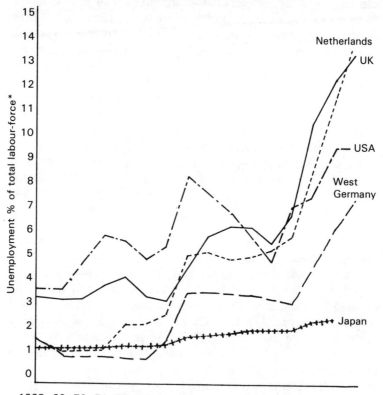

*Standardized rates, calculated on OECD definitions

Figure 1.1 *Rising trend of unemployment in selected industrial countries, 1968–83*

Source: *OECD Economic Outlook*, 35, July 1984, Paris.

Some of the smaller Western European countries appear to have much lower rates of unemployment than the major EEC and North American economies, and Switzerland is a notable example. On closer examination, however, this apparent immunity from the problems faced by other industrially advanced countries turns out to be largely an illusion. In Switzerland, employment in the production industries has been declining since 1971, and the end of the period of very low unemployment came in 1975 with a rapid rise in registered unemployment. The actual unemployment rate continued to be understated, as a result of repatriation of foreign workers, short-time working, and women remaining at home but not being registered as unemployed. It has been estimated that, if these factors had been taken into account, the rate of unemployment would already have been close to 7 per cent by 1976.[1] Similar statistical problems apply to other cases where 'official' unemployment is relatively low; it has been estimated that, on USA concepts, Japan's unemployment would be twice as high as the published figures.[2]   *but still very low*

Moreover, Japan's apparently exceptional position has little relevance for other industrially advanced countries. It started from a much smaller industrial base, and in terms of household consumption levels is still generally below the UK; in 1983, Japan had 185 passenger cars, 460 telephones and 239 television sets per 1000 population, compared with the respective figures for the UK of 256, 480, and 324.[3] Japan also had fewer doctors per 1000 population (1.2, compared with 1.5 in the UK). During the post-World War II period, Japan was able to achieve remarkably high growth rates, based on the use of the latest technology, a massive unfulfilled consumer demand at home, and a rapid growth in exports to the existing industrialized world. Such an experience is by its nature only a temporary phase and, as other yet more *Not necessarily* recently industrializing nations such as South Korea and Brazil start to succeed, even Japan will move gradually into a position of being one of the 'older' industrialized nations. Certainly, a country like the UK cannot retrace its steps, nor reproduce the different institutional and social contexts which further differentiates Japan from Western Europe and North America.

There is no doubt that the industrially advanced capitalist economies in general had been persistently failing to generate enough jobs even before the decline in investment and output at the end of the 1970s, which sent unemployment rates escalating to even higher levels.

17

The effects of depression

The investment decline which initiated the depression occurred more or less simultaneously in the major capitalist countries (see Figure 1.2), leading to a self-reinforcing process of decline in output, employment and purchasing power. Factory closures and redundancies followed in varying degrees throughout these

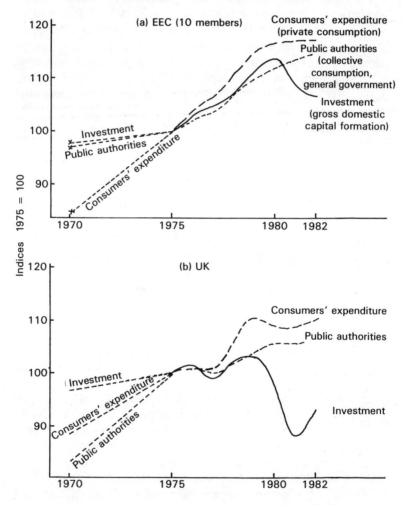

Figure 1.2 *Investment and consumption expenditure, EEC and UK, 1970–82*

Source: *EC National Accounts Statistics*, Aggregates 1960–82, Eurostat, Luxemburg, 1984.

18

	1929	1930	1931	1932	1933	1934
Investment goods	100	74	51	31	41	50
Consumer goods	100	90	85	75	85	87

Table 1.1 *Indices of investment goods and consumer goods output, UK, 1929–34*

Reproduced from Lewis, W A (1949) *Economic Survey, 1919–39*, p54, by kind permission of George Allen & Unwin, London.

economies, and restrictionist government policies worsened the situation, particularly in the UK. Table 1.1 charts the slump in output of both investment (capital goods) and consumer goods in the depression of the 1930s; although the magnitude of the falls was much greater in the 1930s than in the 1980s, the parallels between 1979–82 and 1929–32 are strikingly apparent.

Depression and mass unemployment have previously occurred within economic systems in which the overall level of investment is not planned, but left to the outcome of market forces. Underlying the slump in production and investment is a crisis of profitability, and such crises have recurred at intervals in all capitalist economies. For this very reason, there is a strong temptation to believe that nothing is new, and that today's unemployment poses problems that are no different in character from those faced in the 1930s. For socialists, the tendency is to assume that in an economy with planned investment and social ownership of the means of production, full employment would be assured; thus, the unemployment problem is seen uniquely as a feature of capitalism, which 'solved' the 1930s' unemployment only through rearmament and war. For others, the expectation is that a new economic boom comparable to the post-1945 era will wipe out mass unemployment and restore near-full employment within capitalist economies. In later chapters, we question both these assumptions and argue that technological change poses problems to which both socialists and non-socialists have given insufficient recognition.

A receding summit

Starting from current levels of unemployment of about 32 million for the OECD countries in 1983 (9 per cent unemployment), even to halve this would require 16 million new jobs. Such a vast turn round would itself take several years, during which time more jobs would be lost from traditional industries. For example, the UK, with three million registered unemployed in 1983, was even before the depression losing jobs in industry at the rate of over 200 thousand per year. This was because productivity was growing faster than output. With similar rates of growth, those industries which currently constitute the production base will continue to lose jobs. If a path to full employment is to be found then the generation of new jobs will have to make good this rate of loss, as well as making inroads into the already huge unemployment totals.

The true extent of the problem tends, moreover, to be masked by official statistics. Registered unemployment invariably understates the actual shortfall in job opportunities because it excludes many people, particularly married women, who would be part of the work-force if sufficient jobs were available. Many do not appear on the register because they are not eligible for benefits, and may not choose to describe themselves as 'unemployed', despite having had a previous job and wanting to work if jobs were to be found. In the case of the UK, the government's method of counting minimizes the unemployment figures which are published. In 1984 it was reduced from 3.4 million on the standardized OECD definition[4] to 3.0 million on the government's new counting method. In addition there were almost 500 thousand removed from the register by virtue of their involvement in 'special employment and training' measures, and perhaps as many as 400 thousand other unregistered unemployed,[5] so that the jobs deficit is effectively at least four million.[6] This statistical understatement of the problem occurs to some extent in most countries, and this hidden jobs deficit tends to grow when the rate of unemployment is increasing; substantial numbers of people disappear from the published estimates of the total work-force because they are neither in jobs nor on the unemployment register.[7]

Trying to move towards full employment simply by relying on market forces to generate new job opportunities, to reabsorb the unemployed into the old work pattern of a 40-hour week for life, is therefore like climbing towards a continually receding summit. The more jobs that are created the more people will come forward to fill them, thus raising the total in employment but not giving a corresponding reduction in unemployment. This can be seen in the case of the UK, where the employed labour-force plus the self-employed rose from 23.6 to 24.0 million between March 1983 and June 1984 as the output of the economy started to recover from depression; yet, far from falling, the total registered unemployed rose slightly from 2.98 to 3.03 million.[8] The same effect can be observed in the USA, where the number in employment increased by five million between November 1982 and April 1984 but unemployment fell by only two million (from 10.7 per cent to 7.8 per cent). Moreover, this fall in unemployment in the USA during this period was aided by a reduced inflow of young persons and women into the labour-force.[9] The reverse must be anticipated in many countries. The upward trend in the proportion of women in the work-force is evident in varying degrees throughout the OECD countries, and is reflected in the ratio of the economically active population to total population. This ratio increased from 42.7 per cent to 45.4 per cent between 1965 and 1981 for the OECD as a whole, and for the USA (where the increase was magnified by the changing age structure of the population) the proportion rose from 39.5 per cent to 48.3 per cent over the same period. In the UK the working, or economically active, population — the total of employed, self-employed and registered unemployed — increased steadily during the 1950s and early 1960s and after a fall in the late 1960s resumed its increase in 1972 (see Figure 1.3).

This increase since 1950 has been the result of both the increasing size of cohorts entering the labour market and of the increasing proportion of their lifetime for which women have been employed. The impact of demographic factors will be to continue to increase the number in the 16 to retirement age[10] group until 1991, after which it will go into decline at least until the year 2001. The lower, post-1979 projection in Figure 1.3 represents this 'demographic' effect but the upper projection takes account of the expected increase in women's lifetime employment rates. Such changes of social behaviour introduce major uncertainties into the forward planning process — by 1995 the two projections are over one million apart. The eventual size of the working population will be a product of the availability of jobs as well as the size of the population of working age and the preferences of the people concerned. There are also problems of definition; since 1979 there has been growing use of special training measures which keep young persons, in particular, from being counted as part of the working population; since November 1982 the exclusion of 400 thousand from the unemployment register has further depressed the recorded working population. It can thus come as no surprise to find that the values for working population fall below the 'demographic' projection. If the 400 thousand excluded from the unemployment total are included, the 1984 working population would rise almost to the upper projection; and the additional

21

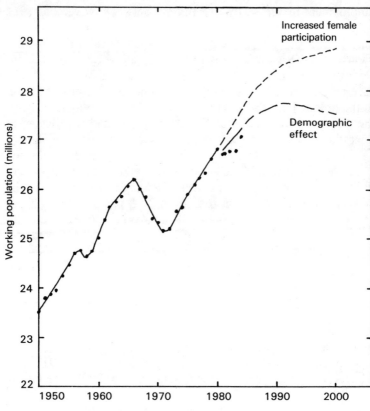

Figure 1.3 *Working population (UK)*

Source: *Annual Abstracts of Statistics, Monthly Digests of Statistics*, and Ermisch, John F (1983) *The Political Economy of Demographic Change*, pp159–62, Heinemann, London.

inclusion of the 500 thousand in special temporary measures would give a total of about 400 thousand above the upper projection.

As growth in the population of working age has risen to a large degree because the number of people retiring is less than the number of young persons entering, it is hardly surprising that it is among the young that unemployment is concentrated. In general, unemployment is not as bad as in the 1930s, when it peaked at 25 per cent (1933) and 22 per cent (1932) in the USA and UK respectively, but it is at these levels among the young in some countries, as is shown in Table 1.2. On the figures in this table only Japan has time to take avoiding action — for the rest the problem varies from urgent to one of crisis proportions.

	Proportion % (up to age 24)
Spain	38.9
Italy	32.0
UK	23.2
Canada	19.9
Australia	18.0
USA	16.4
Finland	12.5
Germany	10.8
Norway	9.8
Sweden	8.0
Japan	4.5

Table 1.2 *Youth unemployment in 1983*

Source: *OECD Economic Outlook*, 35, p44, July 1984.

Whereas the number in the working-age population registering for employment in the UK has increased, that in West Germany has, in declining, moved against the demographic trend; and the large foreign labour-force, still 1.7 million in 1983, has also been declining from a peak of about 2.0 million. It may well be that West Germany's own unemployed, and those who are presently discouraged from entering the labour market, would not wish to do the jobs taken by the 'guest workers' if the latter were not available. Such complex interactions between available jobs, the size of the working population and the level of unemployment, indicate that the 'fit' between these three elements which held for some 25 to 30 years after World War II was a historical peculiarity, held together by women staying out of the labour force and the retired welcoming their 'well-earned leisure'. There is a very wide gap between present female economic activity rates and possible upper limits, and we can also note that many persons past retirement age are no longer 'old age' pensioners but are still capable of work. Both these factors could destroy the old constraints which kept the balance between the three elements. If the present boundaries of participation in the labour-force are broken it is a long way to the next equilibrium point, indeed, so far that forward estimates of job requirements and resulting unemployment rates would be rendered almost uncomputable. The number of jobs required would have proved to be a receding summit which had vanished into the clouds.

Economic growth and employment

The experience of the 1970s was that growth rates approaching or exceeding 4 per cent per year failed to prevent rising

Country	Rate of growth of GDP, 1967–80 % pa	Unemployment as proportion of labour-force % (OECD definition)		
		1970	1979	1982
UK	2.0	3.1	5.6	12.5
Other large EEC countries				
France	4.1	2.4	5.9	8.0
West Germany	3.7	0.8	3.2	6.1
Italy	3.8	5.3	7.5	8.9
Smaller EEC countries				
Belgium	3.8	2.1	8.4	13.0
Denmark	2.7	0.7	6.0	10.3
North America				
USA	2.9	4.8	5.7	9.5
Canada	3.6	5.6	7.4	10.9

Table 1.3 *Rates of growth of GDP and unemployment in industrialized countries*

Source: *OECD Economic Outlook*, September, 1983, and *OECD Historical Statistics 1960–1980*.

unemployment in a number of Western European countries (see Table 1.3) and everywhere the creation of new jobs fell behind the rate required to sustain previous participation rates. In West Germany, unemployment quadrupled between 1970 and 1979 despite a growth rate of 3.7 per cent per year. A quadrupling of unemployment at gross domestic product (GDP) growth rates similar to West Germany's also occurred in Belgium, where the resulting unemployment rate was among the highest in the industrialized countries. In France, during the same period, unemployment rose from a percentage that was lower than in the UK in 1970 to one that was higher in 1979, despite a GDP growth rate of over 4 per cent, which was double the UK growth rate. Of the major industrially advanced capitalist countries, the USA showed the smallest proportional increase in unemployment and a much larger number of new jobs than in the EEC, but its economy was at a comparatively high level of unemployment at the beginning of the period. The growth of the population and labour-force exceeded the growth in number of jobs, with the result that the USA unemployment rate remained higher than the UK's up to 1979. Thus, growth failed to prevent rising unemployment in the USA, as in the OECD as a whole.

The true significance of these trends is now beginning to be realized as high unemployment persists despite a recovery of output. In the UK, the Confederation of British Industry (CBI) anticipated a 4 per cent growth rate for the economy in 1985, continuing on from growth that started in 1982. Yet the CBI expected manufacturing industry to continue to shed labour, and foresaw no decline in unemployment.[11] The prospect of a substantial decline in unemployment through growth alone is also increasingly recognized as unrealistic by economic forecasters using macroeconomic models. For example, by the autumn of 1984, the London Business School was forecasting that Britain's economy would 'enjoy steady growth and low inflation for the next 4 years', but this would 'not help unemployment, which will go on rising'.[12] A similar conclusion comes from another independent group, ITEM, working with the Treasury model of the UK economy. ITEM forecasts an underlying growth rate of around 3 per cent, but a growth rate for 1985–86 closer to 2 per cent: a rate of expansion which 'will not be sufficient to bring unemployment down'.[13]

Economic stagnation?

According to the 'growth means jobs' view of the world, unemployment is supposed to be the outcome of economic stagnation. Various external factors, such as the oil price increases of the Organization of Petroleum Exporting Countries (OPEC) and the ensuing international monetary crises, are then advanced as explanations of why each country's economy did not grow as fast as it would otherwise have done. Yet by any reasonable historical standard, the performance of the industrially advanced economies between the mid-1960s and the end of the 1970s seems to be a very curious kind of stagnation. Even the UK's supposedly 'low' growth rate of 2 per cent would mean a doubling of output in a generation! Over the 15-year period prior to the depression of the early 1980s, such growth rates brought an impressive increase in the availability of consumer goods and levels of comfort enjoyed by ordinary households.

Between 1965 and 1979, the number of households in the UK with cars increased by more than 50 per cent.[14] The proportion of households with refrigerators rose from about one-third to more than 90 per cent. The number with a telephone increased from little more than one-fifth in the mid-1960s, to two-thirds in 1979. Over half of all households had central heating by the early 1980s, compared with under 10 per cent in the mid-1960s — a period in which the average real incomes of those in employment rose by about 30 per cent. Yet while production increased and living

25

standards for most people rose, unemployment had trebled by 1979. Despite a 30 per cent increase in national output and an increase in the economy's estimated gross capital stock of more than 60 per cent, the number out of work increased by over a million.

Even during the worst period of the post-1979 depression, when industrial production was declining in absolute terms, the consumption levels of those in work in most cases held steady, or even increased. Between 1979 and 1982, the average earnings of those in employment in the UK continued to rise (by nearly 4 per cent over the three years) and the number of licensed cars rose from 14.7 to 15.7 million. Between 1979 and 1981, the percentage of households with a car rose from 57.9 per cent to 61.8 per cent; with central heating, from 55.0 per cent to 60.5 per cent; with a telephone, from 67.2 per cent to 75.8 per cent. The decline in aggregate spending which triggered the fall in production was almost entirely the result of the slump in investment, and not a decline in current expenditure of households or public authorities (see Figure 1.2). This was true even in the UK where government policies made the severity of the depression much greater than in most other countries in Western Europe, and brought a decline of industrial production of 14 per cent in the UK compared with about 6 per cent in the EEC as a whole. The government's determination to cut expenditure did not actually produce an absolute decline in current spending by public authorities, but only a reduction in the rate of increase. There was, however, an absolute cut in public investment, which compounded the effects of declining private investment on the level of economic activity. The costs were borne overwhelmingly by the unemployed,[15] and it was the loss of their purchasing power which put a brake on total consumption. This serves to underline one of the most important points about depression in contemporary capitalist economies; there are still enormous numbers of people doing extremely well in material terms, and the costs are born by particular communities and particular groups of workers.[16] It is clear that it is not the production system, despite its hiccups, that is going most drastically wrong but the distribution system. Lewis[17] similarly noted that, in the 1920s and 30s, the standard of living of those in employment rose over the period; in the UK, real wages were about 10 per cent higher in 1929 than in 1913 and, despite the depression, they rose another 10 per cent by 1938.

The human costs and deepening social divisions occasioned by depression have already been well documented,[18] but in terms of production it is important to keep the magnitude of failure in perspective. In a majority of the industrially advanced capitalist countries, the fall in production wiped out only the equivalent of some two or three years' growth at previous rates of expansion, and this loss was rapidly recovered when growth resumed. For the UK, the equivalent loss was nearer to a decade's worth of growth, yet even in this case the pre-depression level of industrial output had been regained by the beginning of 1985.

There is, manifestly, plenty that is wrong with the economic system we live in, but a failure to produce goods can scarcely be reckoned as one of them. Indeed, it is the outstanding success of capitalism in delivering mass-produced goods in the advanced countries, compared with any other historical or contemporary experience, which undoubtedly accounts for its continued support despite its injustices and its failure to provide the basic assurance of an ongoing livelihood through employment to a significant proportion of the population.

Technological change

The future prospects for jobs through growth appear even less promising than in the 1970s because the 1980s' depression comes at a time when the nature of new technology is less labour-intensive. The new wave of investment associated with recovery is at a higher capital intensity, at best creating fewer jobs per million pounds, dollars, Deutschmarks or yen invested than previously, and at worst leading to a net loss of jobs. This contrasts with the earlier postwar period, in which new manufacturing industry was recruiting additional labour. At that time, there was a growing use of unskilled manual and clerical labour, a growing proportion of whom were women. From 1945 to the mid-1960s, employment grew faster than the population of working age; this situation was reversed in the mid-1960s. Over the next 15 years, total employment showed no upward trend while the population (aged 16 to 65) seeking work continued to grow. This decline in employment opportunities is in striking contrast to the first 20 years after World War II.

The reversal coincided with the beginning of the decline in manufacturing employment, which in the UK dates from 1966. Again, this 'de-industrialization' is not simply a British phenomenon arising from declining competitiveness in international markets, but is a characteristic of the stage of economic development reached in the industrially advanced countries. We argue in Chapters 3 and 8 that this decline in manufacturing employment is an irreversible historical process, which invites comparison with the beginnings of the absolute decline in agricultural employment that commenced in Britain in about the middle of the last century. Such a turning point would have major significance, and calls for a reappraisal of traditional thinking about the ways in which employment opportunities are to be assured, and the ways in which income is distributed in society.

The distribution of benefits

It is a truism that, on paper, technological change can make possible not only a great enlargement of the scope of activities which society is able to undertake, but also a beneficial reduction in working time. It is not technology as such which creates unemployment, but the inability of the economic system to translate the fruits of innovation into shared benefits. Labour-saving technical change in the production industries, which make it possible for fewer people to produce more goods, ought to enable society to have more home-helps for the elderly, more nursery school teachers, more national park wardens, and massive programmes of public expenditure to rehabilitate inner city areas and to remove industrial dereliction. Again, higher productivity ought to enable everyone to work fewer hours, and still enjoy as high a level of consumption as before. We live in a society that is able to produce more goods with less labour time than ever before, and which in historical and global perspective is in the midst of a veritable orgy of consumption — of colour TVs, hi-fi sets, home computers, video recorders, food mixers, dish-washers and deep freezers. Yet governments proclaim that we 'cannot afford' more public services, and industrialists insist that we 'cannot afford' a 35-hour week. Why, in practice, do the obstacles to enlarging social provision in a market economy, and to a drastic reduction in the length of the working week, appear to be so formidable? These are the questions which we address in Part 2 and which form the starting point for any genuine attempt to come to terms with the long-term employment problem in the industrially advanced countries. The obstacles in both cases lie in the system of distribution of corporate and personal incomes, and the way in which entitlements are perceived by society at large. Solutions will therefore not be found without radical changes in the 'rules of the game' by which firms and individuals operate, and new attitudes to income and work on the part of society as a whole.

Notes and references

1. Lloyds Bank Economic Survey, Switzerland, 1978.
2. Taira, K (1983) Japan's low unemployment; economic miracle or statistical artifact, *US Monthly Labour Review*, 106, 7 July. Taira's estimates are challenged by Sorrentino, C (1984) Japan's low unemployment; an in depth analysis, *US Monthly Labour Review*, 107, 3 March; but the non-comparability of Japan's official unemployment statistics with those of Western European countries is upheld.
3. OECD Economic Surveys, 1983, for Japan and the UK.
4. This figure is similar to that expected from the method used by the Department of Employment prior to November 1982. The present method includes only people able to claim benefits and thus excludes many who are seeking work. See Taylor, David (1984) *The Unemployment Numbers Game*, Unemployment Unit Bulletin, 11, January, and note on *Old Count Unemployment Figures to May 1984*, Unemployment Unit Bulletin, 13, June 1984.
5. Note on *Old Count Unemployment Figures to May 1984*, Unemployment Unit Bulletin, 13, June 1984.
6. This agrees with estimates by the Manpower Services Commission, which in 1982 estimated that these adjustments added 'at least another 1 million to the jobless total, which it then estimated as 4 million' (*Financial Times*, 4 February 1982). Other estimates are higher: the Economic Development Unit of the West Midlands estimated UK unemployment in September 1982 to be 4.5 million, compared with the registered unemployment of 3.3 million, before the revisions to the criteria for registration were introduced (*Tribune*, October 1982).
7. UK Department of Employment figures showed, for example, that the drop in employment between mid-1979 and January 1981 was more than 250,000 larger than the rise in registered unemployment over the period (*Financial Times*, 26 February 1981, p44).
8. *Monthly Digest of Statistics*, p18, November 1984, HMSO, London.
9. *OECD Economic Outlook*, 35, p40, July 1984.
10. Taken as 60 for women and 65 for men.
11. *Financial Times*, 1 April 1985.
12. *Guardian*, 29 October 1984.
13. *Guardian*, 8 January 1985: 'Is Sustained Growth Enough?'
14. UK Department of Employment, Family Expenditure Survey (annual).
15. The burden of the loss of employment has been reinforced by the failure of benefits to keep pace with inflation, which was acknowledged by the UK Minister of Social Security in Parliament in June 1984. (See Townsend, Peter (1984) Why are the many poor?, *Fabian Tract No 500*, p27.)
16. Some writers see this as only part of a historically consistent trend. Thus, even in the early 1970s, a study comparing the real purchasing power of the lowest fifth of household incomes in 1972 with the lowest fifth in 1938 suggested that the poor were worse off than before World War II, given

that £1 in 1938 was equivalent to 18½p in 1972 (Clark, George (1974) *Whatever Happened to the Welfare State*, City Poverty Committee, London). More recently, Guy Routh has pointed out that the relative earnings of the lowest tenth of manual workers (ie compared with the mean) were virtually the same in 1979 as in 1886 in the UK (Routh, G, Wedderburn, D and Wootton, B (1980) *The Roots of Pay Inequalities*, p5, Low Pay Unit, London, October).

17. Lewis, W A (1949) *Economic Survey, 1879–1939*, p139, George Allen and Unwin, London.
18. Eg Marsden, D and Duff, E (1975) *Workless*, Penguin, Harmondsworth; White, Michael (1983) *Long-Term Unemployment and Labour Markets*, Policy Studies Institute Report No 622; Sinfield, Adrian (1981) *What Unemployment Means*, Martin Robertson, Oxford.

Chapter 2

Current Responses

The responses of society and government

The dominant mood of society at large, confronted with continuing mass unemployment, is undoubtedly one of pessimism. The feeling is that 'we can never get back to full employment', and that society must somehow learn to live with this reality. Such feelings are strongly influenced by a deterministic — indeed, almost fatalistic — attitude to technological change, in which unemployment is seen as an inevitable consequence of 'machines replacing men'. Many people fear what may happen to a society that offers the empty prospect of joblessness to so many of its youth, and which allows the economic life of whole communities to be undermined. But the belief that 'nothing can be done' leads to a resigned acceptance and frustrates any determination that things must change.

For governments, however, there remains a political necessity to be seen to be doing something to try to ameliorate the situation, and to encourage those directly affected to believe that the situation is only temporary and that the problems will go away 'when the economy recovers'. It is the notion that the unemployment problem is a temporary one which underlies the practical aspect of the current responses to unemployment — the multitude of youth employment programmes, training schemes, and marginal employment subsidies which have been introduced by governments throughout Western Europe and North America.[1] Although these measures are undertaken by governments in response to unemployment, they all seem to be conceived as adjustments at the margin.[2] They reflect an assumption that the problem will gradually pass, so the schemes introduced are a succession of temporary measures and palliatives. This has been well illustrated by a recent UK government publication, *Employment: The Challenge for the Nation*, which includes a note of policies for France, Italy, Germany and the United States,[3] as well as the UK, and the

31

descriptions below are largely based on this.

France

France has almost 30 different measures which have changed and developed over the period of growing unemployment but 'have never been less than considerable in scale and scope'. These measures are summarized as 'shaping labour supply, encouraging work sharing and influencing labour costs and recruitment'. The main element of policy in the early 1980s was to reduce working time: a 39-hour statutory working week was complemented by subsidies, overtime limitations and early retirement. These schemes have been modified: the early retirement scheme was expensive and has now been followed up by lowering the age of retirement to 60. The scheme to get the working week even lower than 38 hours is now seen as directed at maintaining existing employment rather than creating new jobs, and 'de-regulation is now at the centre of French employment policy'. De-regulation means that worker-representation procedures, social security requirements and taxes on jobs have all been reduced with the aim of securing greater flexibility in working practices. The intention is to reduce constraints on employment and achieve faster introduction of new technology. There is also the usual emphasis on the training of young people but with the responsibility lying primarily on the shoulders of employers rather than on state provision. It is interesting to note that in 1980 trade union members rejected proposals to reduce employment constraints further and to encourage new technology, which had been provisionally agreed between Mitterand's socialist government and leaders of the trade union confederations.

Italy

Among the OECD countries, Italy has one of the highest levels of youth unemployment (see Chapter 1) but is one of the few countries without government programmes to assist this group. Those measures which are taken are of the 'de-regulation' type, typically the removal of contractual obligations from employers undertaking training of young persons, and there are moves to reduce youth rates of pay. A key feature which differentiates Italy from other countries is that until 1984 there was growing employment in the public sector — by 1.6 per cent in 1983. There are also employment subsidies in the south and for 0.5 million workers on short-time, and, like the French, there are measures for early retirement and reduced working time. In addition, Italy has a flourishing informal economy, presumably not an intended result of government policy, which may mean that unemployment is not as high as the recorded 10 per cent. The other side of the coin is rigidity in the formal employment sector — firms cannot readily undertake large-scale redundancies — and measures are proposed to give greater flexibility.

West Germany
The most significant feature of the West German policy is the programme providing two years of integrated vocational training and job experience for 1.7 million young persons. Apart from this, other provisions, such as job creation schemes, are small in comparison to those of other countries. Despite its recent sharp increase in unemployment, the remedy seen by the Federal Republic of Germany is 'better working of the market'. Labour legislation has been relaxed: extending the use of fixed-term contracts, reducing the consultation and protection rights of part-time employees, further relaxations affecting female employees, and increased flexibility in working hours. The latter change resulted from the 1984 industrial action led by the metal workers, which achieved a reduction in the working week to about 38½ hours; extension of this to other groups of workers is anticipated.

United States
In the USA the main locus of employment measures has been at the state or city level rather than at Federal level. The Job Training Partnership Act offers training and assistance with placement to the young and other long-term unemployed, but apart from this most effort is directed at special groups in a specific locality. These local measures include community projects — 'Youth Service Demonstration' and 'Work-fare' — which aim to develop the motivation and potential of young unemployed volunteers. In the 'Cleveland Tomorrow' initiative many ideas are brought together to provide inner-city development and to counter urban decline as a means of improving employment, but even such a major effort is left to city or state administrations. The one matter on which the Federal Administration does have a policy is on pay. It believes that 'lower pay means more jobs' and it has in mind a 'Youth Opportunity Wage' — a sub-minimum wage for young people.

33

United Kingdom

The UK government's policy is seen in its White Paper as consisting of three elements:

1. *Financial and economic policies:* keeping inflation under control, restraining public expenditure, removing 'distortions' of the tax system, and lifting 'bureaucratic' controls;
2. *Industrial policy:* helping small firms, giving support to innovation and new technology, reshaping regional policy, simplifying planning, fostering competition, and privatization of nationalized industries; and
3. *Labour market policies:* improved industrial relations, removing impediments to employment, reforming the education and training systems, and special programmes to help the unemployed.

The main components of the labour market policy actually implemented are the Youth Training Scheme and the Community Programme. The Youth Training Scheme has provided some 350 thousand places of one year's duration in each of the years 1983 and 1984, and it is to be expanded in 1986 so that 'every young person under 18 will have the choice of staying on in education, taking a job, or receiving training'. The Community Programme for the long-term unemployed has been providing one year's employment for 130 thousand people, and this is to be increased to reach 230 thousand places in 1986–87. For men and women within one year of retirement there is the Job Release Scheme, and 280 thousand have taken advantage of this opportunity during the eight years of its operation. Perhaps the most interesting scheme of all has been the Enterprise Allowance Scheme, which has provided £40 per week for up to a year to unemployed persons willing to start up their own business. Awards have been running at the rate of 50 thousand per annum and in 1985 this will increase to over 60 thousand. A limitation is that applicants must have at least £1000 available to invest in their business. However, it is claimed that 70 per cent of the businesses created are still operating six months after the end of receipt of the allowance, and that for every two businesses set up another job is created.

The implications of the policy

Two features arising from this survey of governmental policies need to be highlighted. First, in certain aspects 'labour market' policies are euphemisms for cutting the income of those at the bottom end of the system on the pretext that they will then 'price themselves into work'. 'De-regulation' is seen as a tool to help achieve this, and to encourage employers to 'hire' because they can just as easily 'fire'. These policies clearly have strongly anti-trade union undertones. Even if successful in their own terms, the result would be that instead of the misery of economic depression being confined to those currently unemployed, it would be shared more widely — by reducing the standard of living of those already at low wage levels. This policy of spreading poverty is a short-sighted and unimaginative monetarist reaction to continuing high levels of unemployment. Second, 'special' employment measures and training schemes are of value only if they are seen as sensible adjuncts to other policies[4] which are more central to tackling the underlying problem. For example, the philosophy of 'work sharing' in the broad sense of a general reduction in working time, more flexible work arrangements, and a more equitable distribution of employment opportunities is of considerable importance for future employment and this is fully recognized in Part 2 of this book. We draw attention to the limitations of the present schemes only in order to emphasize that a much bigger shift in thinking about employment and income distribution is needed if the desired changes are to come about. One of the most important obstacles to such change is the hold exerted over current policy debates by existing economic orthodoxies. This is why there is at present little, if any, sign of the necessary degree of radicalism. Schemes such as those to encourage job sharing are destined to remain ineffective unless they are part of a much deeper rethinking of the whole basis of the distribution of income and work in society, which will require a re-examination of many basic economic assumptions. An assessment of the strengths and weaknesses of existing theories of unemployment is thus the first step to new thinking.

The rival orthodoxies

The deepening employment crisis has thrown into sharp relief the issues which divide the adherents of rival economic orthodoxies. Neoclassical economists reaffirm their faith in the market as a mechanism for bringing about adjustments. The remedy, according to this view, is for workers to 'price themselves back into jobs' by accepting wage settlements below the rate of inflation and allowing the gains from productivity increases to accrue to capital to finance further investment. In contrast, Keynesians reassert the importance of public expenditure as a tool for assisting economic recovery and the growth of employment. The blame for high levels of unemployment is seen as lying largely with governments, for pursuing the wrong monetary and fiscal policies — in particular, for attempting to cut public expenditure in response to recession. Marxists, on the other hand, reiterate that capitalism is inherently incapable of avoiding recurrent crises and periodic mass unemployment, and attempts to blame either trade union bargaining power or mismanagement by governments are misplaced. Change is seen as requiring a political movement committed to public ownership and control of industry, with economic planning constituting an essential prerequisite for full employment.

The period since the late 1970s has certainly generated vigorous economic debates. It has, however, produced much less in terms of new economic ideas; relatively little innovative thinking has taken place within the three main traditions of economic thought, and current responses have closely followed established ideas.

Neoclassical and monetarist economics

Neoclassical economics is founded on the notion of a competitive market equilibrium, with price as the principal mechanism through which economic adjustment is brought about. In any market, there is held to exist an 'equilibrium' price at which supply and demand will be brought into balance. Inspired by the earlier classical economists, the neoclassical economists affirmed their belief in the 'hidden hand' of the market, which in their eyes made state regulation and co-ordinated economic planning unnecessary. Writing during the heyday of competitive capitalism in the nineteenth century, when European imperialism (under the guise of 'free' trade and the 'free' movement of capital) was extending its domination across the globe, these economic doctrines were found very convenient by those who held political power. The neoclassical teaching on wages and employment was similarly convenient for the owners of capital. The wage rate was viewed simply as the price of a commodity and, like any other commodity, there must, neoclassical economists argued, be a price which would bring supply and demand into balance — that is, a wage rate at which unemployment would not exist. Unemployment is, in these terms, the result of a 'disequilibrium' price — a wage rate that is 'too high'.[5]

The argument in fact had to become a good deal more sophisticated once it was recognized that an economy is not static, but continually undergoing change through investment and technical innovation. Neoclassical theory therefore had to shift from the model of a static equilibrium, to a model of an equilibrium growth path for an economy.[6] However, at the end of a lot of algebra, it remained possible for neoclassical theorists to arrive back at their initial proposition that there will always exist an 'equilibrium' wage rate that facilitates full employment. Their theories still permitted unemployment to be blamed on 'excessive' wage demands. It is argued that a lowering of the wage rate would make possible a higher profit share, which would facilitate a higher level of investment. This, in turn, would lead to a higher rate of growth of capital stock, and it is assumed that the utilization of this additional capital stock will require more workers. At the same time, a lower wage rate would mean a lower cost of employing labour relative to capital. This would, according to neoclassical theory, normally favour the adoption of more labour-intensive techniques. Thus, not only would more investment take place as a result of the higher profit share, but the investment would be more labour-demanding, thus reinforcing the employment-generating effects of growth.

There are, in fact, many logical objections which can be raised against this line of reasoning,[7] but the arguments remain extremely convenient for their proponents. This is because the particular set of assumptions adopted means that the possibility of full employment equilibrium is always found to exist — on paper. At the same time, neoclassical doctrines allow those wishing to mount a political attack on trade unions to blame unemployment on the unions' monopolistic power, which is seen as forcing wages above their supposed 'equilibrium' level. Neoclassical arguments about wages and employment have therefore been resurrected time and again in the face of depressions and mass unemployment in capitalist economies. Thus, the International Monetary Fund (IMF) puts the blame for high unemployment in Europe on the rapid rise in real wages since the 1960s and argues that 'until real wage levels fall, making employers more willing to take on new workers, there is little real chance of substantial inroads against unemployment'.[8] These arguments of the 1980s tend to reproduce those of the 1930s — and indeed those of the nineteenth century.

Monetarists are also inclined to argue that measures designed to control inflation will help rather than hinder efforts to reduce unemployment. Once more the IMF — in the restrained tone of an annual report by an international organization — gives support

37

to this view: 'Effective control of inflation would help to restore domestic investment incentives and maintain international competitive positions that would permit domestic producers to share in the cyclical upswing in world markets.'[9] The near coincidence of the increase in rates of unemployment and the acceleration of rates of inflation throughout the industrialized countries in the 1970s has lent a superficial plausibility to the thesis that inflation contributes to unemployment. The orthodox theorizing of the 1950s and 1960s, on the other hand, saw the rate of inflation and the rate of unemployment as *inversely* related.[10] A straightforward explanation of the chain of events in the 1970s is that governments faced with the OPEC oil price increases were bound to take measures to control the resulting inflationary pressure, despite the negative effects this would have on output and employment in their domestic economies. In practice, however, the debate about inflation and unemployment has now become a straightforward political struggle between 'monetarists' and 'Keynesians'. Monetarism rests essentially on the simple proposition that the rate of inflation is directly associated with the rate of growth of the money supply.[11] Politically it has come to be associated with a policy of trying to hold down the level of public expenditure and the level of public borrowing, in the belief that this will control inflation which, in turn, is held to constitute the foremost objective of government economic policy. At a time when inflation coincides with high rates of unemployment, this leads to an approach to public spending which is diametrically opposed to that of Keynesian economics.

Keynesian economics and aggregate demand

Born in the 1930s' depression, Keynesian economics set out to tackle the manifest failure of neoclassical economics to address itself to the characteristic problem of cycles and periodic slumps in capitalist economies.[12] It attacked the absurd irrationality of simultaneous mass unemployment of labour and gross underutilization of existing productive capacity. Whereas neoclassical theory was concerned with the type and quantity of productive capacity being created, Keynes focused on a different problem — the failure to use existing assets.

Keynes was inclined to the view that anything which created purchasing power, thus stimulating the production of goods and services and putting people back to work, must be better than doing nothing. The emphasis, therefore, had to be on the generation of demand. Increased government expenditure was seen as one way of doing this, and so were government policies to stimulate private spending, such as easing of credit and lowering of interest rates. This invoked a barrage of protest from orthodox monetarists, who argued that such expansion is inherently inflationary. Keynes replied that measures which would undoubtedly cause inflation when the economy is working at full capacity can, in the midst of depression, bring forth an increase in the real volume of goods and services to match the increase in purchasing power. An increase in public expenditure would have a positive impact which would be larger than the initial outlay itself, because it would have a 'multiplier' effect through the incomes it generated, which would in turn lead to further spending, and another round of income generation. The increase in money incomes would serve to generate an increase in real incomes, by putting the economy back to work. Even if some inflationary pressure is unavoidable, this is seen as decidedly preferable to continued mass unemployment.

The theoretical basis for these arguments lay in Keynes's analysis of effective demand. While neoclassical economics had tried to couch the problem of unemployment solely in terms of demand in the labour market, Keynes insisted that the question must be approached in terms of the demand for goods and services as a whole, or 'aggregate demand'. Neoclassical economics was preoccupied with the wage rate as a price, and the wage bill as a cost of production. Keynesians, on the other hand, emphasized the twofold nature of wages: they are simultaneously a cost of production for the individual firm, and the major source of purchasing power for the products of the market sector as a whole. To realize profits, it is not enough for firms to hold down costs in order to increase their potential profit margin. They also have to sell the goods in order to realize these profits. Without buoyant consumer purchasing power, it is difficult to see how the economy could grow, because firms will not automatically reinvest past profits simply to produce growth for growth's sake. Firms' investments are governed by what they anticipate profit rates will be on new investment, and this depends on their sales expectations. Since household expenditure is such an important component of final demand, if this purchasing power is undermined by growing unemployment, then the familiar downward cycle of depressions in capitalist economies is reinforced. Contracting markets lead to further closures and redundancies, entailing a further loss of purchasing power, and further decline in sales. Because wages have a dual role, as a cost and as a means of distributing purchasing power, the wage rate cannot be treated in the same way as other commodity prices.

In a depression, Keynesians argued, what is needed is not a cut in the wage rate but a stimulus to demand. It is the responsibility of governments to manage the level of effective demand to ensure full utilization of capacity. The Keynesian orthodoxy held its place in the corridors of power for over 30 years until the post-1979 slump shattered the consensus of the post-World War II period. During these decades, Keynesians had arrived at a slightly uneasy truce with neoclassical economics. While left-wing Keynesians (notably Joan Robinson) had tended to move closer to Marxism, the version of Keynesianism which became embodied in the actual policies of governments was further to the right. By drawing a clear divide between the 'microeconomics' of resource allocation on one hand, and the 'macroeconomics' of aggregate demand-management on the other, orthodox Keynesians could stake their claim to the 'macroeconomic' sphere while avoiding conflict with neoclassical economists when dealing with 'microeconomics'.[13] Keynesians found they could still affirm the virtues of the market economy and the pursuit of profits, thus achieving respectability and influence in the capital cities of Western Europe and North America.

Marxist economics and the contradictions within capitalism

Marxism had never been able to come to terms with its opponents in this way. While neoclassical economics portrayed the market economy as a stable and self-regulating mechanism, Marx saw it as inevitably unstable and torn by inherent contradictions.[14] In response to Keynes, Marxists insisted that demand-management, while it might mitigate temporarily the consequences of investment cycles, could never resolve the fundamental contradictions with capitalist production, which repeatedly gave rise to crises and slumps. These crises had occurred throughout its history, and were part of the nature of the system. Prophetically, Marxists warned that the comparatively long period of fairly steady growth following World War II was only a phase, and that the system remained inherently crisis-prone. These crises are not to be seen simply as crises of 'insufficient aggregate demand' (as Keynesian economics seemed to imply). They are therefore not regarded as avoidable through wiser economic management on the part of government but arise from the nature of the process of capital accumulation and the logic of 'production for profit rather than production for need'. A period of sustained capital accumulation is seen as leading inevitably to a falling rate of profit,[15] and sooner or later a crisis point will be reached when the pace of investment slackens, leading quickly to aggregate 'demand deficiency'. Firms then fail to realize expected profits, and as firms' sales decline, the result is business contraction, bankruptcies and the start of recession. Depending on the specific historical circumstances, this may or may not develop into a full-scale slump.

Recovery depends, in Marxist terms, not on the manipulation of aggregate demand through monetary and fiscal policies, but also on the re-emergence of the conditions under which private capital accumulation can again proceed. These conditions relate to the realization of profits, and paradoxically come about through the very process of asset destruction, business bankruptcies, and job loss during depression. This destruction 'clears the way' for a greater share of total profits to accrue to surviving firms and to newly created assets. This may be reinforced by a tendency for real wages to rise less fast, or to fall, in the presence of mass unemployment. At the 'frontier', with the newest techniques associated with new investment, the rate of profits may then rise, even though total profits in the economy as a whole will have taken a plunge in the downswing of the depression. The re-emergence of profitable investment opportunities from an economy laid waste by factory closures, redundancies, mass unemployment, urban decay and deepening social divisions, is no accident; for this waste is precisely the price paid under the system for the restoration of conditions under which private capital once again makes the level of profits which is deemed sufficient.

Some non-Marxist economists have also emphasized similar points. Joseph Schumpeter, an American economist writing in the 1940s, referred to the 'great gale of creative destruction' which accounted both for the dynamism of capitalism and its apparent irrationality and gross wastefulness.[16] But these two faces of capitalism were never more clearly perceived than in Marx's own writings, where he is as impressed by the astonishing material achievements of the system as he is angered by what he sees as its irrationality and injustice.

For Marxists, it is no use looking for 'solutions' to unemployment under capitalism, because insecurity of employment is its normal condition. Recurrent crises with attendant mass unemployment are an in-built consequence of the very logic of capital accumulation, when it is based on private profit and destructive competition. Solutions must be sought instead in the building of an economic system in which investment is planned, rather than left to the chance decisions of individual firms guided only by profit expectations that are notoriously volatile. A primary goal of such a planned economy would be that people must not be treated as dispensable commodities to be discarded when the system has no need of them, but must instead be assured of the right to work. If a gradual path of transition to this goal exists, then it is generally perceived by socialists to lie through a progressive extension of the sphere of state ownership and public regulation of the economy.

A shared assumption

The contrasts between these three traditions of economic thought are obvious enough, and the political standpoints deriving from them remain largely irreconcilable. Yet in one important respect there is common ground: the belief in economic growth as the pathway to full employment. In this respect, the dispute is more about means than ends. The expectation of those schooled in neoclassical economics is that market demand will generate jobs through growth, as long as the adjustment process is allowed to work itself through. From a Keynesian standpoint, the necessary growth will not come automatically, but must be facilitated through demand-management by governments. For Marxists, on the other hand, regular sustained growth is achievable only in an economy where investment is planned, rather than left to a host of unco-ordinated decisions based on the profit expectations of individual firms. The shared assumption is, nevertheless, that jobs come about by producing more and investing more.

Attitudes to technology and employment

Closely related to this growth assumption is the reluctance among orthodox adherents of each economic tradition to give serious attention to the employment implications of technological change. In neoclassical models, prices can always adjust to bring about a new equilibrium, so 'technological unemployment' tends to be treated as a very temporary adjustment problem. The Keynesian thinking, which prevailed in Western Europe and North America until the late 1970s, rejected the neoclassical faith in the market alone, but assumed that demand-management policies were in principle capable of keeping the economy on a full-employment course. It was only the emergence of inflationary pressures which were seen as limiting the implementation of full-employment policies. Technological change was recognized as an important factor in unemployment in regions where older industries were in decline, but was not seen as standing in the way of near-full employment at a national level. Marxists have approached these questions in a quite different way, and in one sense have accorded technological change an extremely important place, not least because Marx's theory of the falling rate of profit was predicated on capital-using technical change. Yet in practice Marxists have, like other economists, often side-stepped the question of technology and employment because they have treated it as a problem specific to capitalism, implicitly assuming that a planned economy would ensure full employment.

Technological change is often portrayed in economic models as smooth, continuous, and automatic. 'Technological progress' is treated like manna from heaven; it is exogenous, obtained without effort and without delay. In retreating in this way from any analysis of the real process of innovation, economic models fail to take account of the episodic and unpredictable nature of technological change, while at the same time ignoring some of the imperatives which particular technologies impose on the economic and social organization of production. These problems, which are discussed in Chapter 8, impose constraints on the process of economic growth which are absent from abstract mathematical models of growth based purely on 'economic' variables.

In such models, growth is usually governed solely by investment and technical change. The faster the pace of technological change, the higher the attainable rate of growth and, as long as a sufficient share of gross domestic product (GDP) is invested, the rate of growth in the model can be increased to match the rate of technological change.[17] The 'required' investment share may rise, if technological change is capital-using, but as long as this 'correct' amount is invested there can be no such thing as 'technological unemployment', except as a localized and temporary adjustment problem. This mechanistic view of the process of growth, in which the economy can be accelerated merely by pushing the investment pedal down harder, is woefully inadequate in the real world. The pace of technological change and the amount invested are not the only constraints on growth. Abstract growth models by their nature ignore totally both the everyday 'nuts-and-

43

bolts' organizational problems of business life and the overall historical context in which economic change occurs. They are presented to students as timeless principles, supposedly applicable in all circumstances. The constraints left out of such models are apparent enough in any real economy. At the business level, growth is not just a question of how much can be invested. It is also a question of how quickly new skills can be acquired, or people with those skills recruited. It further depends on how quickly changes in working practices can be introduced in ways that are both practicable and acceptable, and how quickly managerial time and capabilities can be extended to new ventures.

At the level of the whole economy, as we discuss in Chapter 8, there are important constraints on economic change which may arise from the rate at which the community at large is prepared to adapt, reflecting the preparedness of society at large to make the effort and sacrifice involved in rapid change. It is possible to see how, under the compulsions of the factory system in nineteenth-century Britain, under Stalin's industrialization drive in the Soviet Union in the 1930s, or during Japan's 'great leap forward' to catch up with the West after World War II, a greatly accelerated pace of economic change may be achieved in certain circumstances over a decade or even a generation. It is not nearly as obvious why an already industrialized society, in which the majority of people have an abundance of goods compared with any previous period of history and where poverty is not the result of a lack of sufficient capacity to produce goods, should see the reason for human existence as lying in greater growth of gross national product (GNP). It is suggested in Chapter 7 that, although people want the status of a job and lack a sense of identity without it, there is not necessarily a desire to have to work hard on the job — and what is actually produced is much less important than the fact of having a job. Economic models which ignore motivation are a somewhat limited tool for understanding real constraints on growth.

Another major limitation of many economic models is the assumption of continuous and freely available substitution between capital and labour in all branches of the economy. This is another example of the unrealistic treatment of technology in much economic theory; it fails to recognize that the very imperatives of technology which endow it with apparently autonomous behaviour also closely constrain the choice of forms that are realistically available at any given time. The more sophisticated the technology that is incorporated into a country's economy, the more entrenched these technologies become and the more difficult is the exercise of choice, because alternatives would involve such extensive destruction of existing methods of working as well as business capital and economic infrastructure. Whereas it is true that cotton clothing can either be made by hand, from the growing and harvesting of the cotton crop through to the finished product, or be produced through highly mechanized agriculture and automated factory production, there is no way in which plastics can be made 'by hand'. At least, in theory, an economy can choose the technology for cotton processing — even if, in practice, the social and institutional structure built around mechanized agriculture and automated factories would make a 'reverse' substitution towards more labour-intensive techniques untenable in any conditions other than catastrophe. But for synthetic polymers, there is no 'craft' technology, even on paper, which could be substituted. The products of the petrochemicals industry are inherently capital-intensive.

Of course, an economy could in theory dispense with petro-chemicals technology and revert to the alternatives of natural rubber or steel for its buckets, but such substitutions are not simply matters of choice of production technique in response to 'factory prices' and again are extremely improbable. Newer technologies such as silicon chips involve yet further constraints. Not only is there no 'craft' element, but their conception, design, and manufacture require sophisticated facilities and sophisticated personnel. Moreover, silicon chips are an intermediate product which would be pointless without equally sophisticated end-users and end-uses. So highly structured is a technology of this type that even a change from using one manufacturer's range of chips to another's is non-trivial and requires major investment spread over a substantial period. Thus, the notion of a high degree of flexibility in the combinations of inputs which firms use, typically implied in elementary micro-economics textbooks, can be highly misleading if used to suggest that the decline in production industry employment might be averted by choosing less capital-intensive techniques. In general, substitu-tion of labour for capital is limited to overtime and shift working on existing plant, to spread capital costs over a larger output.

In addition to the increasing number of these inherently high-technology processes, there is also a growing range of components and finished goods in which precision and standardization require the removal of the undependable human factor in the production process. There is an even wider range of tasks where, as we argue in Chapter 11, it is in no sense desirable to perpetuate the direct use of human labour in repetitive, tedious, and sometimes hazardous jobs. A rational use of technical capabilities demands that the ratio of capital to labour cannot be treated simply as a variable that responds to their respective prices, but is governed by a complex set of social, technological, and market considerations which severely constrain actual business decisions. Any notion that the loss of employment in such processes ought to be counteracted by workers 'pricing themselves into jobs' implies a view of the world in which men are treated as mere appendages of machines, whose cheapness as commodities alone governs whether they are to be kept or discarded. A socially responsible view requires not the perpetuation of this 'machine-slave' status of labour, but that it be transcended. The problem is not how to maintain a demand for industrial labour artificially through the under-pricing of work, with either obsolete technology or overmanning of new technology. The maintenance of traditional forms of manufacturing employment has ceased to be either desirable or possible. The challenge is to find alternative ways of distributing the benefits of industrial progress.

In the rest of Part 1 of this book, we examine the adequacy of existing responses to this challenge in the industrially advanced countries, with particular reference to the UK. The belief that the process of market adjustment is in itself capable of generating large numbers of jobs from new technology and jobs in the service sector is considered in Chapters 3 and 4. In Chapter 5, we enquire into the potential for creating jobs through increased public expenditure, and the limitations that are likely to be encountered. The relationship between economic planning and the goal of full employment is investigated in Chapter 6.

A retreat from full employment?

In marked contrast to the faith of each main economic tradition that solutions to unemployment exist in economic terms, if only the necessary political conditions could be created, many other commentators present the problem as insoluble. Technological change is seen as responsible for the underlying trends, and is widely believed to have made full employment an impossible goal. Some commentators go further still, to argue that the goal is not only unattainable, but no longer relevant. The attachment to the right to work as a political objective is seen as a legacy of a Victorian work ethic which is increasingly out of place in a world in which machines are capable of doing so much of the work.[18] It is suggested that society should be affirming the right to leisure, rather than the right to work. In Chapter 7, we set this prescription alongside the realities of mass unemployment, by reporting on expectations and attitudes to work in one of the communities in Britain which has been worst hit by the decline in industrial jobs.

Industrial renewal?

In such communities, the rejuvenation of manufacturing and the creation of new jobs in industry still remain the image which many hold as the prospect for the future. The hope is that a new economic boom will occur, comparable in scale to the industrial growth which followed World War II and which drew into employment the millions who were demobilized from the Armed Forces, who left the armaments factories, or who entered the labour-force for the first time. In Chapter 8, we consider the phenomenon of economic growth, and the characteristics of late twentieth-century technologies which would underpin any new economic boom. A set of alternative scenarios of growth and employment is sketched in Chapter 9, indicating the kinds of outcome which could be expected on the basis of relying on traditional mechanisms for generating jobs.

Notes and references

1. These are summarized in OECD (1982) *Marginal Employment Subsidies*, Paris.
2. For example, the UK government's White Paper, *Employment: The Challenge for the Nation*, Cmnd 9474. See also Van Ginneken, W (1982) *Unemployment in France, the Federal Republic of Germany and the Netherlands*, International Labour Office, Geneva.
3. *Employment: The Challenge for the Nation*, reference 2.
4. However, in some cases the actual results are so trivial in comparison with the level of unemployment as to raise doubts about their worth — the UK Job Splitting Scheme, launched in January 1983, has in two years led to the splitting of just 1000 full-time jobs into part-time ones (ibid., p37). In other cases, there is doubt about the extent to which participants in the government's training or temporary employment schemes are assisted beyond the period of the scheme itself. Jackson, M P and Hanby, V J B (1982) *British Work Creation Programmes*, Gower Press, found that the proportion who were subsequently helped to find employment might range from about 16 per cent to 35 per cent for the sample they studied (which covered both types of scheme). Many participants had the kind of

47

characteristics that 'suggested they might be able to find employment in a reasonable period of time' — whether or not they participated in the government's programme.

5. The most famous of these writings was Clark, J B (1899) *The Distribution of Wealth; a Theory of Wages, Investment and Profits*, Macmillan, London. A recent statement of the view that there is a unique 'equilibrium' rate is Pearce, I F (1979) A theory of money, capital, general equilibrium and income distribution, in Patterson, K D and Schott, K *The Measurement of Capital*, Macmillan, London.

6. Von Neumann (1945–46) A model of general economic equilibrium, in *Review of Economic Studies*, XIII.I, presented a model whose treatment of growth was described as 'ultra classical' and 'brutally simple' by Robinson, Joan (1971) *Economic Heresies*, p109, Macmillan. Von Neumann's equations describe the equilibrium conditions of an optimum growth path; they cannot, in the nature of the case, say anything about what happens to an economy when it is out of equilibrium (Robinson, op. cit., p41). The neoclassical tradition later found expression in Meade, J E (1960) *A Neoclassical Theory of Economic Growth*, George Allen and Unwin, London.

7. Many of these concern the problem of measurement of capital, and the impossibility of finding a measure which is itself independent of the distribution of income between wages and profits; see for example Robinson, Joan (1956) *The Accumulation of Capital*, Macmillan, London, and Harcourt, G C (1972) *Cambridge Controversies in the Theory of Capital*, Cambridge University Press. An important part of the argument (the 'reswitching' controversy) concerned the rejection of the earlier neoclassical assumption that a continuously increasing capital-output ratio would be associated with a progressively increasing real wage rate.

8. *Guardian*, 18 April 1985.

9. International Monetary Fund, Annual Report, 1984.

10. The view that there is a trade-off between the rate of inflation and the rate of unemployment is still embodied in some models which focus on the wage bargain, eg Layard, R and Nickell, S (1985) The causes of British unemployment, *National Institute Economic Review*, pp62–85, February, who have a 'non-accelerating inflation rate of unemployment' built into their model.

11. The modern version of this proposition is usually associated with Milton Friedman, eg, A theoretical framework for monetary analysis, *Journal of Political Economy*, Vol 78, 1970.

12. Keynes, J M (1936) *The General Theory of Employment, Interest and Money*, London.

13. This separation into two spheres of economics has been evident in a whole generation of textbooks for students of economics, in which 'microeconomics' is virtually synonymous with neoclassical economics, and 'macroeconomics' with Keynesianism.

14. Marx indeed wrote that 'capital is itself contradiction in action', *Grundrisse*, 1857 (London, 1904, pp592–4), because it sought to reduce labour time to the minimum, while establishing labour time as the sole source of wealth. The fundamental contradiction, underlying all the others, is normally understood by Marxists to be the contradiction between the *social* nature of production and the system of *private* appropriation. The resulting conflicts are seen as more and more inescapable the more highly developed

our industrial technologies and large-scale production become.

15. There is considerable dispute among Marxist economists, as well as between Marxists and non-Marxists, over the theoretical basis for the falling rate of profit; Marxists themselves not infrequently reject Marx's own theory. See, for example, Glyn, Andrew and Harrison, John (1980) *The British Economic Disaster*, Appendix 'The Profits Squeeze', p175f, Pluto Press, London; or Aaronovitch, S and Smith, R (1981) *The Political Economy of British Capitalism*, p295, McGraw Hill. There is, however, no disagreement over the existence of profits crises, neither among Marxists nor among writers in the *Bank of England Quarterly Bulletin*, eg Clark, T A and Williams, N P (1978) Measures of real profitability, pp5123–527, 18.

16. Schumpeter, J A (1943) *Capitalism, Socialism and Democracy*, George Allen and Unwin, London; quoted in Robinson, Joan and Eatwell, John (1973) *An Introduction to Modern Economics*, p132, McGraw Hill, London.

17. This is the implicit assumption which allows Layard and Nickell, for example, to conclude that the effect of technical progress on employment 'is negligible' (op. cit., reference 10).

18. These arguments are reflected in a number of books including Clemiston, I and Rodgers, G (1981) *A Life to Live*, Junction Books, London (Chapter 1 'Work Ethic v. Life Ethic'); and Jenkins, C and Sherman, B (1979) *The Collapse of Work*, Eyre Methuen, London. Efforts to give practical expression to an alternative ethic include two business ventures: Leisure Consultancy (Bill Martin and Sandra Mason, Sudbury, Suffolk) and Redundancy Workshops (Ashburton, Devon).

CHAPTER 3

Jobs from Industry

The role of industry

'Production' automatically conjures up images of factories with masses of employees, each with their own allotted task; an image combining both Adam Smith's theory of the division of labour and F W Taylor's theories of mass production and scientific management. It is part of general knowledge that in these factories many jobs have been rendered unnecessary by automation and that more are due to fall to the robots. Somehow jobs in industry are special. These are 'real jobs', at the core of the economic system, seen as producing real wealth which can then be used to pay for other activities, whether of a frivolous leisure-centred nature — the candyfloss of life — or for more desperate matters such as medical care. That industry is special is confirmed by the flattery of imitation. Other activities bid for legitimization by tagging on the vital noun 'industry' — hence we now have the catering, tourist, banking, insurance and health-care industries. In contrast, we are also told that we cannot expect to maintain a lifestyle based on the material products of 'industry' by living off foreign tourists and exported financial services and computer software. This move to become part of 'industry' brings with it an internal ideology of efficiency which reinforces its power through mechanisms of social control; nursing is not just a caring profession but one subject to staffing norms with associated work measurement techniques. Similarly, the productivity of lecturers and teachers must be measured through student:staff ratios, and home-helps must report to, and be controlled by, the management structure of a social work department. The resulting 'efficiency' becomes a matter of dispute, with which we are not concerned here, but the reinforcement of the importance accorded to industry helps add to confusion about sources of future employment.

This perception of the special nature of industry arises in part from the historical role of the industrial revolution in rescuing most of us from poverty; and it persists because industry provides us with the most prized of our possessions. Taking family, friends and health for granted, most people want a Porsche — or at least a Ford — and regard this as central to their life and ambitions. Simpler lifestyles just do not appeal. Non-volatile, substantial property is the cornerstone of economic achievement, both for the individual and the economy. The connection between these attitudes and the economic growth paradigm is examined in Chapter 8, but first the path from science and technology, through innovation to employment, must be followed.

Not only are definitions of progress firmly tied to the performance of industry, but also this performance is seen to be directly linked to national achievements in science and technology. The hope is held out that, through successful policies to encourage appropriate science and its use as technology, we can accelerate the transfer from invention to innovation, and thus get rich quicker and provide more jobs in the process. Of course, no self-respecting science or technology policy expert would be happy to allow such a grossly over-simplified description of the purposes of public policy, let alone the interaction of science, technology and industry, to remain uncorrected. No matter, the point at issue is only whether the process of technological advancement, however achieved, leads to more jobs or fewer. Unfortunately, the discussion of this issue is too often non-quantitative or, if quantitative measures are given, they are disaggregated to a point which defies meaningful analysis. Two hundred new jobs in microelectronics cannot be set against 200 jobs lost in coal mining, in either a quantitative or a qualitative sense, and it is a meaningless comparison in an analysis of overall job gains and losses. The boundaries and time relationships of the analysis must both be clearly defined.

Employment in industry

To determine the overall effect of technological change on employment in industry requires, in the very beginning, an acceptance that industry now is not the industry of 30 years ago. In 30 years, the mix of industry in a country will undergo substantial changes: the colour TV set arrives and linoleum almost vanishes. But more subtle changes also occur: for instance, if catering services for staff are provided in-house, the numbers in industry are higher than if this is bought in from a service organization, and the same applies for management and design services. None the less, it is

Country	Employment index in 1978	Production index in 1978
Belgium	77.8	102.6
Denmark	81.9	107.8
Switzerland	84.8	93.6
Australia	86.6	100.0
Japan	87.5	104.9
Germany	88.3	102.7
Netherlands (1977)	89.2	106.7
France	92.5	105.8
Austria	92.6	110.4
UK	93.7	97.3
Italy	95.5	108.4
Sweden	96.5	95.5
Ireland	96.6	121.8
Finland	96.7	102.5
Canada	97.4	97.8
USA	100.8	110.9
Norway	100.8	101.7
Spain (1976)	104.4	127.7
Greece	113.7	123.1
Yugoslavia	120.5	144.0

Table 3.1 *Employment and production in manufacturing industry in 1978 (1973 = 100)*

Source: Rothwell, Ray and Zegveld, Walter (1979) *Technical Change and Employment*, p19, St Martin's Press, New York.

instructive to note the comparison of indices of employment and production, for 1973 and 1978, made by Rothwell and Zegveld for manufacturing industry in 20 countries (Table 3.1). Over this short period 15 countries show a decline, two a negligible change and only three, Spain, Greece and Yugoslavia, a growth in employment. When the change in production index is taken into account it can be seen that only in the case of Switzerland, the UK, Sweden and Canada was any of the loss of employment related to a fall in production. Further, the increases in production for Spain, Greece and Yugoslavia more than outweigh the increase in employment. It is especially interesting to note the relatively high falls in the employment index in Japan and Germany, showing continued improvement in productivity but equally showing that the manufacturing sector of the economy in these nations, as in most of the rest of the advanced industrial nations, was a declining source of employment.

Rothwell and Zegveld identify three phases in relation to industrial output and employment in nine EEC countries for the period 1950 to 1978 and this is shown in Table 3.2. These figures show that output growth never at any time in the whole period produced a proportionately large growth in employment, and that as the high rates of growth have passed job losses have occurred.

Period	Output change per cent per annum	Employment change per cent per annum
1950–65	+7	+1
1965–73	+6	0
1973–78	+1	−1.8

Table 3.2 *Industrial output and employment phases in nine EEC countries*

Source: Rothwell, Ray and Zegveld, Walter (1979) *Technical Change and Employment*, p18, St Martin's Press, New York.

An analysis of the relationship between capital investment, output and employment in manufacturing industry, based on UK and West German data, is contained in Appendix 1. This shows that:

1. Output generation relative to capital investment was lower in the 1970s than in the 1950s and 1960s;
2. Capital investment in the 1950s and early 1960s was employment-increasing; in the 1970s it was employment-reducing.

Our interpretation of the outcome of investment is that it has had two phases. In the first phase, investment in those industries which provided the post-1945 economic boom led to the mass production of cars and other consumer goods, to market expansion and to increased production capacity. In the second phase, investment in these industries was not used to replicate capacity but to refine the production technologies, to improve design and to reduce costs.

The technological causes for these phases of investment will be developed in Chapter 8, but we now turn to a more detailed analysis of these changes by examining output and employment for the UK Index of Production (IOP) industries.[1] The IOP industries include not only manufacturing but also mining, quarrying, building, construction, gas, electricity and water: the entire group on which it is so often maintained that the future of an industrial nation depends. The changes for industrial employment since 1959 are shown in Figure 3.1 and this repeats the pattern of Table 3.2. There are fluctuations but, since 1966, these are clearly around a trend of falling employment, latterly at a rate of 220 thousand jobs per year, 18 thousand per month. This pattern of

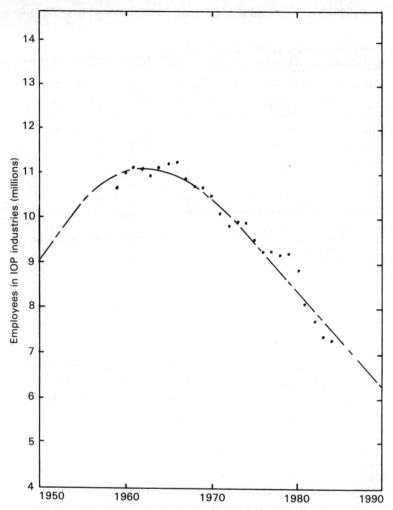

Figure 3.1 *Employment in Index of Production industries*

Source: *Annual Abstracts of Statistics* and *Monthly Digests of Statistics*.

behaviour — for employment to pass through a maximum — requires a divergence in behaviour between production and productivity (defined as production per employee). The humped shape of the employment curve results from three growth phases:

1. production growing faster than productivity; employment-increasing;
2. production growing at the same rate as productivity; employment-static;

3. production growing more slowly than productivity; employment-decreasing.

The reasons why production can be expected to behave in this way are discussed in Chapter 8, and the mathematical modelling which lies behind the curve in Figure 3.1 is outlined in Appendix 2. However, acceptance of the exact shape of this curve is not critical to acceptance of the implications of a fall in industrial employment from 11.23 million in 1966 to 7.66 million in 1982. If this fall is projected on the basis of the trends in production, productivity and working time which generate the curve in Figure 3.1, then the employment in the IOP industries would be down to 6.3 million in 1990 and 4.7 million in the year 2000. It is crucial to note that the underlying trend is not related to changes in the rate of inflation, the introduction of monetarist economic policies or to OPEC-induced rises in the price of oil, although some of the short-term trends might be seen to correspond to such events. The fitted curve is based on data series ending in 1972 and is thus caused solely by the underlying fall-off in the rate of increase of production relative to productivity. This tide of declining employment can only be stemmed or turned by a resurgence of growth in production at a rate equalling or exceeding the growth in productivity.

Again it must be emphasized that this is not solely a UK phenomenon. Table 3.3 records the year in which a downward trend in industrial employment commenced for ten other Western 'European nations as well as the UK. In addition, the proportion of decline by 1979 is given and, as might be expected, those countries in which decline started earlier than the UK have, in general, lost a bigger proportion; those countries in which it started later have lost a smaller one. The job losses in industry in these 11 countries prior to the 1980s' recession totalled 5.5 million.

It is useless to look for a growth in employment from those industries which have reached the third phase of (employment-reducing) investment. An example based on car production is instructive. If, in a closed economy, the saturation level of car ownership is 20 million and the replacement life of cars is ten years then a balance will exist at a production rate of two million cars per year. But if the level of ownership in a given year was only ten million cars, then a level of two million cars per year would give a growth of ownership of one million in that year, of 900 thousand in the next and so on. This decelerating growth of car

55

Country	Year in which downward trend in industrial employment commenced	Total decrease in industrial employment by 1979 %
Switzerland	1964	22
Belgium	1964	17
Netherlands	1965	15
Sweden	1965	14
UK	**1966**	**16**
Denmark	1970	10
West Germany	1971	11
Austria	1973	5
Finland	1974	9
France	1974	8
Norway	1976	5
All above		12½

Table 3.3 *Decline in industrial employment in industrially advanced Western European countries up to 1979*

Source: OECD Labour Force Statistics, 1960–71 and 1970–81, Paris. Earlier estimates adjusted to 1970–81 basis.

ownership would give a car population reaching 16.5 million after ten years and 18.75 million after 20 years — still short of saturation level. It can also be seen that the approach to the steady level of 20 million gets slower and slower. (The fall in the number of cars added to the population each year is an example of the exponential decay process, as distinct from the more commonly known one of exponential growth.) In these circumstances, the normal response of manufacturers would be to drive annual production up beyond the two million level so as to achieve full market penetration as quickly as possible. Thus an overshoot in car production is virtually inevitable as the car population approaches saturation. Far from production being open to further major increase, it is to be expected that over-capacity will arise and require the closedown of production facilities. This is just what seems to be happening in 1985. Bob Lutz, Chairman of Ford Europe, believes that 'although a number of European car groups had reduced capacity the industry was capable of making 2.3 million more cars than the market was absorbing — some 18 per cent of European production capacity'.[2] If plants are closed it must be expected that these will be the older more inefficient ones, precisely those which will employ most labour relative to their production capacity.

More seriously, in a period of rapid technological change in production processes, a decline in employment can take place even in industries in which there is a high rate of growth of output. In a study of 'rationalizing industries' in the UK between 1968 and 1973, in which employment in every case fell, Massey and Meegan have drawn attention to output growth of 11 per cent and 17 per cent respectively in grain milling and in the production of insulated wire and cables, while employment fell by 13 per cent and 15 per cent respectively. Our own analysis for the period from 1973 to the beginning of the depression in 1979 points to similar conclusions. Manufacturing industries can be grouped into those which had relatively high rates of growth of output (food, drink and tobacco; chemicals; other manufacturing), and those with low or negative rates of growth (metal manufacture; engineering; textiles). As can be seen from Table 3.4, where output growth was higher, the rate of productivity increase was also higher and so employment still declined, albeit more slowly than for the 'low growth' industries. Employment declined for all industries listed except chemicals, where it increased by a mere 0.7 per cent in a period in which output increased by 18.5 per cent.[3] This further reinforces the conclusion in Chapter 1 that implausibly high rates of growth of output would be 'required' in manufacturing industries if employment were not to decline further, because productivity growth itself tends to accelerate with the higher output growth rate.[4]

Grouping	Output	Productivity	Employment
'Low growth'	100.1	106.7	93.8
'High growth'	111.6	115.3	96.8

Table 3.4 *Manufacturing industry indices (UK) 1979 (1973 = 100)*

This projected decline in manufacturing industry employment is now widely accepted as inevitable. In a UK seminar held by the National Institute of Economic and Social Research, it was noted that 'the Treasury has written off manufacturing as a net source of new jobs', and it was also observed that 'the TUC does not seem to dissent from this view'. Even in those employment projections which showed some overall growth of jobs in the economy, manufacturing employment continued to decline.[5] In reaction to such problems, import controls have been put forward as a means of preventing further loss of industrial jobs. Quite apart from the risk of retaliatory action, this ignores the global nature of the underlying problem. We cannot all export our unemployment, and to seek remedies in economic isolation is to avoid recognizing the changed nature of advanced industrial society.

Reductions in working hours

While there has been a secular fall in employment in industry since the mid-1960s, there has been a much longer established fall in time worked — traceable for the UK and US back to the 1870s.[6] For men, hours per week, weeks per year and years per lifetime, have all gone down, not smoothly, not consistently, but by substantial overall margins. For women, the years per lifetime have been going up since World War II, although hours per week and weeks per year have shown the same general downward trend as for men. Indeed, if the hours worked per annum since 1959 are examined, those for women are falling by 20 hours per annum which is faster than the rate of fall for men of 16 hours per annum. The annual totals in 1981 were 1914 hours for men and 1316 hours for women,[7] reflecting the much higher proportion of part-time jobs held by women. To reduce annual hours at significantly higher rates than those quoted would require a sharp break with a trend which has persisted for over 20 years. The US figures show that from 1860 to 1950 there was a reduction in the working week from 67 to about 40 hours.[8] But although it went below 40 hours during the 1930s, it has shown no tendency to fall since 1950 and was still 41 in 1978. (The perceived need for such a long working week is further considered in Chapter 7.)

If the figures for hours per annum are combined with the other data for the UK IOP industries, then an index of hourly productivity may be derived and this is found to have been rising very steeply through the recent recession. If employment prospects are calculated as hours per year rather than as the number of employees, the peak year can be estimated as 1960 when some 23.6 billion hours were worked in UK industry, and this occurred some six years before the peak of employment. By 1981 the aggregate was down to 14 billion hours, a rather sharper fall than that for the number of jobs. So we can see that sharing of work is taking place to some extent through a fall in working hours, but that it would require a radical rate of fall in annual working hours to balance job losses. If hourly productivity maintains its present high rate of increase, then by 1990 the projected 6.3 million employees in UK industry could be working as few as 10.2 billion hours. Thus by 1990 men may expect a 46-week year of 38 hours per week, including overtime, to come about without any special initiatives being taken to cut work hours. Policy cuts would have to be on top of this.

Jobs from new technology

The argument is often made, of course, that growth will come from new technological innovations and will turn the jobs tide by creating more new jobs than are being lost by the decline of the old industries. Studies in the UK of the employment implications of new technology show that increases in employment in the major growth area of the new microelectronics-based industries is not only currently failing to offset losses in the traditional heavy engineering sector, but also that the jobs are radically different in type. Trends in the US have clearly indicated a shift in occupational structure (see Table 3.5). Between 1960 and 1980 there was a growth in professional, technical and manager occupations of 7.8 per cent, a similar fall in craft, operative and labourer group, and a rise of 3.9 per cent in clerical occupations. Although most of this change pre-dates the impact of microelectronics, it seems that not only will the US economy continue to shift its demands towards people with the higher professional skills, and away from those at craft and lower levels, but also that new technologies will, at the very least, militate against further growth in clerical posts.

| | Proportions of total work-force % | |
Occupations	1960	1980
Professional, technical and manager	20.5	28.3
Craft, operator and labourer	38.6	31.1
Clerical	15.2	19.1
Sales	7.6	6.5
Service	11.7	12.6
Farmer, farm labourer	6.5	2.2

Table 3.5 *Change in US occupational structure, 1960–1980*

Source: Singlemann, Joachim and Tienda, Marta (1985) The process of occupational change in a service society: the case of the United States, 1960–80, in Roberts, B, Finnegan, R and Gallie, D (Eds) *New Approaches to Economic Life*, Manchester University Press.

The UK Engineering Industry Training Board, in its study of manpower in the electronics industry,[9] chronicles the relative disappearance of craftsmen who account for only 5 per cent of employees in electronics compared with 19 per cent in all engineering. Naturally some employees are retrained; for instance, the introduction of numerically controlled machine tools requires a considerable admixture of skills and some of these can be obtained by building on elements of existing craft skill. Such training opportunities enable some craftsmen and semi-skilled workers to keep abreast of changes in job requirements, but such provision is unlikely to have any significant effect upon the majority of employees. The general conclusion is brutal and uncompromising, and common to all researchers in this area. They agree that the structure of the work-force will change considerably, both in terms of industrial composition and in terms of occupational and skill composition:[10] in other words, that large segments of the present work-force will disappear. No amount of wealth creation will restore the demand for the present spectrum of skills. One approach to the problem of assessing the net effect of new technology on employment is to catalogue job types and their rate of disappearance, and to make broad estimates of probable new employment in industries directly related to new technology. But such a method is unlikely to be helpful because it rests on a false premise: that the effects of new technology can be disaggregated and compartmentalized. It ignores the essence of the new technology. For the 'microelectronics revolution' is revolutionizing not only the structure of employment, but also the patterns of production and consumption, of travel, leisure and use of time, which form the foundations of that structure.

Thus it is necessary to examine the background of job loss and job creation a little more carefully. In particular, it is vital neither to underestimate the potential impacts nor to categorize them as merely a continuation of historical trends. This point has been forcibly made by Ray Curnow who has described the present labour structure as a pyramid, with miners, raw materials processors, fabricators and assemblers as the bottom four layers. Microelectronics is radically changing this structure, and will rapidly eliminate many of the jobs in these bottom layers. Only the top two layers — those who design, test, sell and maintain any kind of product — will survive intact. Nor will the service sector survive unscathed:

'Historically, displacement of labour from the manufacturing sector has occurred over a very long period and has previously been absorbed into the so-called service sector, e.g. office or governmental functions. Unfortunately the advance in microelectronics implies considerable advances in the technologies associated with such service functions. Labour displacement is taking place in retail distribution networks, banking, insurance and, with the coming of the word processor, in offices also.'[11]

The impact of microelectronic technology in administrative organizations may be particularly severe on middle grades; if their skills are built into computer programs — especially with the advent of intelligent knowledge-based systems (IKBS) — then there will be few jobs between data entry and management. Hopes are sometimes vested in a growth of employment in small manufacturing businesses, which it is suggested may run counter to the trends in large firms. However, a survey of small businesses in the UK, made in 1982 by the Forum of Private Business, found that businesses in the survey had laid off an average of three workers each during the previous year.[12] The Forum estimated that for the economy as a whole this implied a gross loss of some 800,000 jobs in small businesses, a figure which could scarcely have been offset by new jobs created. At the same time, the Director of the Economist Intelligence Unit recalled that employment in the small business sector had declined for many years prior to 1971 and while there might have been some growth during the 1970s 'this trend seems to have run out of steam'. In considering the future of industrial employment, it is unhelpful to appeal to the notion that 'small is beautiful'. The task is, rather, to identify the types of activity in which new jobs could conceivably come.

The jobs created through the introduction of microelectronic technology fall into three broad categories. The first, represented by the top layer of Curnow's pyramid, comprises the designers, engineers and managers who are both the driving force and the principal beneficiaries of the new technology. In 1985 there are virtually unlimited opportunities for those with skills and training in these areas; and employment prospects for electronics engineers, computer scientists and numerate managers have never been better. The second group comprises those working on the production and assembly of microelectronics devices, and here the picture is much less rosy. This work requires keen eyesight, manual dexterity and, above all, 'industrial virginity'.[13] Few manufacturers are prepared to employ people with previous experience of industrial production. The methods of working and the styles of management in the 'sunrise' industries require a single-minded dedication; employers almost without exception choose young women for these jobs. This is as true in Europe as in Southeast Asia, and of course the high value and low bulk of the products ensures that producers in these geographically widespread locations compete with each other for the world market in microelectronics. The third category includes those involved in dispatch, transport and retail sales of electronic goods. Arguably the largest growth in employment spawned by new technology has been in semi-skilled salespeople for consumer electronic equipment, from TVs and videos to home computers and domestic appliances. Curiously, in Britain at least, these jobs are largely the preserve of men, but are low-paid and involve considerable 'unsocial hours' of working. Consequently such staff have been recruited from among those who left school expecting clerical or administrative jobs in companies or local government — jobs which have already been severely reduced by the impact of new technology. Few have either the aptitude or inclination to grasp the technicalities of the products they sell.

What is not evident in any of these categories is a source of new jobs to replace those lost at the bottom of Curnow's pyramid. Indeed, beyond the massive but short-term task of rewiring cities for cable TV and interactive computing, there appear to be few tasks associated with the new technology that could not themselves be carried out by the new technology. For instance, many of the data-transfer jobs, which today require the keyboard skills which are being avidly pursued in school curricula, could soon be overtaken by direct reading of data from documents. Voice communication with computers and program-writing programs will further reduce the requirement for keyboard skills. On the assembly line, the parallel developments of robotics and artificial intelligence will progressively displace the residue of manual workers who attend conventionally automated processes. As the size of the production labour-force falls, middle supervisory grades may be almost entirely eliminated because the information and instructions for control will go direct to the production machines from the production control manager. And even in the design office, computer-aided design and computerized draughting will replace many of those skilled tasks to which the bright school-leaver might at present aspire.

This trend is confirmed by the levels of investment required for new microelectronic plants. The typical investment for each intended employee is in excess of £100 thousand, and this bottom line can be seen regularly in newspaper reports of new projects. This capital-intensive nature of the new industry is the other side of the lower labour input to production. The message is clear: however many jobs come from new technology, industry is going to be the preserve of two groups — highly skilled technologists and dexterous assemblers — to an unprecedented extent. In those circumstances we are left to seek elsewhere for employment for those who are neither clever nor virginal.

Notes and references

1. Based on Leach, Donald (1985) Production, productivity and employment, *The Journal of Interdisciplinary Economics* **1**, 1, pp29–42.
2. *Financial Times*, 22 January 1985. It is interesting to note that, in 1984, EEC car production at 9.3 million exceeded that of the US and Japan — 7.8 million and 7.2 million respectively.
3. Massey, D and Meegan, R (1982) *The Anatomy of Job Loss*, Methuen, London.
4. The coupling of productivity increases to those of output has been eponymously entitled 'Verdoorn's Law'. See Freeman, Christopher (1984) Keynes or Kondratiev, in Marstrand, Pauline (Ed) *New Technology and the Future of Work and Skills*, pp109–10, Frances Pinter, London.
5. *National Institute Economic Review*, 109, August 1984, Full employment as a policy objective. Report of a one-day conference held at the National Institute, July 1984.
6. Armstrong, P J (1984) Work, rest or play? Changes in time spent at work, in Marstrand, P (Ed) *New Technology and the Future of Work and Skills*, pp26–44, Frances Pinter, London.
7. Armstrong, P J, private communication.
8. Leontief, Wassily, W (1982) The distribution of work and income, *Scientific American*, p155, September.
9. Lawson, G (1984) *Manpower in the Electronics Industry*, Engineering Industry Training Board, May.
10. Williams, V (1984) Employment implications of new technology, *Employment Gazette*, pp210–15, May.
11. Curnow, Ray (1978) Address to Institute of Mechanical Engineers, London, reported in *New Scientist*, p666, 8 June.
12. *Financial Times*, 22 January 1982, p9, 'Small Businesses Failed to Increase Jobs'.
13. Innocence of the practices of other sectors of manufacturing industry.

CHAPTER 4

A Service Economy?

Long-run trends

The relative decline in production industry employment is often regarded by economists as simply a new stage of economic development. The production of goods is seen as giving way to providing more services, which society can afford for the first time. The ratio of jobs in the service sector to jobs in production industries has indeed risen throughout the industrially advanced countries (see Table 4.1). In the UK, the decline in employment in the production industries of some two million jobs between the mid-1960s and the late 1970s was largely offset by an increase in service employment. This increase was not sufficient to prevent a rise in unemployment of over one million. Nor did it prevent the regional and inner-city problems worsening. It did, however, mean that the overall level of employment in the country as a whole was about the same at the end of the period as at the beginning. This appeared to lend credibility to the widely held belief that the future must lie in a 'service economy'.

Following on from the era of industrialization of the nineteenth and early twentieth centuries, the growth of the service sector is seen as a logical development for an affluent society, able to commit more time to other pursuits as it is increasingly freed from the burden of producing goods with manual labour. It is tempting to see services as the 'natural successor' to the production industries and a mainstay of future employment, just as manufacturing was once the successor to traditional agricultural employment as the basis of people's livelihoods. Why, it is asked, need the decline of production industry employment present any special problems? From the point of view of the overall level of employment, it does not appear to matter whether the jobs are in production industries or in services, as long as there are jobs somewhere. It is indeed theoretically possible to envisage an economy in which fully automated and unmanned machines produce all the goods, and

Selected OECD countries[a]	Total in service employment,[b] millions		Proportion of total civilian employment %	
	1960	1980	1960	1980
USA	37.00	65.46	56.2	65.9
Netherlands	2.07	3.17	49.7	63.6
Austria	2.06	3.90	50.1	62.4
Denmark	0.90	1.54	44.8	62.4
Sweden	1.58	2.63	44.0	62.2
UK	11.26	14.90	47.6	59.6
France	7.15	11.69	38.5	55.3
Japan	18.31	30.03	41.3	54.2
West Germany	10.14	12.95	39.1	50.3
Italy	6.79	9.85	33.5	47.9
OECD total[c]	113.13	183.73	43.0	56.4

a Ranked by percentage of civilian employment in services.
b Branches 6, 7, 8, 9 and 0 in the International Standard Industrial Classification (ISIC).
c 24 countries, including the ten countries listed which accounted for 81 per cent of OECD employment in 1980.

Table 4.1 *Service employment as a proportion of total employment, OECD countries, 1960–1980*

Source: *OECD Labour Force Statistics, 1962–82*, Paris 1984.

almost everyone is employed in 'service' activities. In view of these arguments, it is important to examine why service employment in the industrially advanced economies has tended to increase, and whether it can be expected to continue to increase. This requires an analysis of the origin of the demand for services, and the impact of technological change within the service sector. On both accounts, the convenient belief that future employment will be assured by growth in the service sector is found to rest on very insecure foundations.

Services and consumer spending

One interpretation of the 'service economy' is that people demand more services rather than more goods as incomes rise. The idea is that, as we become better off, we find our desire for goods already satisfied. Instead of buying more goods, it is suggested that we are likely to spend our money going to football matches, to pubs, to the theatre, or to restaurants. Society will therefore need to supply more services rather than more goods. The underlying idea is that, once productivity in manufacturing industry reaches a certain level, we 'outgrow' the need for more goods and the market for industrial products 'saturates'. Hence, it is argued, the pattern of employment moves towards services and away from manufacturing. This is often believed to come about automatically, as the result of market forces led by consumer demand.

The assumption that consumer spending shifts towards more services as a result of growing affluence is not, however, supported by the evidence. Previous studies have effectively shown that the shift in consumer demand has tended to be towards more goods rather than more services (see Table 4.2). People have cars, where they used to use public transport. People have television sets, where they used to go to the cinema. Once upon a time, the upper class employed domestic servants; now, the population as a whole has vacuum cleaners. The rich, because they were small in number, could enjoy the luxury of the stately home by living on the labour of others through purchasing 'services'. Their former patterns of consumption could never be replicated for the majority of the population. An increase in living standards for the whole population has been achieved, not by reproducing the previous service-oriented consumption patterns of the rich, but by producing more goods.

		1954	*1974*		*1954*	*1974*
Services	Cinemas, theatres, etc, domestic help; laundry; transport services	8.5	4.0	As percentage of total in categories	69.7	20.2
Goods	Television (buying and renting); domestic appliances; motor cars	3.7	15.8		30.3	79.8
Total		12.2	19.8		100	100

Table 4.2 *Household expenditure on related categories of 'goods' and 'services'*

Reproduced from Gershuny, J (1978) *After Industrial Society?*, p80, by kind permission of Macmillan, London and Basingstoke.

Differences in rates of growth of productivity are a significant factor in the shift of consumer demand towards goods. It is possible for productivity to increase dramatically in the production of many mass-produced goods — through mechanization and automation, and through the introduction of revolutionary techniques which drastically reduce the number and the complexity of the operations involved. The same does not apply in the case of personal services, such as hairdressing, nor in most repair and maintenance operations. In the long run, changes in relative prices tend to be a reflection of rates of change in productivity. The real prices of commodities tend to fall when the processes which produce them show an above-average rate of productivity increase. Conversely, when the rate of productivity increase is below average, real prices tend to rise. Most mass-produced manufactured goods fall into the first category, while services that consist directly of people's labour come into the second category. Goods become cheaper relative to labour. This is a commonplace observation, familiar through the more obvious cases of the prices of wrist watches and pocket calculators, contrasted with an hour of a garage mechanic's time on a car repair, or calling out the gas man to fix the boiler. One example where it is possible to compare price changes and volume of purchases for a good and a related service is shoes and shoe repairs. In the UK between 1950 and 1971, the real price of shoes fell by 10 per cent, while the real cost of shoe repairs rose by 20 per cent; meanwhile the volume of shoe purchases per head of population rose by 67 per cent over that period, whereas the real turnover of shoe repairs fell by more than half.[1] Thus, consumers increasingly treat the product itself as disposable, substituting goods (a greater volume of purchases) for services (repairs).

For the service sector as a whole, the overall differences are rather less dramatic, because there are a number of factors which blur the goods-services distinction. Some services are highly capital-intensive, and subject to similar kinds of technological change, as in manufacturing processes,[2] because they are based more on 'machine-services' than on direct 'labour-services'. Telecommunications are a clear example. On the other hand, some goods (by the time they reach final consumers) may embody a considerable 'service' component, particularly if (like motor cars) they require a substantial degree of individual handling in the distribution network. Despite such qualifications, goods generally can be observed to decline in price relative to services, even when aggregated statistics derived from the national income accounts are used as a basis (see Table 4.3). Between 1973 and 1983 in the UK, the volume of purchases of consumer durables[3] rose by 71 per cent as real prices declined by almost 40 per cent. This decade included the OPEC oil price shocks and one of the two deepest depressions of the century. This upsurge in sales of hi-fi sets, video recorders, home computers and a multitude of household gadgets is an eloquent testimony to the force of technological change. By comparison, the volume of output of services in total rose by only 16 per cent. In absolute terms purchases of goods measured at 1980 prices rose by £9.0 billion, while services rose by £5.0 billion. There was thus a relative increase in the consumption of goods compared with services, which confirms Gershuny's findings.[4]

		Index of relative prices, 1983 (1973 = 100)
Goods		
Consumer durables	(Not elsewhere specified)	61
Furniture	(Including floor coverings)	84
Cars	(Including motorcycles and other vehicles)	112
Food and drink	(Including alcoholic drinks)	94
Miscellaneous goods		89
Services		
Catering	(Meals and accommodation)	117
Recreational services		112
All services[a]	(Including catering and recreational services)	107

a Also includes telecommunications, where the price index fell to 96.

Table 4.3 *Changes in relative prices of consumer goods and services, UK 1973–83*

Source: Based on Tables 4.6 and 4.7, *National Income and Expenditure*, 1984 edition, HMSO, London. Index of relative prices calculated by dividing expenditure at current prices (deflated by the general consumer price index) by expenditure at constant prices.

The pressures resulting from relative price changes thus create a tendency for the labour-intensive 'service' element in the economy to be squeezed out. Services often have to be reorganized to make them at least partly customer-served, in order to compete at all in the market economy. Examples are pay-on-entry buses in place of the driver-plus-conductor system, and 'fast food' self-service cafes in place of waitress-served restaurants. There is a consequent reduction in employment per customer served. Many service sector activities face an inherent competitive disadvantage compared with the alternative of privately owned goods which provide similar services to the user, because the price of marketed services must embody time as a cost (in the form of the wages and salaries of employees). For example, about 70 per cent of the cost of running local bus services in the UK is wages and salaries, while the driver of a private car is 'unpaid'. Consequently, the price of public transport without subsidy is rarely low enough to be attractive when set against the convenience of the private car, despite the greater number of passengers carried per vehicle mile and per litre of fuel, and the much fuller utilization of the 'capital stock' of vehicles. In the UK, the number of passenger journeys by public transport fell by one-third over the decade 1964–74, (12.3 billion to 8.3 billion journeys), while the number of car-owning households rose by 60 per cent during the same period (6.4 million to 10.3 million households). In a market economy in which costs are dominated by wages and salaries, the maintenance of services, such as public transport, is often found to be increasingly difficult. The provision of these services is assured only if social needs are placed above profitability as the basic criterion in decision making by government and public authorities.

The weak competitive position of services involving a high direct labour component is a major factor perpetuating the low rates of pay which characterize many service activities. A comparison of the rates of pay of those who serve in hotel restaurants, cocktail bars or kitchens with the average incomes of their clientele illustrates that in the market sector the 'service economy' often consists of a low-paid, non-unionized work-force providing services to a highly paid and privileged section of society. It is no accident that private domestic service in Britain declined — it did so as the position of the old aristocracy was weakened and former levels of professional status were eroded. It has been suggested that, at some points, recent trends reinforce a new pattern of a class differentiation. 'Child minders', who may in effect be private domestic servants, are employed at rates which no organized group of workers would conceivably accept. They may be employed by a couple receiving two full-time professional salaries in order to attain a lifestyle free from some of the drudgery associated with the running of the household.

For a significant expansion to occur in employment in consumer services, while at the same time enabling those employed in these jobs to achieve a decent standard of living, there would need to be radical changes in the relationship between business costs and the incomes of employees. There are many reasons for seeking ways of bringing about such changes, which we discuss in Chapter 12. Meanwhile, the upward pressure on real wages drives us, not towards a service economy, but towards the 'self-service' economy.

This is the economy of hypermarkets with automated stock control, which sell customer-assembled furniture kits, loaded and driven home by the buyers in their own cars, which they maintain at the weekend. The economy it is replacing was one with specialist furniture shops, where the customers received individual attention. They may have got to one of these town-centre shops by bus, driven by a driver and served with a ticket by a conductor. The furniture they bought may have been delivered by van, with a driver and mate. The bus and the van would have been maintained by professional mechanics. Evidently, this self-service economy has significant implications for future employment patterns. It is also an outcome of social trends which, in certain respects, are more egalitarian then those which shaped the former service economy. If unemployment is to be reduced by an increase in marketed services, then the distributional implications need to be considered very carefully.

Three categories of service employment

It is important to examine the reasons why total service sector employment has been rising. Gershuny emphasizes that a significant proportion of the apparent growth in 'service' employment is in fact associated in some way with the production, distribution, and consumption of goods. Two examples are the supply of banking services to manufacturing firms and the insurance of goods in transit and in store. There may also be a statistical illusion of an increase in 'services' if activities once classified within production industries are subsequently reclassified to the service sector. Catering in factory or office canteens is a straightforward example. A reclassification may occur because a higher degree of specialization of activities between firms has actually occurred, such as an outside caterer providing what was previously done 'in-house', or simply because government statisticians choose to reclassify certain activities when drawing the boundary between the production industries and the service sector.[5] Many service activities can therefore be regarded as an indirect 'input' into the goods economy, and in Table 4.4 these are described as 'intermediate services'. The other main categories of service employment shown in this table are consumer services and public services. There is in addition a 'service' element associated with construction-type investment, analogous to the intermediate services supplied to the goods economy, and an 'invisible' services component in the economy's exports, which have both increased.

The estimation of the numbers in each of these three categories of service employment is far from straightforward, because the purpose is not to establish what kind of jobs people do, but what types of *expenditure* give rise to these jobs. The categories shown in Table 4.4 do not therefore consist of straightforward groupings of industries or occupations, but involve allocating the employment in each service industry in proportion to the share of its output which goes to each type of final buyer. For example, part of a bank's business is providing services to manufacturing firms, which counts as intermediate services within the goods sector in Table 4.4. Another part of a bank's activity is servicing personal accounts, which are a 'consumer service' in Table 4.4. Public authorities also use banking services, however, and this fraction of bank activity is thus treated as part of the employment associated with providing public services. Because services such as post and telecommunications also use banking services (and vice versa), a technique known as input-output analysis is required to deal with the problem. Input-output tables show the network of flows of goods and services between industries, and from industries to final consumers. By tracing through these flows, it is possible to calculate the output of each industry which is needed in order to provide a certain volume of final purchases of any particular good or service. From estimates of the share of wages and salaries in total value added, and the average earnings per person employed in each industry, it is then possible to attribute service sector employment approximately to categories of demand.

Analysis of service employment in the UK

Table 4.4 gives the results of an analysis of UK employment over the period 1963–79, allocating service sector employment to three major categories:

(A)   services associated with the production and distribution of goods,
(B)   services sold to consumers,
(C)   services provided by or purchased by public authorities.

The use of input-output methods to make these estimates is described in Appendix 3.

A major component of the apparent growth in the 'service' sector is attributable to the intermediate activities involved in the production and distribution of goods, as Gershuny suggested. Most of the growth in intermediate services attributed to the goods

71

Sector	Employment (employees and self-employed) millions			
	1963	1968	1974	1979
Direct 'goods' employment	10.33	9.70	9.01	8.60
Intermediate services (A)	4.60	4.49	4.85	4.91
Total 'goods' economy	14.93	14.19	13.86	13.51
Consumer services (B)	2.92	2.77	2.72	2.38
Public services (C)[a]	3.99	4.66	5.30	5.79
Other employment	2.90	3.23	3.24	3.35
Total in employment	24.74	24.85	25.12	25.03
Registered unemployed	—	0.55	0.55	1.30

a Including employment in the private sector attributed to public expenditure.

Table 4.4 *Summary of employment in the UK economy by 'goods' and 'services' sectors, 1963–79*

Source: Appendix 3.

economy has been in insurance, banking and finance. This was indeed the only 'industry' in the UK apart from public administration and defence which showed continued employment growth after the mid-1960s. However, employment in insurance, banking and finance showed signs of levelling off before the post-1979 depression. This is reflected in the estimates of intermediate services; the rate of increase in employment in these services was 60 thousand per year between 1968 and 1974, but only 12 thousand per year between 1974 and 1979. Moreover, it is widely accepted that computer- and microprocessor-based automation is about to have a major impact on employment within the types of office occupation which characterize this industry.[6] An unusually frank admission of the prospective job loss from new technologies introduced in the service sector came from the management of British Telecom when it announced in May 1984 a £100 million investment in computerization to 'improve efficiency in dealing with customers and to reduce staffing needs'. British Telecom admitted that a major goal is to use advanced technology to replace labour-intensive activities and it told the trade unions concerned that it could not guarantee that jobs would not be lost.[7] In other words, this type of employment may be expected to follow the pattern of decline already seen in the production industries since the 1960s. Table 4.4 shows that total employment in the goods economy (after the inclusion of goods-related services) plus construction fell by 1.42 million between 1963 and 1979, compared with the decline in direct employment in the Index of Production industries of 1.77 million in the same period. This overall decline in the goods economy, despite the growing contribution of intermediate services, must remove the last vestige of comfort about the future prospects of employment in the goods economy.

The second main conclusion from Table 4.4 is that, by the mid-1960s, employment in consumer services was in decline. Growth of employment in the service economy (excluding goods-related services) is found in practice to have depended primarily on public expenditure. This is abundantly clear from the analysis of actual sources of demand for services. Given this evidence, set alongside the importance of the employment problem, how do those who have attacked the level of public expenditure as a burden on the rest of the economy justify their stance? Their argument is that public expenditure has 'crowded out' other activities and thus hindered market sector growth which, they imply, would have provided alternative employment opportunities. There are grave theoretical weaknesses in the underlying assumption that the expansion of public sector activities is in direct competition with that of the market sector, so that the more society has of one, the less it must have of the other; Keynesian economics certainly involves a rejection of that assumption. However, let us for the moment imagine that this part of the argument were valid, and that a reduction in public spending would permit an equivalent increase in private spending on a pound for pound basis. What would be the predicted effects of such a reallocation of purchasing power on the level of employment? Although this type of question cannot be answered precisely, the methods used in deriving Table 4.4 are again useful in providing some broad indications of the impacts of different kinds of expenditure.

Public and private spending

Public expenditure accounted for 21 per cent of the increase in total domestic expenditure, measured at 1975 prices, between 1968 and 1979 (see Table 4.5, column A); consumers' expenditure and total investment accounted for 69 per cent and 10 per cent of the increase respectively. In assessing the employment impact of the increases in each category of expenditure, the distinction between the goods economy and the service economy is highly instructive. The estimated changes in service employment, derived from Table 4.4 and Appendix 3, are shown in column C. Construction, and hence the change in construction industry employment, is attributable mainly to investment (column D). In column E, a notional allocation of the changes in employment in the goods economy is made, according to the proportions of final output of goods to the domestic economy (column B) which go to each of the three categories of final demand. Even if the absolute decline in goods sector employment were to be arrested and column E were to become zero, consumers' expenditure would still not appear as 'employment creating'. In our view employment in the goods economy is irreversibly in decline and it is quite unrealistic to regard expenditure on goods as employment-generating. If this is accepted, then neither consumers' expenditure nor investment as a whole has provided a net addition to jobs since the mid-1960s, because both kinds of expenditure have tended to be 'goods-oriented'. Although some additional employment has resulted from 'invisible' (services) exports, public expenditure alone has provided an estimated net addition to employment from within the domestic economy.

Trends in the USA

Similar factors underlying employment trends are evident in other industrialized economies, including the USA. Although, in the latter case, population increase tends to disguise the effects, it is possible to isolate a 'population-related' component of employment change from the structural element. Urquhart[8] has calculated what 1979 employment would have been with the 1967 industrial distribution of employment, and compared this with actual 1979 employment. The difference can be interpreted as the relative 'gain' or 'loss' of employment in the respective branches of the economy. Manufacturing 'lost' 5.0 million jobs in this reckoning while 'services' in total 'gained' 6.2 million jobs. The main difference between the experiences of the USA and UK, which has meant a larger growth in market-sector service employment in the USA, is the absolute increase in employment in wholesaling, retailing and catering which can again be related to the effect of urban growth and consequent expansion of the number of trading outlets accompanying population growth. In the industrialized countries of Europe where population growth is at most very slow, this factor in employment expansion is not present. The pattern of change within the service sector otherwise parallels fairly closely the UK experience. Finance, insurance, and real estate 'gained' 1.2 million jobs, while by far the largest relative increase was in public services

Category of demand	A Proportion of total increase in domestic expenditure[a] 1968–79 %	B Estimated share in domestic expenditure on goods[b] %	C Change in service employment[c] (millions)	D _Estimated employment changes_ Change in construction employment[d] (millions)	E Notional change in goods economy employment[e] (millions)	F Combined effect C + D + E (millions)
Consumers' expenditure	69	62	−0.39	−0.05	−0.42	−0.86
Public authorities' current expenditure	21	14	+1.13	−0.02	−0.10	+1.01
Investment[f]	10	24	(+0.02)	−0.22	−0.16	−0.36

a Total expenditure arising within the UK, ie excluding demand for UK exports but including UK demand for imports.

b Based on 1968 and 1979 input-output tables, averaging the two years' results. Excludes the effect on demand of the visible trade balance, ie the difference between imports and exports of goods.

c The first two rows are derived directly from Table 4.4; the estimate for investment-related services is implicit in Appendix 3, Table A3.3 but is subject to a larger percentage error.

d Allocation based on value of construction industry output going to the three categories final demand in 1979.

e Allocations of the decline in goods sector employment, according to the proportions of column B.

f In column B (denoting expenditure on goods), vehicles, plant and machinery only; in column D, construction only.

Table 4.5 _Changes in expenditure and estimated changes in employment by category of final demand, UK 1968–79_

75

(especially health and education) which in total 'gained' 4.6 million. Meanwhile, personal services 'lost' 2.0 million jobs, which adds further confirmation to the thesis that, as far as the consumer economy is concerned, industrialized societies move away from, rather than towards, a 'service' economy. In the 'raw' data for the US economy this trend is hidden by the overall growth in total population and employment, but Urquhart's straightforward arithmetic is sufficient to uncover it once more.

The employment consequences of expenditure patterns

The analysis of expenditure patterns and their employment implications made in this chapter can be summarized as follows. First, with a rising average income level people buy more goods, rather than more services. Second, the production of more goods has ceased to require more people. Thus, rising productivity makes higher wages possible in the production industries, for the smaller number of people they employ, but the spending of these extra wages does not create extra service sector jobs to compensate for the employment opportunities lost in the production industries themselves. The extra spending merely provides the market for the extra goods output and the money circulates preferentially within the goods economy through the pockets of those employed within that sector.

Three conclusions can be drawn from the study of changes in service employment:

1. Consumer spending is not the main source of growth in service employment. Indeed, the number of jobs in providing consumer services in the UK has declined.
2. The growth of employment in business services was already beginning to level off before the present depression. The pace of labour-displacing technical change in these types of activity is accelerating.
3. Public services have been the only employment growth within the 'service economy', if goods-related services are excluded.

The service sector provides no automatic employment growth to offset the decline in industrial employment. The market mechanism does not in itself provide the necessary mechanisms of adjustment, and indeed works in many ways against the growth of services rather than for it. Service employment growth sufficient to compensate for other job loss will not come about of its own accord, but has to be brought about through policies which facilitate such expansion. In general, the declining employment resulting from production industry productivity growth has been offset by new job opportunities only to the extent that the fruits of these productivity increases have been transferred by taxation to the community as a whole. Without the resulting growth in public service employment, the jobs situation in the 1980s would unquestionably have been even worse.

Notes and references

1. Estimates based on consumer expenditure data (National Income and Expenditure bluebooks and *Annual Abstracts of Statistics*), and on Censuses of Distribution.
2. Kutscher, R E and Mark, J A (1983) The service-producing sector; some common perceptions, *US Monthly Labour Review*, 106, 4 April.
3. Excluding furniture and cars, which are separately classified.
4. The rising real cost of services means that an increase in the volume of services, measured at constant prices, contributes more to employment than an equivalent increase in volume of purchases of goods, but the subsequent analysis in Table 4.4 shows that consumer demand cannot be relied upon to generate service sector jobs.
5. This occurred in the UK in 1958, with the introduction of a new Standard Industrial Classification in place of the 1948 Classification.
6. Brand, H and Drake, J (1982) Productivity in banking: computers spur the advance, *US Monthly Labour Review*, 105, 12.
7. *Financial Times*, 5 May 1984.
8. Urquhart, M (1984) The employment shift to services — where did it come from? *US Monthly Labour Review*, pp15–22, 107, 4 April.

CHAPTER 5

Public Expenditure and Community Initiative

As we have shown in Chapter 4, public services were a major source of jobs which, in the UK, prevented a downward trend in total employment until the end of the 1970s. It is also clear that government policies aimed at restricting total public expenditure and cutting back capital spending were an important reason for the greater severity of the 1980s' depression in the UK compared with most other West European countries (see Chapter 1). Moreover, demand-management by governments can still bring significant gains at least in the short run. This is illustrated by the reduction in unemployment in the USA from 9.5 per cent in 1982 to 7.8 per cent in early 1984, achieved by a boost to public spending and an increased budget deficit in the run-up to President Reagan's 1984 election campaign. The evidence clearly points to the major role of public expenditure in influencing numbers of jobs, both in the long and short runs, and any government which took seriously the goal of full employment would be bound to find itself committed to increased levels of spending.

Our purpose in this chapter is not to question this need, but to investigate the extent of the employment gains which might be expected from extra public expenditure, and the obstacles facing governments when attempting to implement a programme of expansion. The role of public expenditure in combating unemployment may be viewed in two ways: first, as a boost to the overall level of activity of the economy and, second, as a direct contribution to jobs through public employment. Considered from the first of these standpoints, the problems are seen as ones of financing government expenditure, its impact on the economy as a whole, and the political feasibility of the tax levels envisaged. From the second standpoint, the issues relate to the needs which require to be met, the kinds of employment which would be involved, and the institutional, social and practical obstacles that are liable to be encountered. Accepting that the public purse should be used as a means of increasing employment, the question is whether the attainable degree of expansion is commensurate with the scale of the contemporary employment problem.

Constraints on Keynesian demand-led growth

In Keynesian terms, the significance of public expenditure is not only the direct public sector employment that it generates, but also that it acts as a lever to raise the level of activity throughout the economy. Although measures, such as interest rates, credit, and investment incentives, can also be used to try to influence the level of market sector spending, these are much less certain to have the desired effect on aggregate expenditure. However, Keynesian economists themselves are compelled to recognize important limitations on the extent to which governments can rely on demand-expansion to try to stimulate growth. A reminder of this is the recent experience of France, where the expenditure policies of the Mitterand government have not been sustained. In the case of the UK, the tendency for additional demand to translate itself into increased import demand has always featured prominently in discussions of demand-management. Some would seek to counter this with import controls,[1] but such controls in themselves do not automatically overcome the underlying problem of a failure of domestic production to rise at the 'desired' rate. Inflationary pressures may result from attempts to generate rapid demand-led expansion, and this has been the major plank in the monetarist attack on Keynesian policy prescriptions. While there is little justification for the view that public expenditure *as such* is inflationary, the use of budgetary policies to stimulate aggregate demand through deficit spending and increased public sector borrowing remains open to this charge. In our view, an acceptance of some inflationary pressure as the price of economic expansion is justified. However, even the most fervent 'demand side' economists are bound to acknowledge that their policies will sooner or later run into 'supply side' constraints, and these ultimately govern how much expansion is possible.

The scope for demand-expansion in the short run is largely dependent on assessments of the degree of 'excess capacity'. There is a strong temptation to assume that, in the midst of a depression in which output has contracted by some 15 to 20 per cent, there must exist massive industrial capacity which is simply waiting to be brought back into use following a boost to demand. This was

79

indeed the impression that Keynes himself conveyed in discussing the slump of the 1930s. The extent to which the excess capacity assumption holds in the 1980s is highly questionable. Much of the plant has been physically scrapped, factories closed that will never reopen, and the techniques previously used consigned to the past. In this environment of exceptionally rapid technological change, the past cannot be recreated. In general, new output will have to come from plant using new techniques rather than from their use of old underutilized capacity.

It is arguable that in some countries, such as the UK, much of the loss of capacity was unnecessary. A larger steel industry, a larger car industry and a motorcycle industry could in principle have been sustained. However, the re-creation of lost capacity in these branches of industry now seems largely unrealistic. The focus of technological activity has moved on, and attempts to relive the past would come into conflict with the social and institutional change associated with the incoming technologies. Expansion is therefore subject to all the time-lags inherent in the investment process, with a considerable gestation period between plans on paper and actual commissioning of plant. While there may be some scope in the short run for 'taking up slack' in the economy, which could mean a brief period of exceptionally rapid growth, such growth rates are necessarily short-lived. The 'excess capacity' assumption has relatively little mileage when set in the context of the need for sustained growth of employment over a period of five to ten years. Without excess capacity, Keynesian economic policies in themselves contain no magic formula for accelerating the overall rate of economic growth.

The importance of the public sector

The significance of public expenditure within a long-run strategy for increasing employment, therefore, needs to be seen primarily in terms of the jobs created directly within the public sector, or directly associated with it. A high proportion of current public expenditure is direct outlays on wages and salaries, implying that an increase in this expenditure will lead to a predictable increase in the number of jobs. This could be contrasted with a situation where, for example, extra investment by a firm might be spent largely on imported equipment, which might in turn facilitate a reduction in the work-force required on the production line. An emphasis on public expenditure in generating employment has not, however, gone unchallenged by monetarists, who have argued that there is also an unsatisfied demand for private services and that these, not public services, should expand. It is suggested that if only governments would 'get off the backs of the people' then jobs would be generated through the unleashing of the energy and initiatives of the people. The implication of this is that a reduction of public expenditure would be compensated by an increase in private expenditure. However, the evidence clearly shows the reverse: a reduction in public expenditure tends to initiate or reinforce a downturn in total economic activity, with private investment also falling. For example, in the UK, the index of public sector housing construction fell from 78.6 to 33.0 between 1979 and 1982. This was not compensated by an increase in private sector activity; on the contrary, the index of private housing construction also fell, from 105.4 to 83.0.[2] Over a much longer period (1968–79) prior to the present depression, we found no evidence from the analysis of jobs provided by industry and marketed services (see Chapters 3 and 4) that the private sector could be viewed simply as an alternative to the public sector as a source of employment. The indicators derived in Chapter 4 tended to confirm the view that public expenditure is a more certain source of employment growth than is market sector spending. If this is so, then the stimulus to total demand emphasized by Keynesian economics is reinforced by the greater employment-generating effects of each £1 million spent. The issue then is not whether public expenditure is capable of providing a net addition to jobs, but how large this increase might be in relation to the existing scale of unemployment.

It is useful to approach this question from the standpoint of the needs that require to be tackled and the kind of jobs involved. These needs may be considered under two categories:

1. *Provision of infrastructure:*
   Including — building, rehabilitation and insulation of housing
   — building, extension and maintenance of hospitals, schools, colleges and universities
   — construction and improvement of roads, bridges and railways
   — removal of industrial dereliction
   — rehabilitation of inner urban areas
   — maintenance and replacement of sewers and water mains.

2. *Public services:*

Including — support in the home for the elderly, sick and disabled through the provision of more home-helps
— social provision for groups such as pre-school age children and the elderly
— staff in the health service
— staff in primary and secondary schools
— staff in further and higher education.

Provision of infrastructure

In the UK, public investment fell by 38 per cent between 1979 and 1982, and construction industry employment in 1983 was 28 per cent (390 thousand employees) lower than its peak level of the 1970s.[3] Maintenance work, as well as new building, has been neglected. The need for a major programme of work on infrastructure is recognized not only in the political programmes of the Labour Party and the Social Democratic Party (SDP)/Liberal Alliance, but also in a report by the government's National Economic Development Office (NEDO).[4] The report finds that 'present systems and levels of resource allocation have led to failures to maintain the fabric of buildings and structures, to remedy structure faults, to renew worn out components and to remove obsolescent features', so that in many instances 'the quality of services provided has fallen below statutory or minimum acceptable standards'. The report points to local roads which are deteriorating to a level where they are in danger of requiring complete renewal, and several county surveyors reported that expenditure of around two to three times the current annual maintenance provision was needed to prevent further deterioration. Serious shortfalls in the maintenance of school buildings are also reported, in some cases up to 40 per cent. The NEDO report places greater emphasis on the need for a major programme of repairs and maintenance, including an estimated £2 billion on hospitals alone. Spread over five years, we estimate that this could represent employment of about 40,000 workers for that period. Other essential facilities identified as requiring investment are the water and sewage systems. Estimates of water leakage range from 20 per cent to 40 per cent of the total supply; internal corrosion is resulting in some areas in water of unacceptable quality; and, without the necessary remedial action, it is estimated that half the active length of iron pipe mains could fail in a period of 20 years. In the case of sewers,

14 per cent of the system is more than 80 years old and there are many authorities reporting a backlog of renewal work — resulting in an estimated 5000 failures every year (including 3500 collapses). The total renewal cost of the whole system was estimated at £19 billion at 1975 prices (over £50 billion at 1984–85 prices),[5] and replacement of even a modest fraction would involve several billion pounds of investment and tens of thousands of jobs.

Neglect of housing needs has left another major area awaiting new investment. UK public sector housing building has collapsed, from 180 thousand starts per annum in 1976 to 52 thousand in 1983.[6] Even the funds provided from the sale of public sector housing have not been available for feeding back into building new housing stock. At least as important as new construction is the need for remedial work on existing dwellings. The Building Research Establishment has estimated that some two and a half million dwellings in the UK are affected by dampness.[7] The cost of remedial work varies widely, with most cases in the range of £500 to £5000. Taking a notional figure of £2000 per dwelling, a comprehensive programme to tackle the dampness problem would probably exceed £5 billion, which (again spread over five years) could be equivalent to a further 100 thousand jobs.

A programme of public investment, maintenance and rehabilitation, has the important advantage that the employment can be provided relatively rapidly, and a high proportion of the financial outlay would go directly on employing labour. The work is moreover of a kind which can provide opportunities for recruiting unskilled or semi-skilled labour, as well as drawing back into employment those building trades which are always particularly hard-hit in a depression. Although the existing capacity and availability of skills in the building and civil engineering industries might begin to impose some constraints once a major programme was under way, substantial room for expansion is indicated by the gap between current and former levels of activity.

Constraints on public works programmes

More serious limitations on the rate at which public authorities are able to initiate new work relate to the planning procedures which must be observed, and the possibility of public antagonism to certain major public works. Objections on social and environmental grounds to schemes such as urban motorways and airport expansion lead to delays in implementation, even where the proposals finally go ahead, and may result in greater caution in subsequent plans. Even with less controversial needs such as house-building, the scale of new programmes is likely to be moderated by awareness of the major social problems that have arisen from past large-scale schemes carried out unduly quickly. If developments are to be more carefully tailored to specific situations, with greater sensitivity to local needs, longer gestation periods are inevitably involved. Moreover, with an almost stationary population, the requirement is no longer for quantity but quality, combined with a greater emphasis on upgrading the existing housing stock.

Despite these qualifications, a substantial public works programme could certainly be carried out which would bring significant numbers of new jobs. Tackling the two enormous problems of dampness in housing and the replacement of decaying nineteenth-century sewers could alone make up a substantial fraction of the construction industry jobs lost since 1979. Combined with an adequate maintenance programme on the existing stock of buildings, roads and other infrastructure, plus new public sector building, the result could be a demand for construction work which would return employment in that industry to the levels of the early 1970s. If further increases in expenditure to remove urban dereliction, undertake general environmental improvements, and renovate buildings, were envisaged, this figure might conceivably be increased to 500 thousand — which would represent an increase of more than 50 per cent over present employment levels in the construction industry and match the peak levels of the 1960s. Given reasonable assurances of a long-term programme of government investment, the building and civil engineering industries would expand to meet the demand, and training schemes could be established to ensure that the skilled work-force was adequate. In this sense, such a programme can be regarded as feasible — provided there is a preparedness on the part of society as a whole to see a government finance the necessary expenditure.

Public services

The list of unfulfilled needs for public services is similarly extensive. However, the formulation of targets for future staffing depends not only on the level of provision which is sought, but also on demographic factors influencing needs. In Chapter 4, it was noted that between 1963 and 1979 in the UK, employment in medical services and education together increased by about 1½ million. In the case of education, an important factor underlying

Population Group	1963	1968	Populations (millions) 1974	1979	1983	1993 projection[a]
School	5–15	8.84	9.16	10.03	9.64	8.49	7.98
Tertiary education	16–20[b]	4.21[c]	4.05	3.98	4.48	4.78	3.49
'Working age'	16–64	34.06	34.29	34.31	34.89	35.89	36.01
Over 65		6.32	6.95	7.78	8.31	8.42	8.99
Total population		53.76	55.16	56.23	56.22	56.38	57.17

a Based on Government Actuaries Projection, mid-1981, Series PP2 No. 12.
b Also included in total for 'working age'.
c Estimate.

Table 5.1 UK population by age groups, 1963–1993

Source: *Annual Abstracts of Statistics.*

this expansion was the increase in the number of those of school and college age (see Table 5.1). However, in recent years the numbers entering school have declined, and this will continue to work through secondary schools during the next decade.

The need arising from demographic factors is therefore not increasing, and extrapolation of the earlier rate of increase in employment in education would in this sense be unwarranted. Meanwhile, those who went through their schooling during the growth phase are now entering the population of working age, so that the balance between the need for educational jobs and job seekers has changed from both ends. The one area where there is a manifestly unfulfilled need is in pre-school facilities where at present there is provision for only about 30 thousand children in local authority nursery schools.[8] The provision of places for one million children of pre-school age at, say, ten children per supervisor could provide 100 thousand part-time jobs. If this were combined with some reduction in the pupil-teacher ratios and increased support staff in schools, the projected total addition to employment might become 150 thousand, with a possible further addition numbered in a few tens of thousands in tertiary education.

For other social services, needs are far more diverse and much less readily expressed in staffing ratios. In important areas such as care of the elderly, whose numbers are increasing, much could be achieved with relatively modest total additions to local authority staffing. A doubling of present home-help provision, which is estimated at 49 thousand full-time equivalents,[9] could (if undertaken on a less than full-time basis, as frequently applies) contribute to a general expansion of social service provision involving up to 100 thousand more staff. Additional needs in the health service would also add some tens of thousands of jobs.

Problems of public service employment
In advocating the revitalization of public service employment it is necessary to remain critically aware of the employment limitations of this policy. The skill requirements of the social and educational jobs involved often do not match with those available among the unemployed. In relieving unemployment it is not so helpful to provide a post for a school teacher who will enter into employment direct from being a non-employed housewife rather than, say, two posts for school-leaver trainees in the public parks and gardens department. Central government would need guidelines aimed at ensuring that the expansion of public service employment

is used to maximize employment opportunities for the two groups who are suffering most — young people and the unskilled. There are in practice many rigidities within organizations, some resulting from vested interests within established career structures, and unless these can be counter-balanced by policies the ability to concentrate new posts at the lower end of earnings scales will be limited. Possible chains of events can be foreseen clearly. Industrial development is seen by governments as requiring more engineers and applied scientists, and there is already pressure to expand the numbers graduating in these subjects from universities and colleges. Expansion would lead to demands from the higher education institutions for more staff of all grades for posts which are difficult to fill at the requisite ability and knowledge levels. This in turn leads, during the expansion phase, to demands for increases in salaries and for the allocation of posts at higher grades and, if this occurs, it leads on automatically to the upgrading of pay for all comparable posts within the education system: in social sciences, arts and humanities as well as in science and technology.

This arises simply because teaching staff in any given sector of the UK educational system, whether teaching in the shortage area or not, are generally paid on the same scales. A similar chain of events can be seen to be relevant to the Health Service. The creation of more consultant posts is very expensive and there is, in general, a plentiful supply of qualified applicants among senior doctors immediately below consultant level. The appointment of one more consultant may have the net effect of one more junior doctor being employed at the end of the line, and everyone in between being awarded a pay-rise on promotion. The conflict and dilemmas are similar to those in education. Without more consultants there is a limit to certain types of expansion; and yet one consultant post could pay for three or four posts for nurses or porters.

A further limitation is the inability of conventional kinds of public expenditure (whether on infrastructure or public services) to meet the needs of areas whose high unemployment has arisen from the destruction of the old base of manufacturing employment. This is an especially difficult problem as it is usually associated with low levels of skill and training, as is the case in the community which we describe in Chapter 7. Recognition of this has led to increasing efforts to develop new initiatives, often with the assistance of public funds, as described in Chapter 2.

Direct community initiatives

One encouraging reaction to the return of large-scale, long-term unemployment has been the establishment of organizations not only to disseminate information but also to search out and develop opportunities to create new businesses. Thus we find the European Centre for Work and Society, Maastricht, and the Unemployment Unit, London, which are concerned to raise the awareness of the problems and opportunities. Others, such as the Centre for Employment Initiatives, London, the Community Employment Initiatives Unit (set up by the Western Australian Government), radical groups, religious groups, worker co-operatives, further and higher education and business organizations, are all involved in direct action including the creation of businesses.[10,11] Worker co-operatives in the UK are reported to have grown from approximately 20 in the early 1970s to 500 in 1982, and five of these are described in detail in case studies published by the Cooperatives Research Unit of the Open University.[12] In the UK, much financial support has come from the government and has been channelled through the Manpower Services Commission (see Chapter 2), but much of the work generated has been of a temporary project nature. The Community Programme has provided up to one year of temporary work for unemployed people on any tasks having a clear community benefit; examples are countryside maintenance, including footpath and bridleway clearance, draining, fencing and tree planting, and building restoration and conservation. A specific instance is the conversion of a former weaving mill for use as premises for small businesses.[13] The organizing bodies for these projects include public and private organizations which are, in certain instances, set up specifically to promote the economic development of a community.

The Enterprise and Venture Trusts which have been set up in many cities throughout the UK are concerned both with the establishment of new small business ventures and with assisting existing ones. Like other community ventures they depend heavily on a sense of local identity, as well as a belief in an 'entrepreneurial culture'[14] and responsibility, so that existing businesses feel the need to establish an enterprise trust and support it with both money and time. Other support comes from local authorities and government agencies. In their first year of operation new businesses can often take advantage of the government's Enterprise Allowance scheme and, although such schemes are generally only in their infancy, it seems likely that the unsuccessful start-ups will be balanced by additional employees taken on by those businesses which do survive. The enterprise trusts also assist with the provision of training and the establishment of 'Small Business Clubs', through which mutual assistance to new and existing businesses can be developed. There are parallel moves associated with higher education through Graduate Enterprise[15] which gives support to selected graduates and diplomates in the establishment of new businesses — again, generally, involving the Manpower Services Commission's Enterprise Allowance scheme. Such activity has led on to the concept of 'enterprise networks' linking education, business, local initiatives, public agencies, local authorities, sources of funding, and research and development facilities.[16]

Although the role of public expenditure in their activities is crucial, and the source of initiative may be within a public body — a development agency or university — it is equally likely to come from private businesses or a community organization such as the Church. Although there may be umbrella organizations supporting and cajoling the drive behind the activity, it is located at a distance from central government. Thus this upsurge of enterprise groups has the characteristics of a 'movement', a feature which is nowhere better seen than in the concept of the community business. Community business is not about making profits; it is about creating jobs which will benefit the community in which it operates. The people who organize it do not do so for gain (except in so far as they are themselves paid a wage or bonus) and any profits are intended to be used either to create more jobs, or for the welfare of the local community. A community business will be incorporated so that it has limited liability in the same way as most private firms, and thus operates within the normal private enterprise framework. But instead of being owned by shareholders, who would usually have no other connection with the company, it is owned and controlled by the local community.[17]

Examples of community businesses which have been attempted are: printing and packaging, wood stripping, stone cleaning, community farms, local enterprise workshops, home production, market gardening, hairdressing agencies, community launderettes, and house insulation. In practice these projects seem to have all depended on government subsidy — one programme which planned to establish 20 community businesses over six years estimated costs at almost £11 million. It was hoped to provide a total of 1000 jobs at the end of the sixth year, and a total of 4250 man-years of work, ie an average subsidy of about £2500 per year of employment. Alternatively the cost can be viewed as an investment of £11,000 per job — a much lower cost per job than most new investments (eg microelectronics as described in Chapter 3). However, after the clawback of income tax and National Insurance contributions, the net cost to public expenditure would be substantially lower — perhaps no more than the cost of the benefits which would otherwise have been paid out.[18] Even if there was a net cost to government this is likely to be small; and a number of significant advantages would accrue in addition to the permanent jobs which are expected. There can be no doubt that such efforts raise the morale of the local community, and that the goods made and services provided are of value to those who purchase them.

There seem to be three problems:

1. If such schemes provide subsidized competition for existing businesses in or around the community, then they will be opposed as being unfair, and indeed will be in danger of destroying one job to create another. For such schemes to be fully effective there is a need for a shift in consumption patterns towards services, eg more house painting and hairdressing but a lower rate of replacement of motorcycles and cars.
2. The scale of unemployment is enormous in comparison with the number of jobs which could be created through community businesses or local enterprise trusts in the next few years.
3. In areas of greatest need there is a paucity of entrepreneurial drive and managerial competence. It is in such areas that the establishment of community businesses could play a vital role in developing the talents of social groups who have not previously played a significant role in commercial activity. It has been traditional for women and low-income groups to accept employee roles and to look no further. Community businesses provide co-operative environments in which undeveloped talents can grow in mutual support, provided steps are taken deliberately to encourage, train and support selected individuals from these communities. Indeed, community business is a way of shifting the centre of dynamic activity into seriously affected communities; it stands as a model of what can be done through co-operation, and it encourages others to do more: either in a community business or by starting their own business. What is needed is a source of dynamism in areas selected as suitable for community business — perhaps every university and college should be expected to collaborate with a neighbouring community to establish new business ventures.

How many jobs?

Major increases in expenditure on public works, social services and community enterprise raise problems of public acceptability. Even if these can be overcome, the number of jobs generated is likely to be modest in comparison with present levels of unemployment. Table 5.2 shows the employment from an 'intermediate' programme of public expenditure in the UK, as proposed by the SDP/Liberal Alliance. They would expect to create about 650 thousand jobs from additional public expenditure rising to £2.3 billion per annum in 1986 (at 1984 prices).[19]

		Additional employment (1986) thousands
Community programme		370
Personal social services		50*
Public works	— house building	110
	— roads and sewers	40
Small business encouragement Loan guarantee scheme		25
Broadening of enterprise allowance scheme		42
Revised office and services industrial grant scheme		20
Total additional employment		657

* Part-time

Table 5.2 *Additional employment from Alliance programme of public expenditure*

Source: *The Social Democrat*, 19 October 1984.

Only 287 thousand of these would be 'permanent jobs'; 370 thousand would be temporary places at a cost of only £2600 each,[20] and thus are more akin to the measures which we regard as masking the true levels of job needs. On our analysis they are a temporary palliative and not a long-term solution. Nevertheless, in March 1985 the Conservative government stated its intention to increase the present 130 thousand temporary places on employment creation schemes to 230 thousand by 1986–87.[21]

The programme of public expenditure produced by the British Labour Party is more extensive and is intended to be used to stimulate activity and employment in the economy as a whole, on Keynesian lines. An expenditure plan was tested against the Treasury's macroeconomic model in 1982, which (revalued at 1984 prices) would involve an increase in the level of annual public expenditure of £20 billion by the fifth year of the plan.[22] This would represent an increase of at least 15 per cent in the total level of public spending.[23] The projected total increase in employment in the economy as a whole, which would be assisted by the increase in public spending, is about half a million jobs per year; but even this rate of increase in expenditure and job generation

	Basic Projection		Maximum Programme	
	Description	Additional employment millions	Description	Additional employment millions
Infrastructure	Construction industry returns to capacity working	0.30	Expansion of construction capacity; additional training programme	0.50
Education	Nursery provision; higher pupil/teacher ratios	0.15	Includes expansion of higher education	0.20
Health, social services and other public services	More home-helps;[a] some general expansion in health and other services	0.13	More expansion in hospitals etc	0.18
General administration	Eg staff in finance departments	0.02		0.02
Total		0.60		0.90

a Including part-time jobs.

Table 5.3 Summary of employment possibilities from meeting needs for infrastructure investments and public services

would, it is conceded, still leave a level of unemployment of one million at the end of five years. This is a rate of unemployment which, only a few years ago, the entire Labour movement in Britain would have considered totally unacceptable; and could certainly not have been put forward as the intended outcome of a Labour government's programme. Moreover, the estimates themselves may be regarded as optimistic in their assessment of the employment which would result from growth, and this tends to be confirmed by the failure of unemployment to decrease since 1982 despite the increase in output which has occurred (see Chapter 2). This is a measure of just how remote are the prospects for full employment, if sole reliance continues to be placed on the 'spending creates jobs' approach. Other economic analysts sympathetic to the aims expressed in the Labour Party's programme have put even higher figures on the costs of achieving full employment by this route. Desai, reviewing three sets of projections (including the one described above), concluded that 'the results make terribly depressing reading'.[24] His own arithmetic, which was heavily oriented towards regeneration of industrial employment at an average of £20,000 expenditure per job created, indicated an annual public investment programme of £10 billion (£50 billion over five years) and a rate of growth of GDP of 6½ per cent per annum as the 'requirements' for an expansion of half a million jobs per year. Manifestly, to generate enough jobs to wipe out present unemployment through extra public spending alone would require a radical departure from historically precedented proportions of GDP devoted to public expenditure. Such a steep increase in public expenditure could only come about through an equally radical shift in public attitudes. Even then, it appears the unemployment problem would be far from solved.

In the projected requirements for infrastructure investments and for public services given earlier in this chapter, we deliberately set aside the question of achieving acceptance of the increases in public expenditure involved and based the calculations on perceptions of need. The possibilities which we have outlined certainly lie at the upper end of the range of proposals which political groups or parties are prepared to put forward. The direct additions to employment are summarized in Table 5.3 and amount to less than one million in total (the range being 0.6 to 0.9 million). In the assessment of prospects given in Chapter 9, a median figure of 0.75 million is adopted. Thus, even with relatively high rates of increase in levels of provision, the extra employment appears relatively modest beside the four million or more jobs needed to overcome unemployment.

Notes and references

1. The Cambridge Economic Policy Group, directed by Wynne Godley, was a strong advocate of import controls in the UK in the late 1970s and early 1980s; see, for example, *Cambridge Economic Policy Review*, 6.1, Chapters 1 and 2.
2. Department of the Environment, Housing and Construction Statistics, September 1982.
3. National Income and Expenditure, 1985, and *Annual Abstracts of Statistics*.
4. National Economic Development Office, Investment in the Public Sector Built Infrastructure, *NEDC Papers*, 1985.
5. National Water Council, Sewers and Water Mains — A National Assessment, Department of the Environment, Standing Technical Committee Report No 4, 1977.
6. *CSO, Social Trends*, Vol 15, 1985, p131.
7. Evidence to Select Affairs Committee (1983/84) *Dampness in Housing*, II, House of Commons papers 206–II, HMSO, pp1–2.
8. Department of Health and Social Security, Health and Personal Social Services Statistics for England, 1982, p103.
9. Ibid., p58.
10. A list of UK 'organizations that might be useful to groups working with unemployed people of any age' published by the British Unemployment Resource Network, 318 Summer Lane, Birmingham B19 3RL, includes 72 entries ranging from Adult Literacy and Basic Skills Units to the Youth Enterprise Scheme. The same publication, *Action*, lists approximately 1000 local projects and support activities throughout the UK.
11. For a review of initiatives in OECD countries, see *Community Business Ventures and Job Creation*, OECD, Paris, 1984.
12. Cornforth, Chris and Stott, Martin *A Cooperative Approach to Local Economic Development*, Cooperatives Research Unit, The Open University.
13. Pennine Heritage, Annual Report, 1983, The Birchcliffe Centre, Hebden Bridge, Halifax, HX7 8DG.
14. *Year One*, Leith Enterprise Trust, 1985.
15. The first was established by the Scottish Enterprise Foundation, University of Stirling, 1983.
16. Scottish Enterprise Foundation, Scottish Business School, Stirling/University Division.
17. The definition given by the Local Enterprise Advisory Project, Paisley College of Technology, is:

    'The community business brings together social and economic objectives. It is run by a group of people not seeking personal financial gain. The return on investment it seeks is measured in jobs created for local people rather than surplus profit. It sets out to run business activities in the interests of and for the benefit of local residents, but at the same time it endeavours to operate profitably (that is without making a loss) and efficiently.

    'It is possible to list a number of key characteristics of the typical community business:

(a)   the primary objective is to create jobs for local people;

(b)   the company is owned by the local community (or by a community organization on behalf of and in trust for local people) and through this structure control of the company is vested in the community;

(c)   profits are not distributed to individual members (except by way of wages or bonuses for workers) nor are they distributed to other external organizations, instead they are retained for use either within the company (to create more jobs) or within the local community (for welfare or other uses);

(d)   community business will be incorporated and so have limited liability and may well be granted charitable status;

(e)   they may well undertake a range of different trading and service activities as a multi-purpose enterprise.'

18. The £11 million cost was estimated using 1982 rates. The supplementary benefit rates were £967 pa for a single person living at home and £1963 pa for a couple. (The long-term rates were rather higher.) If half the jobs created went to married men and half to young persons the saving in benefit payments would have been £6,226,250 as total wages and salaries and the total NI contribution payment about £1.5 million. Thus the cost, without the revenue from income tax, would be reduced from £11 million to some £3.25 million, or less than £1000 for each year of employment so created.

19. An analysis of the Alliance budget proposals based on a simulation by the London Business School in comparison with the monetarist proposals of Professor Patrick Minford, University of Liverpool, is given in the *Financial Times*, 4 March 1985.

20. The inclusion of this programme brings the average 'cost per job' in the Alliance Plan to below £4000; whereas the figure for permanent jobs is much higher. To achieve a greater reduction in unemployment with more permanent jobs could, therefore, involve a more than proportional increase in the total budgeted.

21. Department of Employment (1985) *Employment: The Challenge for the Nation*, p22, Cmnd 9474, HMSO, March.

22. 'The Party's programme for recovery', *Labour Weekly*, 26 November 1982.

23. Includes transfer payments and capital expenditure in addition to current expenditure on goods and services.

24. Desai, M (1983) Economic alternatives for Labour, in Griffith J (Ed) *Socialism in a Cold Climate*, Unwin Paperbacks, London.

CHAPTER 6

Economic Planning

Awareness of the limitations of Keynesian demand-management has led on the Left to a renewed emphasis on economic planning as an essential condition for overcoming the problems now faced by the industrially advanced capitalist countries, including unemployment. The fundamental debate about ownership of the means of production is also related to this; socialists see attempts at economic planning as inevitably limited in their effectiveness unless there is also an extension of public ownership. Indeed, relationships between technological change and employment are frequently considered to be secondary to the question of ownership. The implicit assumption is that, if the use of resources is planned in order to meet the community's needs, new technology would scarcely pose any problems as far as jobs are concerned; full employment could be assured through planning. Our purpose in this chapter is to show that the impact of contemporary technological change cannot be ignored by those who believe in planning, any more than it can be ignored by those who assert the efficacy of the market mechanism.

Perceptions of planning

Planning is an ongoing process within any large organization,[1] and in this sense the supposed dichotomy between 'the market' and 'planning' is unreal.[2] Some economists have indeed envisaged a 'managed capitalism' of privately owned firms, operating within a framework of state planning.[3] It is generally recognized that there are major economic and social objectives which remain outside the scope of corporate planning, unless government policies can be brought to bear upon them. The attempts at regional economic planning in the UK since World War II, which have relied on a range of incentives to firms, could be seen as a reflection of this consensus. However, the limitations to this approach have also been frequently pointed out, and socialist economists

96

have tended to assume that economic planning would require the largest industrial and commercial enterprises to be run as public corporations, on the lines of British Rail or British Airways. At the same time the need for a multiplicity of forms of social owner-ship, ranging from small worker co-operatives, through local authority ventures, up to nationalized industries has been emphasiz-ed in other discussions of the economics of socialism.[4] Related to this question of ownership is the issue of how to implement plans, and in particular what role the 'guided' market may have in the planning process. This is a vigorously debated issue within the existing centrally planned economies of the Soviet Union and Eastern Europe, which have had such an important influence on perceptions of economic planning in the West. The intention in this chapter is not to attempt to review the vast field of economic planning, but to indicate that there are difficulties relating to future employment which arise under any system, whatever weight is attached to central planning.

Planning agreements

Since the late 1970s, considerable debate has taken place within the British Labour Party and trade unions over what is usually called the 'Alternative Economic Strategy'. The strategy is seen as 'alternative' not only to the version of monetarism pursued since 1979, but also to the approaches previously adopted by earlier Labour governments. The form of planning that is currently en-visaged within the Labour Party rests primarily on securing plan-ning agreements (voluntary or statutory) with the major industrial and commercial companies. The thinking is summed up by Devine:

> 'The principal concept to have emerged so far is that of the planning agree-ment, a tripartite agreement to be negotiated between the government and the management and unions of each major public and private enterprise. The planning agreement system is intended to ensure that the strategic decisions of enterprises are both in conformity with overall national economic priorities and in the interests of the enterprise's workers.'[5]

What is it that is to be planned, and how does this relate to the employment problem? In Devine's discussion, there is an implicit assumption that planning is about the 'allocation of scarce resources'. The need for overall national priorities is emphasiz-ed: *'once full employment is achieved* [our emphasis] choices have to be made between the different uses to which available resources can be put'. There has in fact been little concrete discussion about how planning can be used to ensure full employment, or even to achieve modest increases in employment.

Basically, the intention is to achieve a measure of control over the level and direction of *investment*. The reasons for wanting to bring major investment within a framework of economic planning relate partly to priorities between major areas of the economy, including the geographical spread of new developments. They also embrace the whole problem of maintaining the level of overall investment and aggregate demand in the economy, to avoid slumps in investment and outflows of funds abroad. It is accepted that this type of central planning would necessarily be broad-brush, and not concerned with detail:

> 'as to the scope or range of planning at the centre, it is evident that this cannot cover more than a minute proportion of decisions concerning the economy. Nor would it be desirable to do so . . . Minor investment and current ouput decisions would be taken directly by enterprises and would be unlikely to require government involvement.'

The concern is with the overall direction of development of the economy — with the major structural changes requiring major investment: 'Such major investment needs to be initiated, or at least approved, by the government to try to achieve consistency and conformity with national objectives.'[6]

It can be argued that if an economy were able to regulate better the flow of investment, to avoid major fluctuations, it would not face the same sudden upsurges of unemployment that occur under capitalism at the onset of depression. But this does not justify the assumption that planning of the level of investment would in itself provide the means of ensuring full employment, given an underlying rising trend of unemployment as discussed in Chapter 1. Indeed, there are the counter arguments that by maintaining investment in old technologies, it would drive attention away from the need to shift to new technologies, as described in Chapters 8 and 9, and thus lead to even greater economic difficulties in the future. In the production industries and in a growing number of service activities, investment is as significant for its ability to *reduce* labour requirements, as for its positive effects in creating new ventures. It is shown in Appendix 2 that the balance between the output-generating and employment-reducing effects of investment has been shifting in manufacturing. This is manifested in the decline in number of industrial jobs in industrialized countries (see Chapter 3), and it is in the manufacturing sector that planning agreements are mainly envisaged. Although the tripartite nature of these agreements is intended to lead to a much greater degree of accountability to the workers involved at plant level, and some specific job losses might be prevented if this were achieved, it is not obvious how new employment would be generated by democratization at the workplace. If a reversal of the decline in manufacturing employment implied retention of more labour-intensive techniques, this would undoubtedly run counter to other objectives of planning, and has never been put forward as a part of the Alternative Economic Strategy. Planning agreements would therefore be unlikely to alter underlying unemployment trends in industry, as distinct from levelling out investment fluctuations, unless they were able to influence the type of investment undertaken, including the choice of technologies.

The planning of technological innovation

Far from planning being used to slow down the rate of technological change, the economic exploitation of technology, by transforming research and invention into technological innovation, is generally accepted as an objective of economic planning. Thus, although the UK Conservative government has ended the industrial acquisition activities of the National Enterprise Board, it has combined it with the National Research Development Corporation to form the British Technology Group (BTG). The BTG actively sponsors research, particularly in universities and colleges, and gives financial support to ensure the industrial application of any suitable development. Again the Conservative government's policy of putting microcomputers into all secondary schools was an example of purchasing policy being used to foster the development of a particular company — in this case Acorn Computers with the BBC Model B. Such activities are widespread: MITI and the Fifth generation Computer (Japan); the Alvey Committee (the UK's response to the Japanese Fifth generation); ESPRIT (the EEC's information technology initiative) and the report to the President of France, *Informatisation de la société*. The message is clear: 'If France does not respond effectively to the serious new challenges she faces, her internal tensions will deprive her of the ability to control her fate';[7] or 'the future prosperity of Japanese society requires technical progress';[8] or, more prosaically, 'The rate of technological innovation in United Kingdom industry will need to increase if its products and manufacturing processes are to match those of [our] major competitors. This is the necessary condition of our future survival as a trading nation.'[9] The general strategy is to back specific types of activity which are seen as particularly promising — microelectronics, information technology and biotechnology are common examples. None of this is done specifically to create employment. Where a concern with employment is expressed, it consists of the threat that the situation will become even worse if nothing is done, rather than a promise of a net increase in the number of jobs: 'We have not been able to quantify the likely effects of technological changes on overall employment levels . . . But more unemployment results from loss of market share following a failure to innovate than from introduction of new technology.'[10] It is only by invoking the vagueness of non-specific 'economic growth' that such policies are usually projected as job-creating. We will return to this central issue in Chapters 8 and 9, where the relationships between technology, growth and employment are examined.

Regional planning

The limitations of relying on investment as a means of implementing employment policies is illustrated by the actual experience with regional policies in the UK, where the professed aims of these policies have been concerned with employment. The objectives have been to redress the marked imbalances in employment opportunities between regions, and to tackle the high levels of unemployment which persisted even when national unemployment rates were comparatively low. The arguments in support of regional policies have not been concerned solely with issues of economic justice, but also with stemming the 'anti-Whitehall' feelings in areas remote from London. There was moreover a powerful case during the 1950s and 1960s that regional imbalance meant an inefficient use of resources, resulting in constraints on the overall rate of national economic growth. It was agreed that labour scarcities in certain regions (particularly south-east England and, in the 1950s and 1960s, the West Midlands) led to inflationary pressures which required a brake to be put on the economy. Meanwhile, labour and other resources continued to be underutilized elsewhere. It was argued that a more even pattern of development across regions would ease the 'bottlenecks' which constrained national economic growth, and thus allow more expansionist macroeconomic policies to be pursued.[11]

While the aims have been employment-related, the means have

been almost entirely investment-related. The form of investment incentive has varied through the several decades in which regional policies have operated, with the emphasis being sometimes on tax relief, and at other times on direct investment grants. The 'control' element, which took the form of industrial development certificates, was intended to limit growth in the 'labour-scarce' regions and redirect investment elsewhere, and has now more or less disappeared. But the philosophy running through all the efforts at regional economic planning was always the same: jobs depended on growth, growth depended on investment, and the way to reduce unemployment in a region was therefore to try to induce more investment by some combination of 'sticks' and 'carrots'.

The assumption that higher investment would provide the solution to employment problems has become less and less tenable. There has been a growing awareness among those concerned with urban and regional planning that the approach of providing investment incentives to manufacturing is now extremely inadequate as a tool of employment policy, and is certainly not commensurate with the scale of the unemployment problem in the areas most in need of assistance. Stuart Holland ends a review of UK regional planning with the conclusion: 'The longer term trend to declining manufacturing employment will certainly raise unemployment in the regions, unless new instruments are developed which will transform regional policy as part of a wider economic and social transformation of society.'[12] The magnitude of the regional problem in the UK is illustrated in Table 6.1. In the USA in 1979, even before the depression of the early 1980s, the unemployment rates by area ranged from less than 1 per cent to as high as 40 per cent.[13] National figures mask a huge variation in unemployment rates, and combining male and female rates also understates the true extent of the problem, since many women out of work are not included in the unemployment register. While the overall rate for Hartlepool, for example, is given in Table 6.1 as 23.9 per cent the rate for men alone was 30 per cent. This is despite a significant influx of new industry, and a *Financial Times*'s writer observed how Hartlepool demonstrates the difficulty of reviving employment: its economy has been restructuring for 15 years, yet the job losses have always exceeded the gains.[14] Cases like this, where new industries have been attracted but unemployment continues to rise, reveal very clearly how a 'growth through investment' approach to more jobs is like climbing towards an ever receding summit. The pace of technological change continually

Registered unemployment, males + females, August 1984

Regions	%		%
South east	9.6	North-west England (Special development areas)	19.1
East Anglia	9.7	Northern Ireland (all)	20.9
Areas[a]			
Winchester and Eastleigh	4.7	Liverpool	20.3
Windermere	6.2	Aberdare	20.3
Bury St Edmunds	6.3	Corby	21.1
Aylesbury and Wycombe	6.4	Cardigan	23.2
Cambridge	6.5	Tyneside	23.4
Tunbridge Wells	6.6	Hartlepool	23.9
		Irvine	24.4

a Travel to work area.

Table 6.1 *Unemployment rates by selected regions and areas, UK, 1984*

Source: *Department of Employment Gazette* 92.9, September 1984.

overtakes the efforts at industrial job generation.

One of the specific problems of the investment-based approach is that the incentives offered are liable to be most attractive to highly capital-intensive types of activity, because the saving of capital costs through subsidies is correspondingly greater. Thus, regional incentives were in the past a significant influence in decisions concerning the location of certain types of heavy industry, but such industry often provided notoriously small numbers of jobs for a very large investment. It might be said in defence of regional policies that at least in the past the job generation was a positive number. Now, with many types of industrial investment, the question is not how many jobs are created for a given investment, but how many are saved through survival of an organization when put against the number lost through 'rationalization' and automation. In this climate, the role of regional planning has become in reality the defensive one of stemming the net loss of jobs. This is far removed from 'full employment planning'.

Public ownership

Given these realities, there would seem to be every reason for despairing of policies that seek to induce investors in a capitalist economy to do things they believe that the market debars them from doing. The path to full employment is seen by socialists as leading through public ownership of the means of production, and the concomitant recasting of profit in the modest role of a performance indicator within enterprises, rather than the *sine qua non* of all economic activity. Again, our purpose in examining some of the contemporary proposals relating to public ownership is not to pronounce on the merits and demerits of particular forms of enterprise ownership and organization, but to consider their relationship to the question of employment.

Historically, employment in each of the nationalized industries has declined, in some cases dramatically. Writing in the shadow of one of the most bitter industrial struggles of all time, the strike over pit closures in the coal mining industry in Britain, we do not need to offer any reminder that public ownership of itself does not ensure jobs. While the case of coal raises a host of issues other than employment alone, there are also the circumstances of state enterprise in other sectors and in other countries to be considered. If faced with a pattern of demand and a potential for technological change, it is difficult to see how Renault, Fiat or British Leyland could avoid reduction in total labour requirements per vehicle produced — whatever the degree of state or worker involvement. Similarly, new technology in British Telecom would have been introduced, almost irrespective of ownership. If it is to be argued that public ownership provides in principle a framework in which more employment opportunities can be generated, then it must be shown how the benefits of technological change can be rechannelled, and new patterns of work established.

These issues of technological change are, however, seldom tackled in concrete terms in debates on ownership. The question, 'Where are the jobs to come from?' consequently remains unanswered. Among the most forthright advocates of a major extension of public ownership in the form of nationalization are Glyn and Harrison. Posing the question of the extent of nationalization required for a planned economy, they indicate that this 'would initially need only a relatively small number of companies nationalized'[15] — relative, that is, to the number of firms recorded in the Census of Production. They note that the largest 100 manufacturing companies account for nearly half of all manufacturing output, and the largest 200 for nearly 60 per cent. Allowing for the inclusion of some of the larger commercial companies, they believe that 'the nationalisation of, say, 200 industrial, commercial and financial giants would therefore be sufficient to ensure effective state control over economic activity'. It is clear that the majority of the companies they have in mind are in manufacturing. We have drawn attention in Chapter 3 to the figures showing decline in manufacturing employment across a whole range of industrialized countries, and we have argued that the process of reduction of total labour requirements in production industry is an irreversible historical phenomenon. If planning is to provide a solution to unemployment it must explain how it can reverse this trend but, to date, the level of discussion among socialists on this issue is not impressive.

Glyn and Harrison begin by recognizing a need for higher labour productivity in British industry; job losses are frequently prevented because workers object to them. UK capital has conspicuously failed to rationalize the use of existing plant as effectively as its international rivals in recent years. Resistance from the work-force is the most plausible explanation.[16] They quite reasonably suggest that the resistance would be less if full employment were achieved. How does this full employment come about? Commenting on what they perceive as the need for the reduction in employment in banking and financial institutions, Glyn and Harrison write: 'It would be necessary to provide in advance for alternative employment. An important aspect of the superiority of socialist planning is its ability to do this. But the process does take time.'[17] The point about time is well taken, but the question of the *mechanisms* by which planning will assure employment in contemporary conditions is simply not tackled. These two authors rely on existing figures from the *National Institute Economic Review* to suggest that the output of the UK economy could be raised by 21.5 per cent using existing capacity alone. They also present calculations from which they conclude that the extra production could, on paper, make possible a significant increase in consumption, plus a 75 per cent increase in the rate of house-building, a 20 per cent increase in expenditure on health and education, and a 50 per cent increase in manufacturing and construction investment. Nothing is said here about new approaches to patterns of work, length of working time, or new forms of employment. The belief is essentially that planning will bring an enormous boom in production, whereas the old Keynesian policies will not. These particular authors may be exceptional in terms of the claims they make for the benefits of planning, but the implicit reliance on investment and output expansion as the basis for full employment is not only representative of most socialist thinking, but is in this respect also a faithful reflection of the dominant beliefs of society as a whole.

Employment and planning in Eastern Europe

The question of what can and cannot be achieved by government economic planning is, of course, not merely a matter of conjecture, since there is now considerable historical experience of planning systems of various kinds. This includes not only the various forms of 'indicative planning' and 'planning through incentives' that have been attempted in capitalist countries, but more significantly the experience of comprehensive economic planning in Eastern Europe and the Soviet Union. Does this experience suggest that economic planning is capable of overcoming the problem of unemployment?

At first sight, the answer is a clear 'yes': there has been a general absence of unemployment in Eastern European countries, sustained over several decades. This is acknowledged even in circles which are hardly predisposed to give credit to Eastern European countries where none is due. In a NATO (North Atlantic Treaty Organization) symposium in the early 1980s, for example, it was noted that 'employment as a social problem has not become known in any CMEA country in the 1970s'. (The Council for Mutual Economic Assistance, CMEA, is the group of Eastern European countries, including the Soviet Union, coming within an agreement of trade and economic co-operation.) 'Statistically, all CMEA countries are characterised by full employment. Moreover, measures for the increased employment of pensioners in the USSR, the GDR and Czechoslovakia indicate considerable shortages of labour.'[18] This achievement of full employment is not to be underrated, nor is it helpful to dismiss it (as some Western economists would like to do) by simply labelling low labour productivity as 'disguised unemployment'[19] associated with a retarded rate of technical innovation. While these characteristics of Eastern European countries pose real economic problems, it remains the case that people have secure livelihoods and in general an assurance of continuity of employment — which workers in capitalist countries do not have. This is a challenge which must be met, and not simply side-stepped, either by socialists who do not want to be associated with the repressive and intrusive aspects of the Soviet-type system, or by those who are solely intent on proclaiming the virtues of the capitalist market economy and the ills of Eastern Europe.

The relevance of the experience of Eastern European economies to the issue of future employment in Western European countries is, however, a different question. In many respects, Eastern European countries have yet to encounter some of the problems faced in Western Europe. Not only did their economies start from a lower level of economic development, they have remained at lower levels of economic and technological development. Their economic performance has left much to be desired, and the consumer has tended to lose out. The technological 'gap' between even the more advanced Eastern European countries and the West remains wide,[20] and the poorer quality and availability of household goods is particularly marked. Their economies have been characterized by a lower level of labour productivity, and a diminished capability to export to the rest of the world. In neither of these respects would the industrially advanced Western European economies wish to follow their Eastern European neighbours. As yet, economic planners in Eastern Europe have not had to grapple with a problem of labour surplus, but on the contrary the managers of enterprises have had to contend with labour shortages. Paradoxically, one response to this has been a tendency for labour hoarding to occur, with enterprises keeping more employees on their books than strictly necessary for fear of not being able to recruit when the need arises.[21] Eastern European economies have in fact relied principally on growth and a high level of investment,[22] which have created conditions of labour scarcity.[23] This growth has occurred in a period in which the primary goal was to increase the volume of material production, and matters of quality, efficiency, and technical sophistication have been subordinated to quantity.

Once again, there is a need to bring into the analysis the effects of technological change. If an economy organized on a socialist basis uses similar technological forms to those in a capitalist country, then these forms are likely to create a parallel social and institutional structure in industry. The technological form predicates the convergence of production arrangements. The problems concerning the relationships between investments, technical change, and the demand for labour now facing the industrially advanced capitalist countries would therefore not simply disappear. Conditions more favourable for their resolution might be created through the social accountability of enterprises, but the question of the future of employment — where and in what kind of jobs — would still have to be answered. The problem of the fall in demand for industrial labour at the point of production, which arises from technological change, is largely independent of the ownership of the means of production, even if socialist economies might have available a wider range of measures for organizing the 'sharing' of work and the creation of activities in other branches of the economy. As long as enterprises make their own decisions about the choice of production techniques, and determine the desired number of employees or co-operative members in relation to the activities they undertake, the problem of balancing the demand and supply of labour in the economy would remain. This kind of autonomy of enterprises with respect to the size of their work-force exists in Eastern European countries, and would undoubtedly need to continue in any future socialist economy in Britain or other Western European country.

A vital question is, therefore, the basis on which enterprises make their decisions, and in particular how they view the costs of employing labour. Adam has suggested that, entirely contrary to firms in capitalist economies, enterprises in Eastern Europe have often aimed at maximizing the total pay-roll,[24] and other authors have referred to the 'underpricing' of labour.[25] This is a feature not simply of earnings levels, but of the way enterprises are taxed,[26] the options they have over the disposition of their own funds, and the way costs are accounted. These points are significant in drawing attention to the way in which the structure of in-centives within which enterprises operate is of major importance in determining employment levels. Indeed, the aspect of the economics of employment in Eastern European economies from which something can be learned in the West may lie not so much in their particular systems of central planning, but in the area of business taxation and the costs to the enterprise of employing labour, which has typically been kept low. The problem is how to reconcile this with incentives to use peoples' time effectively, which is a notoriously weak aspect of economic management in Eastern European countries, and the question of reconciling the goal of increased labour productivity with employment incentives is considered in Chapter 11. The environment within which enter-prises in Eastern Europe currently operate may lead them to employ more labour than in an equivalent West European enterprise; but in the long run, the underlying technological changes observable in all industrialized countries can be expected to give rise to similar trends in labour requirements in the production industries. In the existing centrally planned economies, the affirmation of the right to work, and the success in making it a practical reality for the ordinary citizen, remain significant. But a limited amount can be learned about actual mechanisms for realizing these goals in an already industrially advanced and technically sophisticated Western European economy.

The need for innovative thinking

Ironically, the knowledge of the existence of full employment in Eastern Europe is an important obstacle to fresh thinking among socialists on the question of employment. The premise that 'capitalism means recurrent mass unemployment, socialism means full employment' seems abundantly confirmed by events. Thus, it is felt that there is no need to take more than a passing look at the employment implications of technological change, and no need to explore radical ideas about the future of work. It is, however, not possible to step twice into the same river. If a new kind of society is to emerge in Western Europe, it will be very different from the societies born of a planning system that was originally geared to accelerate industrialization in an economically underdeveloped country, where independent trade unions were scarcely able to develop, and where a substantial sacrifice of technological innovativeness was accepted as the price of achieving other more pressing goals. There are abundant signs that new mechanisms requiring new thinking will be more and more urgently required in the existing planned economies, and that the impact of technological change is a significant factor in this. A failure to recognize such a need within the socialist tradition in Western Europe would be remarkably short-sighted.

The amount of debate on employment in most discussions of socialist planning is remarkably limited.[27] Few thinkers have addressed, let alone given an answer to, the question: 'Through what mechanisms would full employment be assured in an industrially advanced socialist economy emerging in Western Europe in the context of the technological developments of the late twentieth century?' An important part of that context is the collapse of traditional types of industrial employment, which formed the livelihoods of whole communities. In the next chapter, the circumstances and attitudes to work of the people in one such community are described.

Notes and references

1. This is emphasized by J K Galbraith (1970) in *The New Industrial State*, Penguin, London.

2. That 'market versus planning' is a false dichotomy has been stated many times in the debates on economic reform in Eastern Europe, and is reiterated by Hodgson, Geoff (1984) *The Democratic Economy*, Penguin, London.
3. The approach to planning in France is often referred to in this context; see, for example, Lutz, V (1969) *Central Planning for the Market Economy: An Analysis of French Theory and Experience*, Longman.
4. This is emphasized in Nove, Alec (1983) *The Economics of Feasible Socialism*, George Allen and Unwin, London.
5. Devine, P (1981) Principles of democratic planning, in Currie, D and Smith, A (Eds) *Socialist Economic Review*, Merlin Press, London.
6. Ibid., p124.
7. Nora, Simon and Minc, Alain (1980) *The Computerisation of Society, A Report to the President of France*, p1, English translation, the MIT Press, Cambridge, Massachusetts.
8. The world view of MITI policies for the eighties (1984), in Turney, Jon (Ed) *Sci-Tech Report*, p217, Pluto Press, London.
9. Advisory Council for Applied Research and Development (1979) *Technological Change: Threats and Opportunities for the United Kingdom*, p7, HMSO, London, December.
10. Ibid., p7.
11. These approaches to regional planning were discussed in Brown, A J (1972) *The Framework of Regional Planning in the UK*, Cambridge University Press.
12. Holland, Stuart (1975) *The Socialist Challenge*, p117, Quartet Books, London.
13. Rosen, R J (1984) Regional variations in employment and unemployment, 1970–82, *Monthly Labour Review*, 107-2, pp38–45, February, USA.
14. Garnett, Nick (1984) Where unemployment is the talk of the town, *Financial Times*, 23 October.
15. Glyn, Andrew and Harrison, John (1980) *The British Economic Disaster*, pp164–5, Pluto Press, London.
16. Ibid., pp170–2.
17. Ibid., p164.
18. Clement, H (1982) CMEA performance in the 1970s, in *The CMEA Five-Year Plans (1981–5) in a New Perspective*, NATO Economics and Information Directorate, Brussels.
19. Sovietologists in the West seem now to have given up trying to estimate figures for unemployment by including, for example, 'disguised' rural unemployment, but a note by Wiles, P D (1971–72) on Soviet unemployment by US definitions, *Soviet Studies*, 23, pp619–28, illustrates earlier attempts to do so.
20. Technology in Eastern Europe in discussed by Wilczynski, J (1974) *Technology in Comecon*, Macmillan, London, especially Chapter 12.
21. See, for example, Adam, J (1979) *Wage Control and Inflation in the Soviet Bloc Countries*, p156, Macmillan, London.
22. A corollary of the high level of investment is the lower share of national product going to wages. Another element, belonging to the phase of basic industrialization in formerly agrarian economies, was the administrative restriction of the influx of rural labour to urban areas. Both these points are emphasized by Ellman, Michael (1979) *Socialist Planning*, Cambridge

University Press, Chapter 6.
23. Growth and investment are not sufficient conditions for full employment, however, as the experience of Yugoslavia (which left the Soviet alliance) illustrates: 'It is noteworthy that this high level of unemployment (in Yugoslavia) has coexisted with a high rate of industrial growth, a large volume of investments, inflationary pressure . . . .', Nove, A (1983) *The Economics of Feasible Socialism*, p139 (reference 4).
24. Adam, J, reference 21, p185.
25. For example, Nove, A (1982) *The Eastern European Economies in the 1970s*, p58, Butterworths.
26. Discussed in Ficzere, L (1974) *The Socialist State Enterprise*, p127, Akedemia Kiado, Budapest.
27. Nove, A (reference 4) *The Economics of Feasible Socialism* is an exception in noting (p217) that 'Among the important innovations to which they (the trade unions), and the management, will have to adjust is work-sharing, if technical progress is of a massively labour-saving kind'.

CHAPTER 7

The Reality of Unemployment

Cauldmoss

Disraeli referred more than 100 years ago to 'two nations' when he spoke of the gulf between privileged Victorian respectability on one hand, and the realities of nineteenth century working-class life on the other. Britain today is still two nations, culturally as well as materially. While more than a quarter of the male workforce is unemployed in some of the areas of grim industrial decline, in the leafy suburbs the effects of depression are not present in this magnitude or form.[1] Yet it is from the well appointed offices and cosy sitting-rooms, whose comfort seems to belie the very existence of economic crisis, that too many of the complacent ideas about the future of employment emanate. Many have pronounced that the age of work must give way to an age of leisure, that the protestant work ethic belongs to the eighteenth and nineteenth centuries, not to the twentieth, and that we should accept the 'collapse of work' as the dawning of a new age of human creativity and self-fulfilment. Our purpose in this chapter is to see how such ideas about the future of work match up to the realities, beliefs and expectations of the world of dereliction, joblessness and subsistence-living.

Cauldmoss is a former mining community of about 1800 people in the central belt of Scotland, in between the major cities of Glasgow and Edinburgh.[2] By 1982 at least 30 per cent of the men[3] were unemployed, and the effects of general economic depression have combined with the virtual disappearance from the area of the industries that once sustained the local economy, to produce an industrial wasteland. The heyday of mining in Cauldmoss occurred nearly a century ago, and today only very small opencast operations continue. The brickworks and the peat cutting which provided the two major sources of employment in the 1960s and 1970s have now largely ceased, and the iron and steel manufacturers in the nearby towns now provide far fewer jobs than previously. Only one-fifth of the work-force are now employed in manufacturing. Communities like Cauldmoss throw into stark relief the issues behind the question: 'Where are the jobs to be found?'

The problems we describe here are not simply those of one isolated community in the industrial belt of Scotland, but are repeated again and again throughout Western industrialized societies. Economic forces have torn away the livelihoods of a work-force which was once the mainstay of the industrial economy, and neither private employers nor government have put anything in their place. Thus, this is not simply a chronicle of a particular Scottish community, but evidence to be set alongside other studies[4] providing a graphic description of the reality of unemployment and its impact on working-class culture in heavy industrial areas.

Work and real work

The essence of work is paid employment, as far as people in Cauldmoss are concerned. When they were asked to classify different activities the vast majority described as 'work' those activities that are paid jobs — coal mining, packing goods in a factory or selling insurance — and the four main characteristics attributed to work largely reflected the realities of wage labour: something that is done for money, involves effort, is unenjoyable or is a necessity. However, the term 'work' seems to have two meanings — work and 'real work' — the former being inclusive of the latter. An unemployed man was asked, 'Is digging your garden work?' to which he replied, 'No — with the garden, you're working for yourself.' What you are not paid for is not 'real work', however much physical effort is involved, and 'real work' normally occurs in a specific place away from the home (which means women's housework is undervalued by definition). For example, cooking meals for one's own children was described by only 25 per cent of respondents as 'work', but preparing school meals in a canteen was called 'work' by 92 per cent of those interviewed.

The effort involved in real work is physical effort. Although non-manual jobs are sometimes termed work, the reluctance to accord this label to office jobs (even if these occupations are recognized as having their own validity) is evident. Asked about designing an office block, it was at best conceded that, 'I suppose I'd call that work'; but sometimes the response was 'pen pushing's not real work'. Real work is manual, arduous, and not enjoyable. In a society in which such real work is rapidly being eliminated, perceptions of what constitutes work appear as yet to have changed little in those communities that are most devastated by de-industrialization.

Few people in Cauldmoss talked of getting any satisfaction from the actual activities a job entails, and satisfaction is never a primary objective when seeking work. Although some had clearly appreciated the less mindless jobs they had done, they rarely said that they would do them for less money than a more monotonous job. It might be thought that this was a legacy of peoples' mining background, where relatively unskilled hard graft for comparatively high wages was the norm, but even skilled tradesmen do not readily talk about their work as bringing them any sense of achievement. This is not unique to Britain; it appears to reflect the realities of industrial society everywhere. The authors of a study on the work ethic and the place of work in the USA today found that: 'while people may not want to labor, they usually want a job. The distinction is not merely semantic — few are compelled by the sheer excitement or challenge of their work.'[5] Again, a review of studies of the experience of manual employment carried out in a number of countries concluded that 'work on these shopfloors was physically exhausting and soul destroying, whether done under a communist or a capitalist regime'.[6]

Jobs wanted

Despite the realities of wage labour, the evidence from Cauldmoss is that the great majority of people do want a job. Organized actions in response to redundancy or plant closure throughout Western Europe reflect this. The hardship and the violence involved in the industrial actions of French steelworkers and in the British miners' strike of 1984–85 are indicative of the strength of feeling behind the right to work, as well as the solidarity felt against attempts to ride roughshod over the interests of whole communities. The interviews in Cauldmoss left no doubt that in this community the vast majority of men and most unmarried women want to work a full working week, and that many married women, especially those with older children, would like part-time jobs. Unemployed teenagers receive much sympathy in the community because their job prospects are so bleak, and they themselves definitely consider that work should be a feature of one's life. Very few in Cauldmoss, even among convicted young offenders, actually say they do not want to work — even though some are accused of it. The very small number who do not want to work are ostracized for this very reason. In the early days of unemployment, at least after the initial period of shock, most people spend a lot of time trying to find work — through newspaper advertisements, the Jobcentre, and most important in Cauldmoss, through their relatives and friends. If they are unsuccessful, guilt and depression usually follow.

The different stages of reaction to unemployment witnessed in Cauldmoss were very like those that have been recorded in previous studies, ranging from Austria in the 1930s to other recent analyses in Britain. Marie Jahoda summed up the stages of demoralization witnessed 50 years ago, and it is striking how closely these resemble the reactions of men today:

> 'The initial response is fear and distress; this is followed by numbness and apathy, gradually replaced by some adaptation and efforts to obtain employment. As the futility of such efforts become obvious, hope weakens. This is followed by complete loss of hope which gradually changes either to apathy or sober acquiescence.'[7]

The demoralizing effects of unemployment may for a time sap the will to work, but this is rarely permanent. When an unemployed man, who has previously held down a steady job and has made efforts to find work, declares that he is not interested in getting another job, this is usually interpreted by others as a temporary fit of resentment: 'Deep down in their hearts they don't mean it.' The small number of people who at some stage told us they did not intend to work again all sought employment at a later date.

Men in Cauldmoss who lose their jobs often seem, especially in the early stages of unemployment, to try to maintain their old routine, leaving a space in their day that they hope a job will soon refill. They tend to get up at the same time, and to carry out all the tasks they used to do before leaving for work according to the old timetable. Many of the unemployed do not seem to want to come to terms with their situation by taking up new activities as an alternative to a job. This is because to do so involves giving up hope of finding work at some time in the future; they prefer to leave the 'job slot' in their lives open.

Money

Surviving on the 'dole' (welfare payment), especially with a family, is hard enough in itself, quite apart from all the other personal and social problems which unemployment brings. The money problem is further compounded by the pressure of society to maintain a certain level of consumption, for oneself and one's family. Consciousness of the lifestyle that others expect one to lead, plus the continual reinforcement of a materialist culture through media advertising, combine with previous expectations and commitments to increase the intensity of deprivation felt. Many of the unemployed whom Dennis Marsden interviewed in Britain in the early 1970s were very conscious of this pressure from society, which adds to the purely material problems associated with loss of earnings.[8] It might have been expected that the workless today, because of the dramatic increase in their numbers, would not feel so keen a sense of failure in this respect. However, our experience is that in a community like Cauldmoss the pressure to spend is as strong among both workers and unemployed as it was a decade ago.

When asked the question 'Why do you want a job?', men almost always say 'for the money'. Many women also give this response. While it is obvious that the majority of men seek a regular income in order to provide an acceptable standard of living for themselves and their family, attitudes revealed in other ways show clearly that their answer cannot be taken at its face value. Money by no means accounts fully for the deeply rooted importance of work, which is evidenced not only in this study but in many others. There is a reluctance within the community to admit this openly, because in our society only something which appears economically rational will pass as a valid explanation. On occasions, the gap between stated reasons and actual motives emerged particularly clearly. Husbands stuck to the line, saying that if they found they were making no more in a job than on the dole, they would stop. But their wives told us that their husbands would never stop working; 'It's built into you, work', said one. Evidence from other industrialized countries shows that this is not just a reflection of the influence in Scotland of the Calvinist tradition, with its austere work ethic. In the US it has been found that 'millions hold jobs in spite of their eligibility for welfare at comparable levels'. The same report emphasizes the findings from labour market studies, which 'have shown repeatedly that three (out) of four workers would continue working even if they inherited enough money to live comfortably in leisure'.[9]

The need to earn

The fact that people prefer to *earn* rather than simply *receive* money reflects one of the enduring psychological needs that work seems to fulfil. (In fact, as we will see later, it appears that, as the role of work has become increasingly important in our society, so these needs have taken on a specificity which means only employment itself can satisfy them.) If the role of work is going to change as a consequence of changing technological conditions, it is vital that the full extent of these needs is properly appreciated. They may be summarized as follows: the need for identity and status; the need to engage in purposive activity, to feel that one is making a contribution in some way; the need for one's time to be structured and to have regularity in one's activities; the need for variety in one's social and physical environment.

It is only when a male becomes a wage earner that he is fully adult, and is capable of becoming a real 'family man'. His contribution to society is twofold in that in exchange for his labour he is paid money which allows him to support an institution (the family) that is central to our communities; the more adequately he does this, the greater is his status. This need to earn money is not so much related to the effort actually expended in the activities undertaken, as to the fact that the cash comes in a wage packet, signifying that what one does is in some sense wanted by society. By the same token, any reduction in a man's wage tells him that his services are no longer as valuable, that he is worth less to society than he was. The value that Cauldmoss folk feel should attach to a worker's skill and experience, and their unwillingness to accept a job offering a wage less than that achieved in the past, are aspects of a conservatism that strategies to alleviate unemployment must recognize. Any attempt to encourage more flexible attitudes to sources of income, for example, must overcome the traditional distinction between wages and welfare payments, which is concomitant with the high esteem given to a 'real worker'.

'You're better earning your money' is the general view in Cauldmoss, and those who receive 'something for nothing' in benefits are condemned, mainly by those who have jobs. Some resent the young unemployed because they have not even contributed in the past by working and paying contributions into the system.[10] Moreover, when unemployed teenagers were asked whether the levels of welfare benefit should be raised, some said 'no, because then nobody would work'. Their conclusion is not actually born out by evidence, but the attitude expressed — that people ought to work — shows that, to some extent at least, the traditional work ethic continues to be held by the young.

A regular pattern to one's life

What is actually done on the job is less important than the routine associated with it, as long as it involves roughly 40 hours per week spent away from home in the company of other workers. When people in Cauldmoss were asked what they would do with the extra time, if they could earn a good wage by working only 20 hours a week, several reported that they would look for another job to fill their day. During the main summer holiday, generally of two weeks' duration, workers sometimes complain, 'it's too long, you get fed up'. The need for a regular pattern of activity, which a job provides, accounts for many of the feelings of disorientation experienced by those without a job. The unemployed frequently comment on how their lives seem to be dominated by boredom and a feeling that they are wasting their time. As one of them said: 'There never used to be enough hours in the day for me when I was working . . . now, I know what an hour is . . . it just drags round.' The discipline with respect to time which wage employment imposes seems to be felt as a need in an industrial society which has been accustomed to imposed work patterns.

It has not always been so. The approach to time in traditional rural societies before industrialization was quite different, and still is in much of the world today. E P Thompson shows how a concern with precise time reckoning, and the belief that time should be spent in purposive activity, had to be positively cultivated by eighteenth century capitalists, in order to get the factory system to work.[11] He describes the struggle the employers had in imposing time discipline on their workers in the early days of industrialization. Ironically, now that automation is at last providing the technological basis for freeing people from these rigid dictates (and on the basis of an immensely greater material prosperity than in any previous period of human history), we find that only a 40-hour working week fits the 'job-shaped space' which people have become used to. If the need to reduce the work any one individual does is recognized at all in Cauldmoss, it is in terms of earlier retirement (which is seen as a just reward for previous hard work), rather than a shorter working week. To what extent the need for a time-structure must continue to be satisfied through employment for a substantial proportion of the population may be left an open question. The need for work as presently experienced is one that has largely been shaped by industrialists in comparatively recent times, but to replace it would require social forces as powerful as those which led to its establishment.

Getting out of the house

In Cauldmoss, the house constitutes the woman's domain and, for men, a crucial aspect of having a job is that it enables them to 'get out of the house' during the day. Unemployed married men usually try to find pursuits that keep them out of the house for as long as possible. There is some evidence that certain men will take a job which pays even less than social security benefits, simply in order to save their marriage, which is threatened by rows when the man is at home all day.

In this respect, having a job has a particular importance for men. It would be wrong to think, however, that the majority of women in Cauldmoss would be happy not to have employment. For married women who do not feel they have full-time domestic commitments and whose husbands work, changing their social and physical environment by getting out of the house is usually the prime motivation for working. Many working women take part-time jobs, having less need to identify themselves as a 'worker' (which is seen as the male role). Money of course remains an important factor and there are many families where the wife works because the husband has an insufficient wage or none at all. In the early 1980s about 40 to 50 per cent of women in Cauldmoss had a job outside the home. Many more would have liked employment, yet in the sample of 10 per cent of households surveyed, not one of the women described themselves as 'unemployed'. This highlights the distinct roles which jobs have for men and women in this community.

Coping with unemployment

'Working on the side' — taking temporary and often part-time work without the employer or the worker paying insurance contributions or tax — is an important way in which some of those on the dole try to cope with their situation. Activities in the 'hidden', or 'black', economy satisfy the moral imperative to be working, and in Cauldmoss men have commented how working a 'shift on the side' (perhaps filling in for someone who is sick) makes them feel equal again to those employed legally. The same has been observed in other countries.[12] There is also the advantage that, as with 'moonlighting'[13] which was common in more prosperous times, the income is undeclared and therefore untaxed. For the unemployed, the relative financial benefit of work on the side is often even greater than for 'moonlighters'. The very complex system of benefits and taxation that has arisen in Britain frequently means that it does not pay to take legal part-time work. For the two-thirds of the unemployed who receive supplementary benefits, declared weekly earnings are (in 1984–85) deducted from benefits pound for pound, after the first £4. Thus, the unemployed typically find themselves on the 'poverty plateau', from which the only ways to ease their situation are illegal'. As one of the men interviewed in Cauldmoss said, 'they're creating the situation for you to diddle them out of the tax and benefit . . . but if I had the choice, I'd rather do it legal'. The situation is not unique to Britain, and in most other nations where the government tries to reallocate resources through income tax the hidden economy thrives.[14]

Obviously it is very difficult to assess the extent of the hidden economy and extrapolation from a detailed study of one village is clearly untenable. The availability of informal employment in a particular region will depend on the nature of the local industry (whether seasonal, small scale, unskilled, etc); the level of skills of the unemployed work-force; the state of the local economy; the way bureaucratic regulations are operated by government agencies, and so on. Many studies suggest that it is far easier for the employed, rather than those out of work, to get involved in the underground economy, because of their social contacts, their financial resources and their access to tools and equipment. Nevertheless, it is evident from nearly all ethnographies and surveys that there are considerable incentives for the unemployed to take work on the side, and these outweigh any moral scruples.[15]

Work on the side is never a satisfactory alternative to a proper job, and the majority of individuals would prefer to do things legally if they could. Fear of 'grassers' informing the Department of Health and Social Security (DHSS) means that people must be secretive, not only at work but also over what they spend, particularly in the pub. Moreover, jobs on the side are rarely regular, and a man may find himself hired in the morning but told he is not wanted later the same day. Work in the hidden economy does little to provide a structure to one's life, which is one of the crucial roles that a job fulfils. The government loses in terms of taxes and benefits, the worker loses in terms of lack of security, legal protection at work, and through the need to lead a semi-furtive existence. The incentives that outweigh all these disadvantages are not only financial; an important motive for working on the side is 'to keep your hand in', to make oneself more attractive to a prospective employer in the formal economy.

To employers, there are great advantages in taking on people unofficially: they can be dismissed instantly, without any trade union being able to act in their defence; and they cost less, because there are no employer's national insurance payments and workers are paid outside of any collective bargaining agreement. All this is just a manifestation of the classic role of unemployment in undermining workers' bargaining power. Thus the situation of the unemployed in the hidden economy is analogous to that of illegal immigrant workers, such as Mexicans in southern USA, who can be grossly exploited by employers. Mass unemployment in a capitalist economy provides employers with a cheap, unprotected labour-force that can be used or ignored at will. It undermines the statutory gains achieved through more than a century of struggle for protection of workers, and agreed working conditions achieved through collective bargaining. In the last century, Marx referred to the unemployed as the 'industrial reserve army', from which the captains of industry could draw recruits at any time, thus undermining the workers' position. In communities like Cauldmoss in the 1980s, this reserve army is now larger than the total remaining in production industry employment, although the firms taking advantage of the situation are in practice local businesses and not the major companies run by the 'captains'.

The hidden economy might provide a clue as to why the unemployed have been so passive in Britain, despite the general belief before the late 1970s that a few million unemployed would precipitate massive social unrest. It should not be thought that, because the only riots we have had that have been ascribed to unemployment were also associated with ethnic minorities, that the majority of those out of work are fairly content with their lot. There are many factors that inhibit the unemployed from protesting violently: the lethargy that afflicts the long-term unemployed, their underlying shame at being workless, and their isolation, which is compounded by involvement in the hidden economy. Working on the side might discourage militancy since the unemployed's moral outrage is compromised when they are 'on the fiddle'.

Fiddling and stealing

If neither regular employment nor work on the side (as a second best) is available, the young in particular may resort to fiddling and stealing as a way of partially meeting their requirements: principally, financial independence from parents, and the ability to maintain themselves. These social norms are largely fulfilled simply through possessing money, not necessarily through having work. Welfare benefits are sometimes supplemented not only by undeclared earnings but by fiddling the authorities in some shape or form. Fixing the electricity meter to provide virtually free energy has its place among the economic survival techniques of the unemployed. Sometimes claimants manage to obtain extra money from the DHSS, perhaps through a fraudulent appeal for special help. Occasionally the unemployed resort to theft. It is clear that it is not simply the poverty of unemployment which encourages crime but an element of playing to beat the system, which is a way of restoring the self-respect which a job otherwise provides. This again has been found elsewhere; in the USA, unemployed blacks in particular feel they can retain their dignity through success in cheating the system.[16] In general the older generation of Cauldmoss is critical of stealing or fiddling the authorities. Among the younger generation the dividing line is less clear, and a big difference is seen between crimes against the rich (including big stores) or the authorities on one hand, and on the other hand, offences against one's 'own kind' (which are universally condemned). In fact, it is probably a minority of the unemployed who actually steal, although few would refuse to buy cheap goods that had 'fallen off the back of a lorry'. Minor thefts such as siphoning petrol are fairly common, and there is the regular temptation to shoplift. Raiding fields for potatoes is barely considered theft — since it involves the work of digging them up. Thus theft merges into self-help activities to alleviate the worst effects of poverty resulting from unemployment.

Do-it-yourself

It might seem from the outside that there is a wide range of legal activities open to the unemployed with which to use the time that is no longer being spent at work. Some writers have even predicted that the old distinctions between 'work' and 'leisure' might begin to break down, simply through the persistent failure of the economic system to provide formal jobs.[17] An important assumption they had was that, with more time not being employed and with less income, people would become more self-sufficient, thus saving money and using their extra time productively.

In places like Cauldmoss this is a pipe-dream, scarcely touching the cultural and material realities of life. There are few activities which are actually possible without equipment and some money, quite apart from questions of motivation. One of the sociologists who previously forecast a great rise in 'do-it-yourself' among the unemployed later carried out investigations on the ground. He found that it tends to be among the wealthiest households, that is those in work, not the poorest, that the most do-it-yourself activities occur.[18] This is partly because one needs tools and equipment to do things: the more one has, the wider the range of activities that are possible, and the higher the returns for one's efforts. The power drill, the sewing machine, the freezer in which home-grown vegetables can be stored, or the barrel for home-brewed beer, all give the affluent middle-class household advantages over low-income households when it comes to doing-it-yourself. On top of this, most people in Cauldmoss live in council houses and therefore have no incentive to do their own plumbing, joining, glazing and other house repairs for which the local authority is responsible.

These material aspects are, however, strongly reinforced by the cultural differences which separate the 'two nations' in Britain. There are important areas where the unemployed could in fact save some money if they had the inclination. All the council houses in Cauldmoss are provided with generous gardens sufficient for growing most of the household's vegetables, if the occupant wished. Yet the few gardens which are actually cultivated usually belong to people with jobs, not to the unemployed. Again, beer is a crucial commodity as far as social life is concerned, and not being able to buy it is one of the greatest hardships for unemployed men. Drinking at home or taking a 'carry-out' to someone else's house is common — yet very few regularly brew their own beer, even though it can be done with just a plastic bin and a collection of bottles saved for the purpose. In Britain, there has been a big upsurge in home-brewing in recent years, which provides beer at a small fraction of the cost of the heavily-taxed commercial product, yet this appears to be a pursuit undertaken mainly by higher income groups.

The differences here are primarily a matter of values. Among at least a section of the middle-class things that are hand-made or home-produced are likely to be valued for that very reason, whereas in working-class communities, like Cauldmoss, only things which are bought carry the respectability which goods provide — based on the fact that one can afford them. Home-made articles which are less well finished and less sophisticated in appearance tend to carry the stigma of poverty. Maintaining self-respect and recognition from the rest of the community is always crucial for people in difficult circumstances. In the context of the cultural values of the communities with massive rates of unemployment, doing-it-yourself, at least at present, does not fulfil that need.

Anything which is done to save money has to fit into these cultural values. This is clearly illustrated by one aspect of self-provisioning which is fairly widespread in Cauldmoss. Several people collect their own fuel, and unemployed men may return with carrier bags or (with luck) hundredweight sacks of low-grade coal from abandoned opencast sites or exposed coal seams. Wood is also collected from nearby copses, which (like the fuel wood supplies in many developing countries) are rapidly being depleted because live trees are cut as well as dead ones. Another source of 'free' fuel is peat, which is still cut and sold as a commercial undertaking in the vicinity; some of the unemployed with access to a car or other vehicle help themselves to the cut peat at night. Most of these activities are technically illegal, but generally condoned in the village, and several people who do not collect it themselves are happy to buy stolen coal. Although not quite respectable, they are recognized as being more like 'real work' than other do-it-yourself pursuits. Above all, collecting fuel accords with the existing traditions of the village, representing a return to a practice well known in the area's history, particularly during the depression of the 1930s.

Traditions in communities in other industrialized countries are sometimes a little more conducive to a self-providing type of economy, geographical as well as historical differences playing an important role. One example is the Newfoundland fishing ports, studied by Wadel, where hunting and fishing are the 'real things in life', whether or not men are in paid employment.[19] Growing all one's own vegetables, cutting all one's own firewood, building and repairing one's own house, are all consistent with the traditional way of living. For the unemployed, all these things not only keep people active but provide a substantial supplement to welfare payments. This situation perhaps approximates to the patterns which some writers have envisaged emerging in what has been called a 'post-industrial society', but it is a far cry from present realities in the old mining and industrial communities with mass unemployment.

In Cauldmoss cuts in expenditure are made by reducing total consumption, rather than by substituting home-made or self-provided goods. Clothes, furniture, food, drink and nights out are all severely cut back, and really heavy expenditure like cars frequently have to be abandoned altogether. For many, the fall in income is dramatic. However, this does not give rise to innovative strategies for coping with unemployment, but to a range of illegal (though often condoned) activities which provide the means which enable people to conform with the dominant traditions of the community. To try to come to terms with the situation in other ways, by seeking to launch out into other activities (even if these were possible), would be to acknowledge the permanency of the loss of paid employment. This would mean abandoning all hope of a return to a job, and would involve a fundamental change of attitude which most would find morally unacceptable; that is, no longer to seek employment genuinely.

Community enterprise

Self-help community projects have been advocated as one means of tackling the high levels of unemployment concentrated in particular localities, as we have discussed in Chapter 5. The establishment of community-owned shops, the formation of workers' co-operatives, and participation in government-assisted community enterprise programmes are the kinds of activities suggested. There have been a few successful and much-quoted examples of such schemes, but these are exceptional cases which perhaps give a misleading impression both of the co-operativeness and innovativeness of working-class people as a whole, and of the real scope for financially viable undertakings. A number of projects have been initiated under government-assisted programmes in nearby towns, encouraged by a local Enterprise Action Trust, but no one in Cauldmoss has yet initiated one. It is in fact extremely difficult to find a potentially profitable enterprise, given the prevailing economic conditions, despite the government-funded Enterprise Allowance Scheme that guarantees a £40 weekly wage for the first year. The Youth and Community Worker in Cauldmoss failed to interest members of the recreational Unemployment Club in schemes where they might provide useful services, because there was no guarantee of cash earnings. To accept any mode of occupation other than paid employment would be another way of implicitly acknowledging that one could not expect ever to work again in the traditional employee role.

The leisure society?

Of the many false notions that exist about what the destruction of work in our society will mean, one of the most pernicious is that it may create a 'leisure society', and that we should welcome the release from 'wage slavery' that it brings. According to this view the main task ahead is to educate people for this new world of leisure. It is no accident that this world of worklessness is seldom seen as encompassing its own advocates. The way people experience leisure is in fact as the counterpart of work, and (quite apart from the income actually needed to enjoy it) the idea of leisure without employment is entirely alien to most people. In Cauldmoss, it is questionable whether the majority of the working population would even welcome any further reduction in their working time, financial considerations apart. Certainly, in the situation where income depends on time worked, people will prefer extra income to extra leisure time and take any overtime they can get. Lip-service is sometimes paid to the leisure idea by people in middle-class jobs in the community. The headmistress at the primary school says 'we've really got to teach them for leisure', but finds, like everyone else, that it is impracticable to translate this into meaningful action. She can 'give them games; badminton, pool . . .' but these activities cannot be satisfactory ways of spending unbounded free time. The headmistress says that very few children in Cauldmoss read for pleasure now, unlike their parents' generation who still 'look at' romantic fiction or detective stories. The television is invariably switched on when children might have been engrossed in a book, and so, in the headteacher's words, 'they've no time to read now'. The function of the school remains largely to instil in people a time discipline, and familiarize them with hierarchies based on perceived merit and the subordination to authority which characterize wage employment. Teachers at the

Cauldmoss primary school largely accept that schooling is to 'fit' people for jobs, and the fact that so many school-leavers face unemployment has not changed perceptions of the role of the school. Of course the school cannot operate outside of the predominant social and cultural paradigms of the larger society of which it is part.

The principal recreations for the employed in Cauldmoss are watching television, drinking in pubs, social clubs or at home, gambling (bingo or at the bookmakers), attending club meetings, playing football and bowls, walking and fishing, and visiting friends and relatives. The unemployed follow the same pursuits, cutting down on those requiring money, watching more television or spending more time just walking. Very few fill their extra time with radically different recreational or money-saving activities, and the time spent on fishing or ferreting is as much to 'get out of the house' as to actually catch anything. For an activity to be real 'leisure', the time involved has to be relished, and not merely wished away: 'It is one thing to come home after a day's work and flop down in front of the television screen, but quite another to watch television during the day because you simply have nothing else to do.'[20] Marie Jahoda came to similar conclusions from her study in Austria in the 1930s, which showed 'that being unemployed is something very different from having leisure time. The unemployed decreased their attendance of clubs and voluntary organisations, their use of the free library, their reading habits. Their sense of time disintegrated'.[21] Employment provides both a time-pattern to life and a freedom from a sense of guilt, which the experiences of the unemployed suggest are necessary to give value to non-working time. The notion that a 'leisure society' might arise out of the failure of the economy to provide jobs has no foundation in the experience of those who suffer the worst of the unemployment.

Signs of change

Most people in Cauldmoss think that a Labour government and the end of the recession, particularly in the building trade, will bring employment back to 'normal' levels. On the basis of the analysis presented in the earlier chapters of this book, there is no foundation for such a belief. In this respect the collapse of traditional work is permanent, and new patterns of employment will have to emerge.

The experience and perceptions which we have reported in this chapter may seem to lead to profoundly pessimistic conclusions, not only concerning the present realities, but also with regard to the receptiveness of people to any possible new approaches to the employment problem. The perception of hard manual labour as 'real work', the insistence on a 40-hour week job, the desire for more overtime rather than a shorter working week, the rigid divisions between male and female roles, the persisting idea that a wage should reflect one's true worth, and the reluctance to regard as an entitlement any form of payment other than the wage received in exchange for labour time; all these bode ill for radical approaches to the future of income and work. These are the values that once had to be thrust on society by the pioneers of industrial capitalism in the eighteenth and nineteenth centuries, as their price of progress, but now they threaten to stifle new thinking and new initiatives in our time.

Societies change despite all the weight which bears down upon them from the past; ideas about the future cannot remain fixed within the perspectives which an analysis of present realities shows to be dominant. One must look instead to the signs of change, however slight, which point to shifts in attitudes that may develop further with changing circumstances. In fact, some changes in people's attitudes to work have already begun to occur. A positive development is that the unemployed are less condemned than they used to be within their own communities, since the lack of jobs has spread in some way to affect almost every family. Few still blame the unemployed themselves for being idle, and unemployment is now seen less as a problem of individual deviancy than as a political issue which it is the responsibility of government to solve. This does not in general lead to political action, and virtually every study of unemployment, both in Western Europe and the US, confirms that those out of work do not entertain original solutions and seldom participate in politics.[22] The government is, however, held responsible.

Among the young, other significant changes in attitude are occurring. They clearly do not feel the moral imperative to work as urgently as their parents, and they increasingly see welfare payments as a right, not as a shameful handout. Also, they will not work for 'rubbish' money, and will refuse to take places on the government-funded Youth Training Scheme for this reason. While they certainly do not enjoy unemployment, they value their time more highly than to sell it for £25 a week in a monotonous

127

job that leads nowhere. The need for a fixed pattern of working time set in the mould of the 40-hour week also shows signs of weakening, and already one or two young men in Cauldmoss say they prefer the flexibility and free time which informal work allows. Indeed, working on the side can, for those lucky enough to get it, habituate people to part-time working. This may accord better with some of the new kinds of employment patterns which we discuss in Part 2. Even the rigid division of roles between the sexes is beginning to show some cracks. Within the household, some men (both in jobs and unemployed) are very gradually taking on the sharing of tasks that were traditionally women's work.

We have argued that work is still as central to people's lives as it was in the past, and the opportunity for everyone to participate in society through employment is a fundamental right. It is a necessity which the economic system as presently constituted is unable to meet. Unemployment is a degrading, debilitating state to which no one should be condemned. To be workless means a collapse of one's notion of oneself, one's time and place, and one's relation to society. At the same time, we believe the realities of economic and technological change throughout the industrially advanced countries mean that the old pattern of all men working a 40-hour week, with a sizeable share of the population in unskilled, manual, industrial jobs, will not be re-established — even if it were desirable. To be explicit, there is a need to allow everyone to fulfil the basic needs which employment now satisfies through *some* work, but through more flexible patterns of employment, new kinds of activities, and for less than 40 hours a week.

A crucial obstacle to such change is the payment of income purely in relation to hours 'sacrificed': the whole basis of the wage-labour contract. 'Work' is identified as the time the worker is selling. Work has been so self-legitimating that the more a man did in overtime the more prestige he earned, both through material consumption and through recognition as a 'good worker'. There was virtue in work, and a man could rarely do too much, especially if he had no family commitments.[23] These are the values which have both been required by the wage-labour system, and highly effectively established through it. The future of employment is going to require changes in that system, and in the attitudes to work which went with it. Among the unemployed and the young in Cauldmoss there are just a few signs that, if support can be established elsewhere for radical change, it will not encounter a totally unyielding conservatism in traditional working-class areas.

What does the future hold for areas where the collapse of industrial jobs has left a huge section of the population without work, and offered virtually no prospects for school-leavers? Not only is the profit-governed economy unable to maintain aggregate investment and so offer any hope of a substantial regeneration of jobs, but it is irrelevant to this economy whether or not the activities are located in areas where jobs are most needed. The problem is also that any renewed industrial growth, which we discuss in Chapter 8, is not going to bring the large number of unskilled jobs which went with previous phases of economic growth.

Notes and references

1. Refer to Chapter 1 for a discussion of the geographical and social distribution of unemployment in Britain.
2. The material in this chapter resulted from a social anthropology research project that started in July 1982, and has been funded for two and a half years by the Economic and Social Research Council (ESRC) and administered by Edinburgh University. Anne-Marie Bostyn and Daniel Wight lived in Cauldmoss continuously for two years, conducting research based primarily on participant observation, as well as questionnaire and interview techniques. Further findings from this research have been reported in:

   Turner, Robert, Bostyn, Anne-Marie and Wight, Daniel (1984) *Work and Non-work in a Small Scottish Lowlands Town*, SSRC Final Report HR7700 F00230066.
   Turner, Robert, Bostyn, Anne-Marie and Wight, Daniel (1985) The work ethic in a Scottish town with declining employment. In Roberts, B, Finnegan, R and Gallie, D (Eds) *New Approaches to Economic Life*, Manchester University Press.
   Bostyn, Anne-Marie and Wight, Daniel (in press) Inside a community — values associated with money and time. In Fineman, Stephen (Ed) *Unemployment — Personal and Social Consequences* (provisional title), Tavistock, London.

3. Our discussion concentrates on men since their sense of identity is largely invested in their role as workers; this is not so much the case with women who, for example, tend not to describe themselves as unemployed. However, this is not to deny the work that women do, both paid and unpaid, of which we will say something later. For an examination of women's unemployment see Coyle, Angela (1984) *Redundant Women*, The Women's Press, London.
4. Eg Marsden, D and Duff, E (1975) *Workless*, Penguin, Harmondsworth.
   Wadel, Cato (1973) *Now Whose Fault is That? The struggle for self-esteem in the face of chronic unemployment.* Newfoundland Social and Economic Studies No 11, Institute of Social and Economic Research, Memorial University of Newfoundland.
   Clarke, Roger (1982) *Work in Crisis: The Dilemma of a Nation*, The St Andrew Press, Edinburgh.

Buss, Terry and Redburn, F S (1983) *Mass Unemployment, Plant Closings and Community Mental Health*, Vol 6, Sage Studies in Community Mental Health, Sage Publications, Beverly Hills.

Willis, Paul (1984) Youth unemployment. *New Society*, **67**, 1114, pp475–7, 29 March; **68**, 1115, pp13–15, 5 April; and **68**, 1116, pp57–9, 12 April.

McKee, Lorna and Bell, Colin (1985) Marital and family relations in times of male unemployment. In Roberts, B, Finnegan, R and Gallie, D (Eds) *New Approaches to Economic Life*, Manchester University Press.

5. Levitan, S A and Johnson, C M (1982) *Second Thoughts on Work*, pp30–1, W E Upjohn Institute for Employment Research, Kalamazoo, Michigan.

6. Jahoda, Marie (1982) *Employment and Unemployment, A Social-Psychological Analysis*, p41, Cambridge University Press.

7. Jahoda, ibid., p22.

8. Marsden and Duff, reference 4.

9. Levitan and Johnson, reference 5, p31.

10. The use in Britain of the term National Insurance Contribution is an anachronistic euphemism for a highly regressive poll tax which helps perpetuate the myth of benefits being a right derived from past contributions.

11. Thompson, E P (1974) Time, work-discipline and industrial capitalism. In Flinn, M W and Smout, T C (Eds) *Essays in Social History*, Oxford University Press.

12. Wadel noted that, among Newfoundland loggers, a temporary job is enough to establish that one is still willing and able to do real work (Wadel, reference 4, p31).

13. 'Moonlighting' means working in the hidden economy while holding a regular job.

14. Italy is renowned for its *lavoro nero* (Merritt, Giles (1984) *World Without Work*, p94, Collins, London), and in France tax losses due to the hidden economy are estimated to be well over £2000 million (Jahoda, reference 6, p10). US estimates of the underground economy in that country are around 27 per cent of GNP (Merritt, ibid., p93), while some people reckon the British figure to be about 15 per cent of GNP (Heertje, A, Allen, M and Cohen, H (1982) *The Black Economy: how it works, who it works for, and what it costs*, Pan, London.

15. Eg Wadel, reference 4, p39.
   Marsden and Duff, reference 4, p182.
   Jahoda, reference 6, p95.

16. Merritt, reference 14, p84.

17. Gershuny, J I and Pahl, R E (1980) Britain in the decade of the three economies. *New Society, **51**, 900, pp7–9, 3 January.
   Clemitson, Ivor and Rodgers, George (1981) *A Life to Live: Beyond Full Employment*, Junction Books, London.

18. Pahl, R E (1984) *Division of Labour*, Blackwell, London, Chapter 9.

19. Wadel, reference 4, p66.

20. Hill, John (1978) The psychological impact of unemployment. *New Society, **43**, 798, pp118–20, 19 January.

21. Jahoda, Marie (1979) The psychological meaning of unemployment. *New Society, **49**, 883, pp492–5, 6 September.

22. Eg Marsden and Duff, reference 4, p259.
   Clarke, reference 4, pp82–6.

Economist Intelligence Unit (1982) *Coping with Unemployment: The Effects on the Unemployed Themselves*, London.

Buss and Redburn, reference 4, p37.

23. A popular folk song from Glasgow illustrates how widespread this ethos is, at least in industrial Scotland:

> *Chorus*
> Three nights and a Sunday double time,
> Three nights and a Sunday double time,
> I work aw day and I work aw night,
> Tae hell wi' you Jack, I'm all right;
> Three nights and a Sunday double time.

> 1. There's a fella doon the road that I avoid,
>   He's wan o' them they call the unemployed.
>   He says its all because of me,
>   He canny get a job and I've got three.
>   Three nights and a Sunday double time.

> 2. The wife came tae the work the ither day.
>   Says she "We've anither wee one on the way."
>   Says I "No wonder you can laugh,
>   I've no been hame for a year and a half."
>   Three nights and a Sunday double time.

> 3. I never miss the pub on a Friday night.
>   And there you'll always find me gay and bright.
>   You'll see me down at the Old Bay Horse,
>   I'm a weekend waiter there of course.
>   Three nights and a Sunday double time.

> 4. There's some will head for heaven when they die,
>   Tae find a Dunlopillo in the sky.
>   But I'll be going to the ither place,
>   For an idle life I couldny face.
>   Three nights and a Sunday double time.

Matt McGinn (1973) 'Three Nights and a Sunday', in Buchan, Norman and Hall, Peter (Eds) *The Scottish Folksinger*, p12, Collins, London, reproduced by kind permission of Janette McGinn.

CHAPTER 8

Technology and Economic Growth

Economic growth assumptions

The assumption of continuous economic growth is one of the in-built beliefs of our society, affecting in a multitude of ways the everyday affairs of business and government. It is taken for granted that, over a period of years, there will be more of everything we want — more cars, more television sets, more washing machines, more education, more health service care, more social services, more holidays and, above all, more in the pay packet. When recovery comes, it will bring not only more goods but more jobs.

The immense success in material terms of the post-1945 boom in the industrialized countries, which brought an unprecedented abundance of consumer goods into ordinary households, led to a faith in economic growth in which rising GNP was readily seen as a panacea for all ills — including unemployment. Growth had enormously increased the range of goods available and the scope of activities accessible to most individuals. Society was also better able to afford improved education, health and community services. Economic growth could surely also be expected in time to overcome poverty, and to provide a path to full employment. If there is widespread unemployment this is attributed to a failure of the economy to grow sufficiently rapidly. With more growth, it is believed that jobs are bound to follow, and thus unemployment must eventually disappear. If growth is not fast enough to create the jobs required, it is assumed that somehow the economy is being 'mismanaged'. Blame is then apportioned for this state of affairs; it is seen as the fault of the government for adopting the wrong policy measures, or the fault of firms for not investing enough, or the fault of the trade unions for making 'excessive' wage demands which are perceived to be undermining profitability. It is a tacit assumption that there is always a potential for higher growth.

The basis for this belief — that any economy is in principle capable of sustaining indefinitely and without interruption whatever rate of growth is 'required' for full employment — is rarely questioned. The idea that growth is the natural state of affairs has become one of the distinguishing beliefs of modern industrial societies. Yet, in a long-term perspective, sustained material progress has, on any reckoning, been a rare achievement of human society. The experience of the last 200 years, during which economic growth has flourished with only interludes of recession, depression and war is itself unique. For most of human history, there has been no expectation that incomes would rise year upon year, nor was it anticipated that each generation would see a momentous transformation of the material conditions of society. Such expectations were born with the progressive extension of the fruits of industrial development to the majority of the population, which has occurred only in this century. Moreover, the magnitude of the rates of growth by which the performance of industrialized economies are now judged is based on still more recent experience. The 2 per cent rate of growth of the UK economy between the mid-1960s and the end of the 1970s, during which period unemployment trebled, is deemed by the conventional economic and political wisdom to be 'too low'. Yet the average rate of growth of the British economy between the 1850s and the 1930s was about 1½ per cent per year — a rate which gave rise to more than a threefold increase of production over those 80 years. It is only by comparison with the experience of other industrialized countries in the decades immediately following World War II, or with a few quite exceptional episodes, like the forced industrialization of the Soviet Union during the 1930s or the 'catching up' of certain developing countries now, that growth rates of 1½ to 2 per cent can be deemed 'low'. A growth rate of 2 per cent sustained over a generation means a doubling of the turnover of goods and services; if sustained over a century, it means almost an eightfold increase. Rates of growth averaging 4 per cent or more, which have been observed in a number of industrialized countries since 1945 (and which 'laggards' like the UK were supposed to emulate) would, if contrived for over a century, give rise to a fiftyfold increase of GNP! If this growth is thought of in these gross material terms, such extrapolations appear quite unreal.[1]

Challenges to growth

The conventional assumption of endless and rapid material growth

133

has not gone unchallenged. Outstanding economic thinkers, from J S Mill in the nineteenth century to J M Keynes in the 1920s, have placed the phenomenon of growth in historical perspective and seen it essentially as a passing phase. Keynes concluded that 'assuming no important wars and no important increase in population the economic problem may be solved, or at least within sight of a solution, within a hundred years'. Reflecting on the consequences of this end of the growth phase, he thought 'with dread of the readjustment of the habits and instincts of the ordinary man, bred into him for countless generations, which he may be asked to discard within a few decades'.[2]

In our own generation concern has not centred on the idea that all human needs will have been satisfied but, rather, on a perception that economic growth brings with it inherent problems which detract from the material satisfactions. Awareness of the costs of economic growth, and recognition of the inability of consumerism to bring all that is expected of it, had by the 1970s developed to the point where it began to find expression in official reports. The 1971 Brooks Report of the Organization for Economic Co-operation and Development (OECD) states:

> 'Yet, in spite of these achievements, concern about the future is widespread in our societies. Faith in economic growth has been replaced by a feeling of unease in the face of the prospects opened up by it and has been shown to be insufficient in itself to respond to the aspirations of mankind for a better way of life. What is more, far from bringing only benefits, it is accompanied by more or less traumatic effects, less and less acceptable to large sectors of public opinion. Finally, the transformations that it engenders throughout the whole economic system increasingly reduce the effectiveness of traditional mechanisms devised to cope with the management of that system. Thus it is, in a sense, that by its very success the economic approach has proved its limitations.'[3]

There are thus not only inherent saturation effects for any product but, long before any theoretical maximum (such as, say, one car per adult) is reached, other objections arise. Such objections to the traditional mechanisms for managing the system have centred on the environmental consequences of industry and its infrastructure, on perceived social limits to growth, and on the wasteful use of natural resources.

The changing perceptions of these problems do have a significant effect on the process of economic change. Sustained opposition to a particular development — whether new airports, major road developments, chemical plants with operation risks of explosion or noxious waste, or nuclear power plants — helps to foster a climate that is hostile to industry with its expansionist demands unless these demands can be carefully regulated and judiciously moderated. This reflects an increasing unwillingness on the part of society to make unquestioning sacrifices for the sake of 'growth' as an end in itself. A further weakening of the drive for economic advancement is seen by Fred Hirsch in his book, *Social Limits to Growth*.[4] Many of the most highly valued privileges enjoyed by those elevated as successful in society consist not in material goods that can be reproduced, but in 'positional' goods which by their nature cannot be indefinitely multiplied in number: the country cottage or the university professorship are obvious examples. Economic growth cannot make it possible for the same *kind* of benefit to be enjoyed by everyone; the country cottage becomes the Wimpey estate on the edge of the town, and the positions of status would be downgraded because, in W S Gilbert's words, 'if everyone is somebody, then no-one's anybody'. As the fruits of growth are spread more widely, Hirsch argues, frustration may be expected both on the part of those who fail to secure the full benefits anticipated, and on the part of those who find their former positional advantage has been eroded. As it comes to be realized that economic growth is incapable of bringing to everyone the same kind of benefits which the privileged had previously enjoyed, the feeling that the competitive rat-race centred on individual gain is really not worth the candle becomes more widespread; and this further limits the sacrifices that people will make in order to drive the economic system harder.

At the same time, there has been a growing challenge to the assumption that living standards can be improved only in proportion to the increase in the material turnover of the economy, involving ever-increasing consumption of energy and materials. Common sense ways in which benefits to the consumer might be achieved with less material throughput include both the increased durability of goods (for example, non-corroding car bodies), and sophisticated technologies such as coated glass to trap the sun's heat in buildings, and microprocessor-controlled heating and ventilation systems to reduce energy losses. In economic terms, there is a unifying principle which runs through all such examples; the gains to the consumer should logically be measured in terms of the utility derived, and not the quantity of goods which have to be purchased. The householder is better off, the *less* fuel he or she has to purchase — provided the building is designed to provide equivalent warmth in other ways — rather than the *more* fuel

135

which the coal, oil, or electricity industries deliver. Thus, 'welfare' might better be assessed by indicators such as warmth in buildings, access provided by transport, and services derived from consumer goods over their lifetime than by industrial throughput. This is in contrast to the actual concepts used in calculating gross national product whose growth economic statisticians are busy measuring. GNP is calculated on the basis of quantities like sales of fuel, sales of cars, car repairs undertaken and the throughput of consumer goods from factories. The distinction between these two approaches, which long ago was recognized as an important theoretical principle by Irving Fisher,[5] underlies Gerald Leach's 'low energy strategy for the UK'.[6] Leach's scenario assumes an increase in living standards comparable to that projected in official energy forecasts:

> 'Houses become warmer so that everyone enjoys the amenities of the better off today. Most families come to own freezers, dishwashers, clothes dryers, colour TV, and other heavy users of electricity. Car ownership grows rapidly so that 72–75% of households in 2000 have at least one car, compared with 58% today. Air traffic grows 2.4–3.0 times by 2025. Total industrial output increases by a factor of 1.7 to 2.2. The area of offices, schools, hospitals, shops and restaurants increase by anything from 30–80%.'[7]

Thus Leach and his colleagues comment that they have 'not supposed a future of material austerity' and go on to claim that all this could be achieved with less energy being used in 2025 than in 1975. The emphasis in Leach's scenarios is on the more efficient use of energy and a shift of the economy away from energy-intensive activities. These changes could lead to the decoupling of energy use from the gross domestic product.[8] The ideas of economy of use which lie behind the Leach energy proposals have much wider possibilities.

If we can use less energy for each unit of GDP then it will constitute an exemplar for other reductions of resource use. The linking idea is the substitution of 'software' for 'hardware'. Software in this context represents the modification of any aspect of design, choice of materials, amount of material, durability, maintenance and running costs, so as to reduce the consumption of raw materials or energy. Thus, not only could growth in GDP be decoupled from energy supply,[9] but, for instance, the growth in number of cars could be decoupled from the supply of steel.

Growth and technology

This raises a fundamental question: what is it that 'grows' with economic growth? What should economic statisticians actually be measuring? There are always notorious difficulties with any index which seeks to aggregate essentially unlike objects. One of the maxims of scientific method — that one should only compare like with like — is immediately broken once the attempt is made. The difficulties are particularly great when making international comparisons, or comparisons over a very long period of time, when the two sets of commodities consumed are so different. These 'commodities' include both goods (with a possible physical unit of measurement) and services (where measurement is normally possible only in money values). This distinction between 'services rendered' and material turnover is of fundamental importance. If 'growth' is thought of in purely physical terms — as a volume of goods, numbers of factories, floor area of warehouses, or mass of machinery — then growth is self-evidently a finite process. No physical quantity can show indefinite exponential increase, whether it be numbers of the human population, numbers of cars on roads, depletion of fossil fuels, emissions of carbon dioxide into the atmosphere, or accumulation of reactor wastes. A moment's reflection on the physical resource and environmental implications of 2, 3 or 4 per cent exponential growth of the material and energy throughput of industrial societies extrapolated over a century, in a world in which the hitherto non-industrialized countries are rapidly staking claim to their share of global resources, is sufficient to make one rethink the idea of exponential physical growth. It does not take sophisticated models of the world's economic system and environment to realize that there is a problem. Thus, it is only realistic to see such growth processes as represented by sigmoid (S-shaped) curves rather than exponential curves. Sigmoids were used in Chapter 3 to model the growth of production and productivity and are used again in Figures 8.1 and 8.2 for the economic growth of the UK and the US.

If growth is thought of primarily as the process of acquisition and use of technological capabilities, however, then the nature of the constraints on growth may be seen rather differently. To understand growth in this sense, it is necessary first to analyse its technological basis. Then limitations on the process of growth are liable to be seen in terms of social processes rather than material resources.

The underlying force behind economic growth, which is technological change, has not operated steadily and smoothly but has come in waves of invention, innovation, diffusion and decay. Major technological achievements have had a period of pre-eminence, when they generate a whole host of engineering developments and lead to a corresponding boom in investment and industrial innovation, before becoming in turn commonplace, then 'traditional', and finally 'old-fashioned'. Wind and water power in their original forms clearly followed such a path, becoming at their height the motive force for the mills and factories which were the very hallmark of the industrial revolution in Britain and continental Europe. Yet eventually they declined until they became relics and museum pieces. A similar path was followed by steam-driven transportation, which once powered not only locomotives but farm tractors, traction engines and a whole range of industrial machinery, but came to be replaced by the internal combustion engine and the electric motor. Steam destroyed wind and water technology, to be in turn largely destroyed as a direct source of motive power by electricity and the internal combustion engine. With the technology went many firms, organizations, skills and careers, all in Schumpeter's 'creative destruction'.[10] For both water and steam, the transformation of these sources of power into electricity through generators or turbines greatly extended their contribution. Of course, some canals survive and water power has transformed into hydroelectric power, but neither is any longer necessary as a major contributor to economic activity and, more significantly, neither of them has 'leading edge' high-technology status, which is now seen as belonging to biotechnology, microelectronics, computer software and robots. More important, these long established technologies, even when revamped with higher technology, no longer bring with them (as they did in the eighteenth and nineteenth centuries) the possibility of a great wave of new investments, taking place simultaneously in a whole range of different industries, so that a new economic boom may be created.

The development of 'clusters' or 'families' of related technological innovations allows the establishment of new industries producing new products of sufficient importance to sustain a long period of economic growth. Freeman has conceptualized the scale of the process involved in his term 'new technology system'; to think of this as simply a major, or radical, innovation would, indeed, mislead. A new technology system must be all pervasive and all important — steam, oil and electricity have the right scale.[11] Such new technology systems will have been established over an extended time-scale and have demonstrated their basic reliability before diffusion can occur on a substantial scale. Moreover, in the diffusion process the underlying technology must give rise to further innovations so that the growth process may be multiplied. New technology systems are propagated by the imitative behaviour of entrepreneurs, realizing the potential for profit from the innovations, which Schumpeter called 'swarming'. If the technology generates such an ongoing series of innovations, for example as with steam in the nineteenth century, then a major growth phase can result and economic recovery can be followed by a period of prosperity.[12] In the past such growth phases have been labour-intensive in their early stages when demand for the new products or processes has been met by replicating production facilities and exploiting economies of scale. An increasing demand for labour thus resulted from a boom in investment. As the demand for labour rises so does the upward pressure on wages; and this, together with any labour or skill shortages, intensifies pressures to introduce process innovations which improve productivity and reduce costs.

For a time, a precarious balance may exist between the drive for labour-saving innovation — which will tend to create a labour surplus — and the continued growth in demand for labour associated with the design, construction, commissioning, supervisory and marketing functions associated with business expansion. However, economic growth has been an uneven process which, in capitalist economies, has consisted of boom and slump, prosperity and depression. Exactly how investment cycles are to be understood is disputed among economists, but it is clear that the onset of recession is related to a falling rate of profit which, in an economic system whose driving force is profit, spells job losses, business failure, take-overs, rationalization and closures. Viewed in terms of technology, this may be seen as arising from an exhaustion of the early profit opportunities open to 'first in the field' investors, when a new cluster of technologies comes on the scene. In the mature phase profits are 'competed away'; they are harder to make because everyone is already doing it, the market is saturated and the cumulative effect of past investments tends to be a lowering of the rate of profit. This is often referred to by Marxist economists as 'over accumulation', but what is meant here is that the accumulation is 'excessive' in relation to that level of investment which would enable higher profits to be made. It does not necessarily mean an exhaustion of the real gains which may accrue to society from the application of the technologies in question, but only a receding of the inducement to private investors. It is in this sense that the term 'recession phase' is used below; Appendix 1 illustrates this behaviour for the UK and West Germany since 1945.

Episodic growth

The relationship between technology and the successive booms and recessions in the course of capitalist development has received only spasmodic attention from economists. Kondratiev in the 1920s and Schumpeter in the 1930s drew attention to the way each 'long-wave' economic cycle appeared to be associated with major technological developments. If we examine the experience of economic growth of the UK and the US, for both of which long series of data are available, we find that the growth phase since World War II can be seen as distinct from that of the previous century (in the UK) or half-century (in the USA). (See Figures 8.1 and 8.2; in the latter per capita values are used for the USA because of the very substantial population growth that occurred throughout the period — from 76 million in 1900 to 216 million in 1977.) Figures 8.1 and 8.2 clearly show that growth after 1945 was at an unprecedentedly high rate in both cases and, in broad historical perspective, continued smoothly until 1979 — although with the signs of a falling growth rate.[13] In whatever way contemporary observers may have perceived the magnitude of the 'stop-go' cycles — the Korean War price boom, the OPEC oil price increases, and about-turns in government policy — the effects on output are scarcely detectable against the background of the secular trends. Similarly, the short-period cycles around the pre-1915 growth era are also of minor magnitude compared with the long-run trend. The crucially different period is that between 1915 and 1940, which not only includes the booms of the two world wars but also the post-World War I slump. The sigmoid curves indicate that both the UK and the US would at best have been in a period of recession from the earlier growth phase but that this recession was allowed to become an uncontrolled boom and slump cycle. Economic growth is not a smoothly continuous process and there are clear signs of repetition in the late 1970s of the rounding out into prolonged recession which occurred at the beginning of the twentieth century.

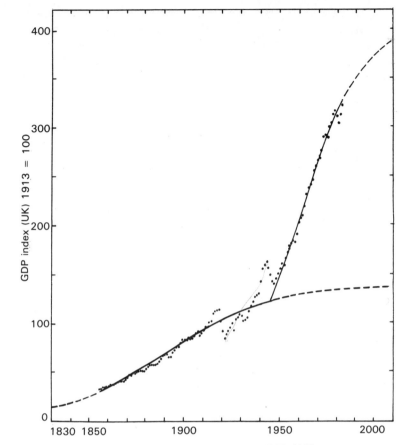

Figure 8.1 *Index of GDP for the UK, 1855–1983*

Source: Feinstein, C H (1972) *National Income, Expenditure and Output of the United Kingdom 1855-1965*, University Press, Cambridge; and *Annual Abstracts of Statistics* and *Monthly Abstracts of Statistics*.

In broad canvas we thus align two main growth episodes with their related 'technology systems': 1850–1910, driven by steam and implemented by mechanical and civil engineering; and 1940–74, driven by electricity and oil and implemented through the consumer goods industries.[14] It is in this general way that we see the value of the 'long-wave' idea and not in any mechanistic notion of a 50-year cycle.

The existence of a technology is only the merest of beginnings and it may take 50 years or more before it burgeons into a technology system able to carry a major phase of economic growth.

141

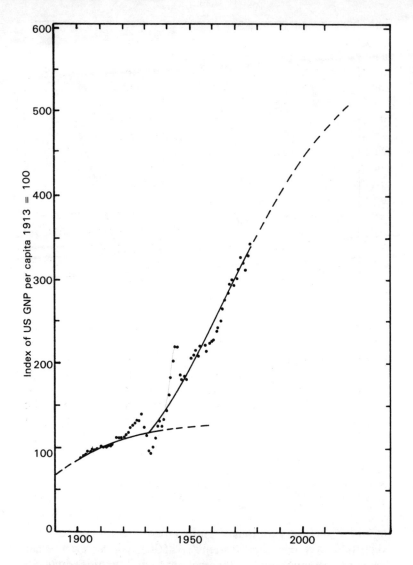

Figure 8.2 *Index of GNP per capita for the USA, 1900–1977*

Source: The British Economy, Key Statistics 1900–1966, for London and Cambridge
Economic Service by Times Newspapers Ltd; *Statistical Abstract of the United
States*: 1978 (99th edn), US Bureau of the Census, Washington DC 1978; and World
Tables, 1980, International Bank for Reconstruction and Development — World
Bank.

The change to a new technology system will thus be a major event, requiring enormous effort and a correspondingly long time to achieve. But one development also facilitates another. For instance, the development of steam power required iron and steel making and machine tools of adequate precision. Again, the petrochemical industry was impelled into being substantially through the demands of, and markets provided by, the automobile industry.

On the evidence of the internal combustion engine and electricity generation, the establishment phase of a new growth period will take place in the recession phase of the preceding wave of growth. It is unlikely that it could have occurred earlier (thus allowing a smooth transition from one prosperity phase to the next), because it is not until the industries based on existing technologies experience the problems of declining profitability of capital investment that the inducement becomes strong enough for attention to be transferred to the new technologies. Moreover, even if the switch of capital and manpower to the new technologies could be achieved earlier, all of the means for the development and implementation of the new technology would have to be already to hand so that this investment could be successfully absorbed. This is rarely the case. Indeed, the magnitude of the task of establishing a new technology system is reflected in the observations of Collingridge[15] who analyses the problem of securing control of technological change. Using the examples of organic-lead compounds in petrol and nuclear power generation, he describes the way in which a technology becomes 'entrenched'. Lead cannot be removed from petrol without consequential changes in the design of internal combustion engines or changes in refinery operation. Such changes would either require the replacement of all existing petrol engines — a necessarily long-term process — or affect the costs of refining and the resulting product mix. But, as Langdon Winner has noted, technological changes also require restructuring of the social environment[16] and will thus be resisted by those who are involved in the status quo. In the same way a nuclear power programme is not merely a choice between that technology and coal but also a choice between the careers, jobs, and skills of those concerned in the two technologies. Thus major technologies become embodied in the economic and social structure, and their removal from pre-eminence is truly an act of destruction but one which is necessary to release the initiative, talent and energy for the creation of new ones.

143

Growth in the twentieth century

In moving on to speculate about the nature and timing of a new economic boom in Chapter 9, it is instructive to examine the well-documented path of economic growth in the twentieth century in relation to the two 'new technology systems' which have been identified as its driving force. The internal combustion engine and electricity generation were both nineteenth century inventions and required several decades in which to become established as major innovations. Thus Edison's Pearl Street generating station was opened in 1882 and alternating current adopted for the Niagara Falls hydroelectric generators in 1893; the Otto cycle was demonstrated in 1876 and Benz's four-wheeled car made in 1893.

Year	Private cars registrations thousands	Goods vehicles registrations thousands	Airlines millions of passenger miles	Electricity consumption megawatt hours (Mwh)
1900	Nil	Nil	Nil	100
1904	8	4	Nil	—
1932	1 128	370	16	12 300

Table 8.1 *Early twentieth century growth in the UK*

Source: *Abstract of British Historical Statistics* and *Second Abstract of British Historical Statistics.*

Table 8.1, which covers the first third of the twentieth century, shows for the UK how slowly the products of the new technology systems came into substantial use. The diffusion of the motor car, the pre-eminent consumer durable, is examined in Figure 8.3 as licensed cars per 1000 population for the UK.[17] This growth may be represented by two distinct curves, separated by World War II. After the War there was both a massive increase in the proportion of population who could afford cars and in the organization of production and maintenance to meet that demand. Then the technologies, the social and organizational infrastructure, and the pent-up demand, were brought together to give the major new growth curve.[18] The motor car affects the economy not only through the production process, but equally directly through its distribution, sales, maintenance, repair and refuelling, and beyond this it extends tourism and aids business. Thus, even when a nation has no motor car production, or ceases (as the UK has done) to produce as many cars as it consumes, the impact on the economy of internal combustion engine technology is still a dominant influence.

Year	Registrations of motor vehicles per 1000 population	
	UK	USA
1909	0.74	0.95
1913	4.6	12.9
1930	33.2	216
1938	51	227
1965	238	458
1980	351	670

Table 8.2 *Motor vehicle registrations for UK and USA*

Source: Adapted from Svennilson (1969) Growth and stagnation. In Landes, David S *The Unbound Prometheus*, p442, University Press, Cambridge; with extensions from *Annual Abstracts of Statistics* and *OECD Economic Survey, 1983–84.*

In Table 8.2 the disparity in the diffusion rates of motor vehicles through the UK and USA economies is evident. From rough parity in 1905 the difference was almost threefold in 1913 and over four-fold throughout the 1930s but has since fallen back to less than twofold. This behaviour is reflected in Figures 8.1 and 8.2; in the 1920s the US economy was clearly expanding at a higher rate and on a higher growth path compared to the UK economy, which was well below its earlier levels of performance. This statistical disparity was matched by the much higher degree of mechanization of production in the US where the ratio of horse-power per operative was four to five times higher, and the productivity in cars per worker, three times greater.[19] There is, of course, no technological reason why one nation should not be able to develop an innovation earlier than another and, hence, climb the growth curve faster and further.

Electricity generation exhibits a similar pattern and required a long period in which to become an established innovation. Figure 8.4 shows how it underwent a period of growth throughout the 1930s' depression and that this first phase was then the basis for much more rapid growth after 1949, leading to generated output in 1980 being five times that of 1950. Similarly, not only does Table 8.2 show that most of the growth in motor vehicle registration in the UK and US occurred after 1938, but it was not until the post-war years that there were major long distance road building programmes — interstate highways, autobahns, autoroutes and motorways. Beyond this, the World War II innovation of the jet propulsion form of internal combustion has provided a major expansion of air travel. Thus the history of the diffusion of the motor car and electricity generation clearly shows that, together with oil,

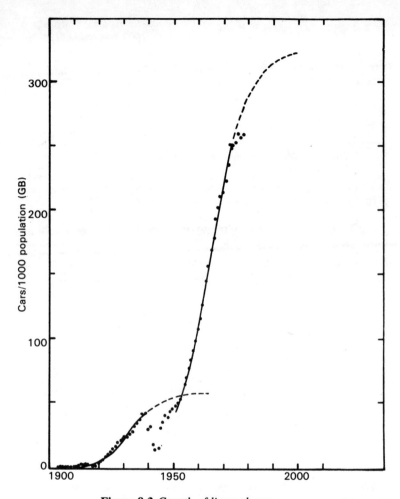

Figure 8.3 *Growth of licensed cars*

Source: *Abstract of British Historical Statistics, Second Abstract of British Historical Statistics* and *Annual Abstracts of Statistics*.

they were the core of the technology system which underpinned the post-1950 growth wave.[20] The increased use of synthetic materials and electronics were led by these more fundamental developments. Indeed, the whole upsurge in innovation tends to become self-reinforcing, as one technical development becomes the catalyst for others. This is not to deny the importance of growth in other areas (such as pharmaceuticals and agro-chemicals) but only to suggest that these were not sufficiently pervasive in the

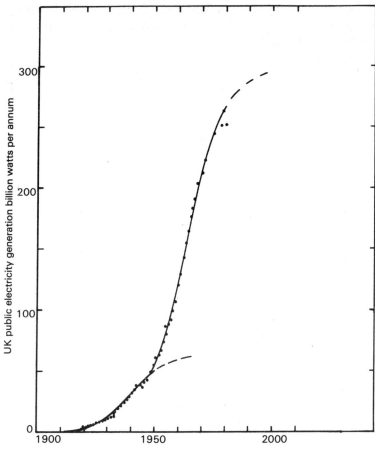

Figure 8.4 *Growth of electricity generation*

Source: *Abstract of British Historical Statistics, Second Abstract of British Historical Statistics* and *Annual Abstracts of Statistics*.

economy, nor of sufficient magnitude, to lead a growth phenomenon on the scale of that which has occurred since 1950.[21]

International diffusion of technology

The diffusion of technologies on an international scale may be likened to the internal process of diffusion between industries within the domestic economy. Throughout the whole of Britain's leadership of the industrial revolution, technology was diffusing to other countries and, eventually, these countries were able to catch up

147

and overtake. Japan is only the latest of a number of countries which have overtaken Britain; it was a process which started in the nineteenth century:

> 'In 1870 Britain mined 50 per cent more coal than the United States, Germany and France together; in 1900 they mined 70 per cent more than Britain. While British output had doubled, the American had been multiplied by eight, the German by four, and even the French by two and a half.'[22]

Thus the laments for the economic performance of the UK in comparison with competitor nations, which have been heard ever since the latter half of the nineteenth century, show a decided lack of historical perspective. As the 'first in the field' in industrial technologies until at least the third quarter of the nineteenth century, the UK was bound to see its relative position eroded as its unique position as 'the workshop of the world' gave way to growth of industry among a wider group of countries. There is no reason either why one nation should absorb as much as another of any particular technology system; for instance, the substantial differences in the number of motor vehicles per 1000 persons shown in Table 8.2 ought not to be seen as indicating that the UK has still to catch up the USA. Rather they should be interpreted in the light of growth curves such as Figures 8.1 and 8.2, as indicating that different economies may well saturate at different levels of penetration.

Whatever view is taken of the causes of such differential absorption of a technology, the changing technological basis of growth eventually presents a new arena of competition. No longer does it matter how many, or how big, steam locomotives a nation possesses. The changing technological basis of growth has enabled the UK to continue to contend among the leading industrial nations and, in some cases (such as personal computers), be in the vanguard. More generally, what is important is the recognition that growth phases are essentially international, even if confined among the limited number of industrialized nations, and that the experience of growth post-1945 is more or less common among all these countries. By the same token, in discussing the future, one is not discussing the prospects for any one economy in particular, but the positive course of development for the industrially advanced nations in general. It is to the present prospects for such a universal period of new growth which we turn in the next chapter.

Notes and references

1. They can, of course, easily exist for a single artefact if comparisons are made with a point early in its lifecycle, eg car production in Britain was 34 thousand in 1913 and over 1.8 million in 1968, a period in which GDP increased only 2.55-fold.

2. National and Athenaeum, 11 and 18 October 1930, reprinted in Keynes, J M (1972) *Essays in Persuasion*, pp326-7, Macmillan, London.

3. *Science, Growth and Society* (1971) Report to the Secretary General, OECD, p26.

4. Hirsch, F (1977) *Social Limits to Growth*, Routledge and Kegan Paul, London.

5. Fisher, Irving (1906) *The Nature of Capital and Income*, Macmillan, London.

6. Leach, G et al (1979) *A Low Energy Strategy for the United Kingdom*, Science Reviews.

7. Ibid., p13. The increase in car ownership appears broadly in line with that discussed later in this chapter.

8. Both gross domestic product (GDP) and gross national product (GNP) are used in this book to describe the total output in a year of goods and services in the economy. GDP is used here because it is the one used by Gerald Leach *et al.* In the context of the concerns of this book the difference between GNP and GDP may be ignored.

9. This decoupling has at present occurred to a large extent in the UK because of energy conservation measures and the changing nature of industrial manufactures.

10. Schumpeter, J A (1939) *Business Cycles*, McGraw-Hill, New York.

11. Freeman, Christopher, Clark, John and Soete, Luc (1982) *Unemployment and Technical Innovation: A Study of Long Waves in Economic Development*, p64 *et seq*, Frances Pinter, London.

12. Thus steam engines, electric motors and internal combustion engines are products in their own right; but they are (or were) also essential parts of process machinery, railway engines, pumps, consumer durables, motor cars, lorries and tractors. Electricity has been an especially potent technology and has led to major electronics and communication industries.

13. These are logistic curves but the saturation levels and growth constants must be treated with caution — relatively large changes in the predicted level, which do not greatly affect the quality of curve fit, can result from minor differences in data.

14. The term 'industrial revolution' is sometimes used to describe such major changes. Thus wind and (particularly) water would constitute the first industrial revolution (a slow gentle process); steam-based technologies the second; and electricity- and oil-based technologies the third. The possibility of a fourth industrial revolution is discussed in Chapter 9. These are not the timings used by Freeman (ibid.) who argues that since the beginning of the industrial revolution there have been four long waves based in turn on textiles and steam power (1780-1830); railways and steel (1830-1890); electricity, the internal combustion engine and chemicals (1890-1940); and synthetic hydrocarbon-based materials and electronics from 1940 onwards. Our disagreement with the particular phases and descriptions which Freeman

uses does not affect the crucial idea of discrete growth phases related to distinctive technology systems.

15. Collingridge, David (1980) *The Social Control of Technology*, Frances Pinter, London.

16. Winner, Langdon (1977) *Autonomous Technology*, MIT Press, Massachusetts.

17. There may be substantially more vehicles in use than those licensed — 10 per cent is one estimate — a factor which would be expected to increase in times of recession, thus putting a question mark on the comparability of the figures for before and after the mid-1970s.

18. A detailed analysis can be obtained in Tanner, J C (1978) Long-term forecasting of vehicle ownership and road traffic, *Journal of the Royal Statistical Society*, A, 141, Part 1, pp14–63. Tanner used a modified logistic curve to give a forecast saturation of 350 cars/1000 population.

19. Landes, David S (1969) *The Unbound Prometheus*, p445, University Press, Cambridge.

20. This is a substantially different view of the relationship between technology systems and growth periods from that supported by Schumpeter and Freeman. (Reference 14 gives Freeman's timings.) Our analysis dispenses with the need to seek 50-year long waves, and is simpler in that the necessary conditions for growth are the availability of new technology systems, the competing away of profits of an earlier system to make room for 'creative destruction', and sufficient time for the new technology to have become established. The problem of the economic logic of long waves is discussed in Rosenberg, Nathan and Frischtak, Claudio R (1984) Technological innovation and long waves, *Cambridge Journal of Economics*, 8, pp7–24.

21. Indeed, it does suggest that without electricity and the internal combustion engine, a consumer goods boom based on gas ovens and gas refrigerators would not only have been smaller in itself, but would have led to a smaller demand for synthetic materials.

22. Derry, T K and Williams, Trevor I (1960) *A Short History of Technology*, p306, University Press, Oxford.

CHAPTER 9

Present Prospects

A new growth episode?

The first question which requires consideration in the analysis of present prospects is whether we can now expect a new growth episode of comparable magnitude to those of Victorian and post-World War II periods. But the prediction of this possibility, let alone its timing and magnitude, is dependent on more than the state of present technological knowledge. In the mid-1980s, we can observe signs of renewed economic growth, but we have no way of knowing if this is merely a regaining of the previous growth curve based on the old consumer goods technologies — which can provide only a modest rate of expansion — or the beginnings of a swarming process creating new products in sufficient volume to establish their pre-eminence over the old. To achieve a new period of boom will require a wave of imitative innovation in products for which the productivity of capital will be at a level that will encourage investment. Experience suggests that this may not be achieved without a massive shift in institutional frameworks and social attitudes. The shift to the production line and the work routines associated with it, which made possible the previous consumer goods revolution, depended on the acceptance of organizational ideas and the imposition of managerial prerogatives commonly known as 'Taylorism'.[1] A new technology system will require a similar transformation of occupational patterns among the work-force and resistance to such change will lead to them being excluded from the process — as well as posing a potential constraint for the rate of change. It is by no means certain that such a new episode is going to happen: the most that can be done is to identify the conceivable technological bases for a new innovative boom, and to consider their implications.

It was argued in Chapter 8 that there is always a considerable time-lag between the first appearance of any technology and its evolution to the point where it can provide the widely diffused swarm of applications and knock-on effects which characterize a distinct growth period. Thus, any possible technological basis for growth in the remaining part of this century must already exist, and already be developed to a point where a multiplicity of applications in a whole range of industries can be perceived. On those criteria certain candidates, which some observers might be tempted to see in the role of 'lead technology', do not qualify when examined more closely. Biotechnology, in the sense of exploiting genetic engineering, is of too recent origin, and its potential contribution — even if acceptable — has yet to be demonstrated. Genetic engineering has not yet undergone the establishment phase through which motor cars and electricity passed long before the post-World War II boom. Nuclear power, even if it remains on the agenda for contributing to energy supplies, does little more in an economic sense than replace present fuels in the supply of electricity, which is an already established motive force in industry and not a new revolutionary development. It is possible to identify only one candidate for a new innovative boom comparable in scale to the post-1945 consumer goods revolution, and that is information technology (IT). The combination of computers, microelectronics, telecommunications, satellites and video systems, and their manifold applications in wordprocessing, electronic offices, personal computers, microprocessor-based controls, computer-assisted learning, electronic games, cable television, viewdata and electronic mail, may indeed constitute a 'new technology system'.

In terms of rates of investment and the general level of business activity, it is possible to consider two alternative scenarios. One is a continuation of the growth of already established consumer goods production, based essentially on the same technologies as now, although with some penetration of new products like home computers, and some adaptation of production techniques. In this case, a great acceleration of the rate of investment cannot be envisaged, because the inducements are not there. This 'low growth' would be at the modest pace characterizing the mature years of the technological cycle and for the UK and US the path, as cumulatively expressed by GDP, would be expected to lie around the extrapolation of the upper sigmoids of Figures 8.1 and 8.2 (shown as dashed lines). On the other hand, there could be the major upsurge of innovation based on the spawning of new products from the microprocessor revolution leading to a new investment boom and 'new growth'. But when is this going to start?

Too much comfort must neither be drawn from the appearance of some new products, such as personal computers, nor from the fact that the telecommunications industry is over 100 years old. Electronic computers have been in use for only about 40 years and it cannot be just assumed that the overall new technology system is sufficiently mature to support a major growth period. Not only is 40 years shorter than the establishment phases of the internal combustion engine and electricity — which lasted 50 to 60 years — but we have, very fortunately, no imminent world war to act as the trigger to growth.[2] It could be starting now, or start in 10 or 20 years; all these timings would be consistent with the analysis of the last chapter. Caution about the timing lends emphasis both to fears of premature expansion generating a boom and slump cycle and to the need for strong science and technology policies to encourage its arrival and underpin its success.

Setting the scenarios

In setting the scenarios there are three overriding factors: the trend in the size of the working population, the number of jobs created by public expenditure and the presence or absence of the 'new economic boom'. Our analysis of the prospects deriving from current policy options and hopes will deal with the UK economy, but it applies to most industrialized nations. As has already been made clear, while it is accepted that there is a range of performance across these nations, we do not believe that this leads to differences in principle, only in magnitude. The starting point is the low and high projections of working population, from Chapter 1, against which can be set the likely job provision under 'low growth' and 'new growth' scenarios, and, hence, allow levels of unemployment to be projected. In doing this it is assumed that public expenditure creates 750 thousand additional jobs (ie about the middle of the range discussed in Chapter 5) and that this does not have any side effects which restrict job growth in the private sector. The two growth scenarios are shown in Figure 9.1; the low growth projection is for GDP to remain on the curve shown in Figure 8.1 of Chapter 8 (c. 1 per cent pa); the new growth projection is for 1984 to have marked the beginning of the IT-based growth period postulated above, and for the growth to be at 3.5 per cent pa (the rate for 1950 to 1970 in Figure 8.1 was 2.7 per cent pa).[3] The projections of GDP for 1985 and the first half of 1986 given in the government's 1985 budget were marginally below this new growth curve.

153

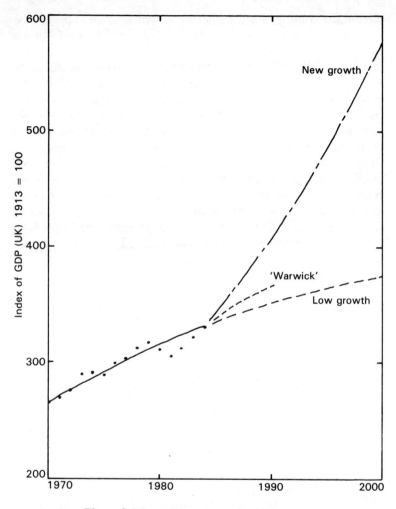

Figure 9.1 *Low and new growth of GDP*

Source: Data as for Figure 8.1; and Institute of Employment Research (1983) *Review of the Economy and Employment*, p16, University of Warwick.

The effect of growth on industry

The effect of economic growth on jobs is most clearly evident in its expected impact on employment in industry. In Figure 9.2 the graph for employment in the IOP industries, first introduced in Figure 3.1 of Chapter 3, is extended to project forward to beyond the year 2000. There are two projections: the lower is a continuation of the trends in production and productivity which were established prior to 1973, ie GDP remains on the low growth path, as shown in Figure 8.1, while productivity goes on rising and hours worked continue their downward drift. The new growth period starting in 1984 gives the upper projection which may aptly be seen as 'jobless growth'. Industrial employment would fall slowly until it reached a low of 6.8 million in the early 1990s and then rise again to about 7.4 million by the year 2000 — a similar level to that of the early 1980s.[4] But by 2000 the IT-driven phase would be expected to be beginning to slacken off and round out along a sigmoidal path and thus, just as happened around 1966, industrial employment would peak in the early part of the next century before rapidly declining as productivity increases overtook production ones. For the UK this must be seen as a good scenario. Of course, a low rate of productivity increase would show somewhat higher employment — about 7.3 million in 1990 — but the lower efficiency would be expected to make the output growth more difficult to sustain by generating inflationary pressures and balance of payments difficulties.

To achieve greater industrial employment through growth of output would require a substantially higher rate of growth, for which there is no historical precedent in the UK. Indeed, far from feeling able to propound a 'solution' based on, say, 6 per cent pa growth of GDP, there must be doubt about the optimism of extending the new growth calculations as far ahead as 10 or 15 years. At the stage of development reached in the industrially advanced countries there appear to be greater constraints on production than on productivity. Thus management are likely to see an easier and less risky task in increasing productivity for the same output rather than the more problematic one of establishing additional production units. Even allowing for the special nature of 'new' IT-led growth providing a sufficient imperative to produce the necessary action, large corporations, working on an international scale, are quite likely to seek to place a new production unit, albeit based on research design and development work carried out in an industrially advanced nation, in one of the rapidly developing low-wage nations of the Pacific basin. Beyond these managerial attitudes lie the longer term adjustments which industrial economies will eventually have to make in their use of energy and other material resources. To this we add the caution of evident social constraints on the rate of change which arise when industrial and commercial interests conflict with community interests and amenities. Indeed, an analysis of employment prospects from the

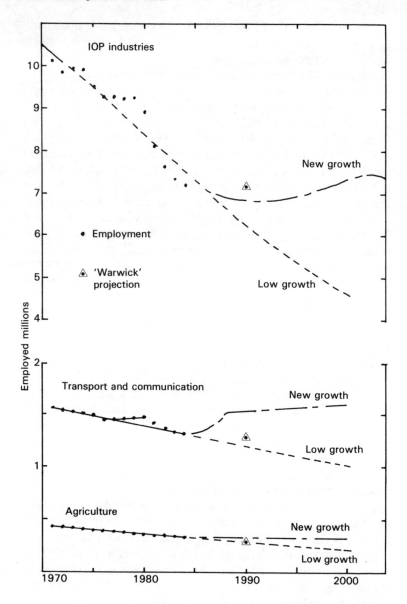

Figure 9.2 *Categories of employment — decreasing*

Source: Appendix 4.

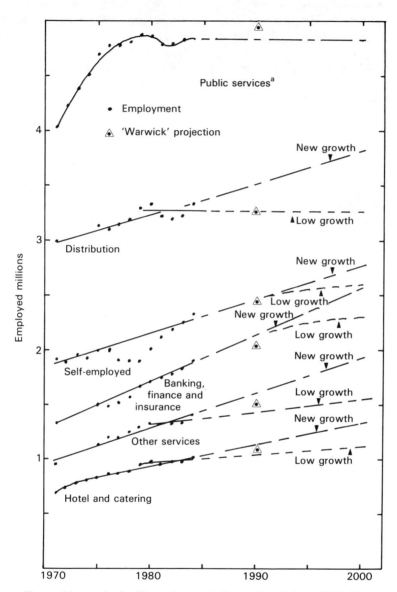

a The possible growth of public employment is discussed in relation to Table 9.2.

Figure 9.3 *Categories of employment — increasing*

Source: Appendix 4.

Institute for Employment Research, University of Warwick, which is discussed later in this chapter, is based on 1.9 per cent pa average growth[5] — the path for which is shown in Figure 9.1.

In addition, the possible impacts of microprocessor-based information technology on employment outside of industry, which were described in Chapter 4, must be remembered. Even with new growth, this could particularly affect jobs in banking, finance and insurance and thus, far from a contribution of new jobs, these activities may have stagnant or declining employment potential.

Other employment changes

The other areas of employment in the UK economy have been disaggregated into those which have declined over the last 10 to 15 years — transport and communications, and agriculture — and those which have generally increased: public administration; education; medical and veterinary services; distribution; self-employment; banking, finance and insurance; other services; and hotel and catering. The decreasing categories are shown in Figure 9.2 and the increasing ones in Figure 9.3. Two projections have been made for each of these employment categories corresponding to the new and low growth scenarios and the assumptions implicit in these are discussed in Appendix 4. It should be noted that in all cases of increasing employment the maximum rate of growth of employment over the period 1984 to 1996 is substantially below that of 3.5 per cent assumed for the economy as a whole — the annual averages being distribution: 0.9 per cent; self-employment: 1.1 per cent; hotel and catering: 1.8 per cent; banking, finance and insurance: 1.9 per cent; and other services: 2.1 per cent — and that this implies an overall improvement in productivity for these areas.

The scenarios

In Table 9.1 the projections for each category of employment are given for both the 'low growth' and 'new growth' scenarios, for the years 1990 and 1996 in comparison with the base year 1984. In this table the number of jobs in the public sector is kept constant at 4.84 million so that the importance of this politically contentious expenditure may be highlighted; everyone is in favour of growth, most on the political right of centre are not in favour of substantially increased public expenditure. The total in employment is crucially dependent on the degree of growth — with 'low

| Category | Base | Employment (millions) | | | | War-wick[b] |
| | | Low growth | | New growth | | |
	1984[a]	1990	1996	1990	1996	1990
Agriculture	.34	.30	.26	.34	.34	.31
Transport and communications	1.32	1.21	1.10	1.54	1.58	1.29
IOP industry	7.22	6.29	5.23	6.85	7.00	7.24
Hotel and catering	1.02	1.05	1.10	1.14	1.26	1.10
Other services	1.40	1.44	1.50	1.61	1.80	1.52
Banking, finance and insurance	1.90	2.14	2.27	2.14	2.40	2.02
Self-employment	2.33	2.47	2.57	2.47	2.66	2.44
Distribution	3.34	3.27	3.27	3.52	3.70	3.26
Public services	4.84	4.84	4.84	4.84	4.84	4.98
Armed Services	.33	.33	.33	.33	.33	.33
Total	24.04	23.34	22.47	24.78	25.91	24.49

a   Actual values.
b   Derived from *Review of the Economy and Employment,* summer 1983, Institute for Employment Research, University of Warwick (see Appendix 4).

Table 9.1 *The employment scenarios*

Source: Appendix 4, Employment Projections, 1984–96.

growth' the jobs total falls by a further 1.57 million by 1996, primarily because of losses of jobs in the IOP industries. Given the 'new growth' scenario there would be 1.87 million more jobs. It is, of course, implicit that the growth from IT industries percolates through into the rest of the economy. However, as was pointed out in Chapter 1, the jobs summit recedes because the more jobs there are, the more people who are not currently registered as unemployed will come forward for them. Thus, in projecting the future level of unemployment, although it is cautious to set a low number of jobs against the low estimate of working population (and thus avoid accusations of exaggeration), it is equally cautious to set the higher projections of jobs against the high estimate of working population. The resulting calculations are shown in Table 9.2.

Thus with 0.75 million extra jobs resulting directly from public expenditure and a period of new growth, sufficient additional jobs would be created by 1990 for job losses to be overtaken, additional entrants to employment to have been absorbed and, hence, for unemployment to be expected to have started to move down. Even if this slow downward trend in unemployment could continue there would still be two million unemployed in 1996. To

	Base 1984	Low growth 1990	Low growth 1996	New growth 1990	New growth 1996	War-wick 1990
Working population (millions)	27.60	27.70	27.63	28.41	28.70	28.05
Projected employment (millions)	24.04	23.34	22.47	24.78	25.91	24.49
Additional public expenditure employment (millions)	—	0.75	0.75	0.75	0.75	—[a]
Total employment (millions)	24.04	24.09	23.22	25.53	26.66	24.49
Unemployed (millions)	3.55	3.61	4.41	2.88	2.04	3.56
Unemployment rate %	14.8	15.0	19.0	11.3	7.7	14.5

a The 'Warwick' scenario includes an increase of public service employment in the 24.49 million from Table 9.1.

Table 9.2 *Projections of unemployment*

Source: Table 9.1 and Figure 1.3, Chapter 1.

aid comparability, a similar calculation has been made for 1984 as the 'base' year, using the high estimate of working population, and this gives 3.56 million unemployed, a value intermediate between that recorded by official figures — 3.03 million — and that of 3.9 million obtained when allowance is made for those excluded from registering for the official figure and those on special employment and training measures. It must be noted that without the additional public sector employment of 0.75 million jobs the unemployment level in 1996 would be 2.8 million — barely lower than in 1984 despite all the economic growth.

For comparison a scenario entitled 'Warwick' is given in the final column of Table 9.1 and is based on the rates of change in the various employment categories expected by the Institute for Employment Research, University of Warwick, applied to the 1984 base (Appendix 4 gives details of the calculations). The 'Warwick' projections for 1990, based on less than 2 per cent pa growth, are similar to the low growth scenario for all categories except banking, finance and insurance, where it is even lower, and IOP industries where it is higher. The latter difference is the crucial one — it projects a growth in IOP industry employment, in contrast to a decline, which is sufficient to compensate for the other categories (Table 9.1) and give an employment total of 24.49 million, which is approaching that for the new growth scenario (24.78). However, the 'Warwick' scenario involves an increase of only 0.14 million in public service employment (Table 9.1) whereas the other scenarios include 0.75 million (Table 9.2) from

public expenditure.[6] To balance this the total employment level
of 24.49 million has been set against an intermediate working
population of 28.05, which puts unemployment at 3.56 million,
a rate of 14.5 per cent.[7]

The 'Warwick' scenario thus has significant differences from
the low and new growth ones, particularly for industrial employment about which we believe it to be unduly optimistic. However,
the comment passed by the Institute for Employment Research on
the significance of their figures is equally applicable to all these
scenarios:

> 'For some years we have stressed the importance of recognising that any
> major policy to reduce unemployment will be chasing a moving target.
> This needs to be appreciated more clearly when estimates are presented
> in political debate. By the same token, the *underlying* (Institute for
> Economic Research emphasis) level of unemployment applicable to the
> 1982–90 period, taking into account the special programmes, is above
> 4 million'.[8]

The depression scenario

If it is possible to feel slightly optimistic about the new growth
scenario promising some reduction in unemployment in a climate
of expansion and relative affluence, it is profoundly sobering to
contemplate the low growth figures of Table 9.2. An unemployment rate rising to around 19 per cent in 1996 would approach
the worst levels of the US and UK at the height of the 1930s'
depression, and this is on the assumption that people are so
discouraged from seeking work that registered unemployment is
held down to 4.4 million. The upper projection of working population in Figure 1.3 of Chapter 1 indicates that one million more
would like work if it were available — giving a jobs deficit of
at least 5.5 million. But the problem is that there would not be
a rapidly growing GDP out of which to finance the extra 0.75
million public services jobs which have been postulated; the net
cost of these jobs would have to be paid by people currently in
employment through their foregoing any increase in real standard
of living over the next decade, and perhaps even suffering an actual reduction in the standard of living. The 'low growth' scenario
is thus more correctly seen as a 'depression' scenario — marking
the continuation and deepening of the present situation into the
late 1990s.

In such circumstances steps to create additional jobs, by whatever policies, would be bound to meet powerful resistance from

those in employment and their political and trade union represen-
tatives. The problem would be so large that if major reform was
not entered into willingly then those dispossessed of their right
to work could come to support subversive forces, leading to disrup-
tion of the normal political processes. Yet, even in this situation
it would be unacceptable to maintain that nothing could be done
and that the unemployed could have no hope. The arithmetic of
the problem puts it into perspective; four million jobs involving
an average of, say, £2500 additional net income (after tax and NI
contributions clawback) over existing social benefit payments
would add £10 billion on the GDP of some £250 billion. It is not
the 4 per cent single step increase in GDP which is the problem
but how to channel this 4 per cent to the presently unemployed
as jobs; and without the presently employed appropriating it to
themselves.

Conclusions

An examination of Figure 9.1 and Table 9.2 shows that before
1990 it will become clear where these scenarios lie in relation to
the unfolding reality. Whichever scenario most closely represents
the future of the UK, it seems evident from the patterns of
unemployment described in Chapter 1 that only a minority of nations, who through fortunate accidents of demography, repatriation of foreign workers, wholly atypical high growth rates, or,
perhaps, a willingness to fund very large measures of public
employment through taxation, will have any possibility of full
employment occurring through 'orthodox' economic policies. In
general such serendipity will not result and, even given new
economic growth, most industrial nations are destined for continuing unemployment at unacceptably high levels. It is this analysis
which leads us to question in Part 2 the theoretical orthodoxies
behind current economic thinking. We feel sure of our position;
those on the political left who advocate even higher public expenditure to create jobs will also demand substantially lower levels
of unemployment as the outcome of policy; those on the right who
reject public expenditure as an option have at least as big a task
even if they countenance higher levels of unemployment. No one
who wishes to reduce unemployment to 'more acceptable levels'
can avoid the conclusion that current orthodox policies, even if
fully implemented, cannot achieve a sufficient improvement and
that new ideas and new policies are essential.

Notes and references

1. Perez, Carlota (1983) Structural change and assimilation of new technologies in the economic and social systems, *Futures,* **15**, 5, October, pp357–75. Perez points out the vital role played by the ideas of Frederick Winslow Taylor which were a 'social and institutional innovation within the production sphere', in providing the seed idea 'out of which continuous mass production evolved as a fully fledged technological style'. This new style required a transformation of occupational patterns among the work-force, not to an immediately apparent new structure but as a dynamic process extending over many years. Not only was it necessary for a new white-collar middle management to evolve but, without skilled electricians and motor mechanics, the products would never have been made, installed or maintained. Perez sees this 'technological style' as beginning its diffusion in the early 1900s and notes that at that time the USA was able to adapt to this new style more readily than Europe. After World War II, 'there was a good "match" between the requirements of a mass production technological style, based on cheap oil, and the social and institutional framework within which this technological style could flourish'. Of course, in the 1930s there was depression and social turmoil and which were appropriate social and institutional frameworks was not obvious; consequently, the solutions which were advocated varied from Fascism to Communism, with the New Deal and Keynesianism in between. It is now the common belief in Western nations that Keynesian policies were an essential ingredient: 'radical demand management and income redistribution innovations had to be made of which the directly economic role of the state is perhaps the most important'. As a result we moved from a heavy equipment market to mass production consumer and defence markets.

2. Indeed, as has been pointed out, such a growth period is unlikely to be achieved without a massive shift in social and institutional frameworks and attitudes, comparable in magnitude to those which occurred in the 1920s and 1930s. In Ralf Dahrendorf's telling phrase it is possible to be very busy 'planning better yesterdays' — planning IT in the context of the social structure of a Keynesian mass production society. If, in order to exploit IT to the extent necessary for a new economic boom, it is necessary to reconstruct our social and institutional arrangements, then there is little sign that the process has started. Our society is still in thrall to mass production consumerism. It is not that mass production consumerism will have to be eliminated — any more than steel works or railways have been — but it cannot remain at the centre of the socioeconomic structure.

3. The choice of 3.5 per cent pa, which is the same as IOP industry growth in the period 1959 to 1969, is thus one of some optimism for the UK.

4. The background to these calculations is fully discussed in Leach, Donald (1985) Production, productivity and employment: models for UK Index of Production industries, 1950–1990, *The Journal of Interdisciplinary Economics,* **1**, 1, pp29–42.

5. Institute of Employment Research (1983) *Review of the Economy and Employment,* University of Warwick, summer.

6. Part of the difference in the IOP industry projections is due to the Warwick anticipation of 174 thousand extra jobs in construction work. In this book any expansion of the construction work-force is seen as arising from public expenditure.

7. The Warwick value for the working population is 27.4 million, but the 0.33 million in the Armed Services is excluded from this. The total of 27.7 million is the same as Ermisch's lower, 'demographic' projection (Chapter 1, Figure 1.3). For 2.9 million registered unemployed the unemployment rate, excluding the Armed Services, is given as 12 per cent.
8. Ibid., p5.

Part 2:

Rethinking Employment Strategies

CHAPTER 10

Employment and Distribution

The goal of full employment

There is a growing awareness of the limitations inherent in established responses to the employment problem. Economic growth cannot be accelerated to the rate that would be required to absorb millions of workers into production. Workers will not 'price themselves into jobs' simply by allowing their living standards to be eroded, their bargaining power undermined, and their purchasing power reduced. At the same time, stimulation of demand led by public expenditure would encounter supply constraints and strong inflationary pressures long before mass unemployment disappeared, and the principal means by which the centrally planned economies have realized full employment are applicable only at an earlier stage of technological development than that of industrially advanced Western Europe. From whichever tradition of economic thought the issues are approached, it is clear that there are dimensions of the problem that are not adequately dealt with in orthodox prescriptions.

There are those who tend to read all this as a counsel of despair. For them, the goal of full employment must be abandoned and the only message offered to young people is that they must look to pursuits other than formal 'jobs'. We find this morally, politically and socially unacceptable. Nothing could be a more certain recipe for increasing alienation, violence and social destructiveness. The challenge of securing the opportunity of employment for everyone must be met, and we must ask why traditional economic thinking has led to such a loss of confidence in our ability to tackle the problem. Economists are often prevented from pursuing the radical lines of thinking suggested by their own traditions, as a result of an undue concern to accommodate to what is perceived as the 'political realism' of the day. One of the necessary tasks is to help to shift the ground of political debate by exposing the false hopes encouraged by the conventional wisdom. The hope which, more than any other, has to be abandoned is the notion that large-scale unemployment will simply disappear with renewed economic growth. Relinquishing that hope has profound implications both for economic thinking and for social attitudes.

Business decisions

The belief in economic growth as a panacea has proved convenient from many points of view, not least because it enabled many awkward questions concerning the social consequences of business decisions to be pushed to one side. Workers might find their factory or their colliery closed because it was deemed 'uneconomic', despite the fact that the closure would add to the wasted assets and to the dole queues which already surrounded it. Economists offering a defence of such decisions would invariably see them as part of the process of 'creative destruction' inherent in economic growth. The social conscience of those directly involved has, up to now, been calmed by the belief that, with due allowance for the time required for structural adjustment in the economy, the people displaced would find jobs elsewhere. While change destroyed many jobs, the process of innovation could be relied upon to generate a whole range of new possibilities which promised to re-employ the labour no longer required in the old lines of production.

The evidence concerning jobs from industry and market sector services reviewed in Part 1 of this book suggests that in the late twentieth century these comforting beliefs are increasingly untenable. If this is so, then there is a need for a reappraisal of the employment implications of decision making at the level of firms and organizations. It is no longer possible simply to regard employment as amenable to 'macroeconomic' solutions such as reflation, increased public expenditure, or faster economic growth. An effective strategy for employment also requires a re-examination of the 'microeconomics' of costs of production and business decisions. The issues involved here apply to public enterprise as well as to the market sector. The changes may be seen in terms of the redesign of the market incentives within which capitalist firms operate, of the specification of cost criteria for state-owned industry and public authorities, or of the establishment of accounting rules for enterprises in an industrially advanced socialist economy. The theoretical considerations, which will be discussed in Chapter 11, can to a considerable extent be treated as independent of the particular institutional framework of the economy in question. An important theme is that concepts of 'cost' cannot be divorced from the distributional implications of the decisions being taken. This question of distribution in fact becomes central to the whole employment problem.

Growth and distribution

As long as economic growth could in itself be regarded as a solution, it was possible for economists to treat the question of distribution as secondary. The basic concern (both in capitalist and centrally planned economies) was with the success or failure of economic systems in attaining economic growth. In capitalist economies, the problem of distribution was seen as significant for the functioning of the system only in as much as the relative shares of 'capital' and 'labour' were thought to affect the rate of economic growth and stability of output. If extra output from the production industries itself generated the extra employment required, the interests of wage and salary earners in these industries in securing increases in earnings in line with productivity increases need not conflict with the objective of full employment. Indeed, the growth in incomes could be seen as necessary for providing the purchasing power for the goods being produced. If, however, the basic assumption of 'jobs through growth' is no longer justified, then future employment will depend crucially on the way in which the benefits of technological change are distributed.

Redistributing the gains from productivity increases

As the labour requirements for production and distribution of goods decline relative to the size of population of working age, so the creation of sufficient job opportunities comes to depend on the redistribution of the gains from increases in productivity which originate in the production industries. The possible mechanisms through which such redistribution can occur may be readily summarized:

1. Growth in employment in marketed services to compensate for relative decline in production industry employment;
2. Expansion in public services and publically financed construction work;
3. A fall in the activity rate, ie a reduction in the percentage of the population of working age who seek jobs;
4. A reduction in working time instead of reduced employment in the production industries.

When each of these possibilities is examined in turn, it becomes apparent that the obstacles to the expansion of employment lie as much in the problems of distribution as in barriers to growth, failures of demand-management, the nature of technology, or unwillingness of firms to invest.

Marketed services

Looking at the supply side in isolation, services may appear to offer a more favourable prospect for employment expansion than does the production of goods. This is particularly the case if a 'service' is defined as a benefit supplied directly by human effort, in contrast to benefits derived from material goods. On this definition, expenditure on 'services' is inherently employment-creating. We have seen in Chapter 4, however, that the tendencies generated by the market are actually away from consumer services and towards goods. Just as machines replace labour in production processes, so do low-cost goods substitute for expensive services in the consumption process. If existing wage and salary earners were voluntarily to 'trade in' part of their additional purchasing power over goods in favour of higher expenditure on services, this extra expenditure would create new service jobs. The extent to which this occurs in practice appears to be extremely limited. Services tend to become more expensive as a result of increases in real incomes while goods such as video recorders, space invader games, and home computers become cheaper in real terms as a result of technological change. People buy more goods, through self-service outlets, and maintain these goods themselves as far as they are able. In the absence of radical changes in the structure of relative prices, making services cheaper, there is every reason to expect a continued movement towards the 'self-service' economy rather than an increase in demand by consumers for marketed services.

Public services and public investments

Let us imagine a government which fully grasped the absurdity of mass unemployment in the midst of urban dereliction and neglected needs, and which set out to tackle these problems through a bold programme of public works and expanded services. What economic problems would face a contemporary government intent on making public expenditure a weapon against unemployment? The arguments in many ways parallel those relating to marketed services. The feasibility of creating additional employment again depends on the distribution of the extra goods being produced within the production industries. Whereas the growth of marketed services was shown to require a 'voluntary' redistribution through choices over household expenditure, the growth of public services is dependent on a redistribution of output from the goods sector through taxation. Nurses and doctors in the National Health Service consume goods, but do not in any direct sense add to the production of these consumer goods. It is of course equally true that everyone else benefits from medical services while few contribute in any direct sense to their provision, and the services provided are in common sense terms far more valuable than many of the things promoted by the market sector. The problem is that there exists an in-built asymmetry, rooted in market power, which allows transfers within the market sector to go unnoticed or to appear as 'natural'. Meanwhile, transfers to the non-market sector require extra taxation, and typically involve an ongoing political struggle to secure the expenditure needed. In real terms, the growth of public service employment depends on the rate of growth of material consumption by those engaged in goods-producing industries being less than the rate of increase in productivity. Although society as a whole would be manifestly better off with the extra public employment and services than with mass unemployment, there is no escaping the fact that employment outside the market sector does have to be paid for. Achieving acceptance of the distributional implications is the fundamental economic constraint on the growth of public employment.

Reduction in economic activity rates

Sometimes commentators have suggested that the unemployment problem would be 'solved' if the proportion of the working-age population seeking work could be reduced by, say, 10 or 15 per cent. On some occasions, the 'labour supply reduction' approach has taken the form of progressive thinking about the possibilities for extensive early retirement or even 'sabbaticals' from work. At other times, far less progressive notions creep in; that if women went back to housework, or Yugoslav workers in West Germany went 'home', the unemployment statistics would be reduced. There are in fact many economic difficulties with the underlying notion of a fixed 'pool' of jobs to be filled, but what concerns us here are the distributional obstacles to achieving any voluntary change on the 'supply side' of the labour market. All available surveys of household income and expenditure in the UK show clearly that the level of real personal income is strongly correlated with the number of earners in the household. Conversely, deprivation and family poverty is typically associated with lack of regular earned income. High income households tend to be those with more than one regular earner, while poverty is most frequently found among pensioner households and among single parent families.[1] The pressures to secure paid employment have never been stronger, and the costs of exclusion from it are all too evident. Anyone who wishes to propound a reduction in economic activity rates must therefore ask whether society is willing to provide sufficient income in lieu of formal employment — and if so, how?

Shorter working time

Not surprisingly, the idea of a fairer distribution of employment opportunities through shorter working time has been put forward in every crisis of mass unemployment, and has been debated by generations of economists. The fundamental distributional obstacles are always recognized; Gregory in 1930 emphasized that the issue is how new gains are distributed: 'Growing productivity, in fact, gives society a margin to "play with", and this margin is the source out of which unemployment can be relieved' — by allowing the extra income to accrue to those drawn into employment.[2] Beveridge, considering in 1936 whether it would be a good plan to reduce hours of work with a view to absorbing some of the unemployed into work, asks 'when you shorten the working week, what do you mean to do about wages?'. He observed that there is all the difference in the world between leaving *hourly* rates unchanged and *weekly* rates unchanged, and was pessimistic about the prospects for what might be called 'work sharing' arguing that the reduction of working hours ought to be put forward for its own sake, rather than as a cure for unemployment.[3] Trade unions justifiably resist attempts to force cuts in earnings during depressions, particularly when they can point to an increase in the rate of growth of productivity, which has been the case in Britain in the 1980s. There is, nevertheless, a conflict between the interests of employees on one hand, in securing the largest total increase in earnings that technology-derived productivity increases might afford, and on the other hand the maintenance of employment opportunities for the whole work-force. Let us consider two outcomes of a situation in the production industries where hourly productivity is increasing at 3½ per cent per year and output at 2 per cent per year:

Case 1

Hourly pay and weekly earnings both rise at 2½ per cent per year but there is no reduction in the working week. Employment declines at 1½ per cent per year in these industries. If real prices remain unchanged, increased profits arise from the margin of 1 per cent between productivity growth and the growth rate of earnings. The workers' share of the value added by industry falls, but their incomes rise faster than national output.

Case 2

Unions and management negotiate a 2 per cent per year reduction in the working week, with no change in the rates of growth of output and productivity. On paper, this not only enables retention of the existing work-force but also requires an addition to the work-force of 0.5 per cent per year, thus absorbing new entrants to the labour market.

If, in Case 2, the unions were to accept the 2½ per cent rate of increase in *hourly* pay of Case 1, then the decrease in hours would mean an increase in total earning of only 0.5 per cent per year. Such a settlement would almost certainly be unacceptable to the unions' members with output growing at 2 per cent per year. If hourly earnings were increased by 3.5 per cent, then total earnings would rise by 1.5 per cent per year which, although still less than output growth, might be acceptable to the employees. However, this would wipe out the employer's margin which provided the profit-inducement to firms to innovate in the first place.[4]

The machine economy

To highlight the growing conflicts associated with the potential of modern technologies, when adopted within a market economy, it is useful to imagine an economy with two sharply contrasting types of activity. On the one hand there are 'pure' services, which consist solely of labour time and require virtually no equipment. In principle, these services can be expanded without investing in new buildings or infrastructure. The park attendant, or the house-to-house window cleaner who already has a ladder, may be taken as illustrating the 'service' economy. On the other hand, the economy also has major, highly capital-intensive production industries with fully automated, computer-controlled factories which produce goods, supervised at the push of a button by one person.

173

The goods, in other words, are *machino*factured and not *manu*factured. Moreover, they involve technological processes which make it impossible for them to be produced 'by hand' and the concept of 'capital-labour substitution', beloved of neoclassical economists, no longer has any relevance. Alongside these gleaming computerized and robot-operated factories with their handful of technical and managerial staff there are millions of people unemployed. In this dual economy of machine-made goods and pure labour services, how are these millions of people to get a livelihood? What kinds of economic structures and economic policies are needed to bring about the opportunity of employment for everyone?

Let us suppose that, due to a clever bit of computerized rescheduling and fine-tuning in the factories, the output of the production industries increases. This extra output does not require any more people to produce it. Now it happens that the machine supervisors are tightly unionized, with well-organized bargaining power as a result of the immense economic damage that would result from a shut-down (even for a short period) of the plants they supervise. They have also lived through long and bitter struggles with management over the terms on which computer-age technologies were to be introduced, and are not disposed to give up lightly the concessions they have won. They have managed to hold on to the notion of 'productivity' as a description of the relationship between the output of an industry and the number employed in it, and in this way are assisted by the economic statisticians who calculate 'productivity' indices and by the journalists who use them in economic commentaries in newspapers. The society remains caught in the cultural lag between the changed technological realities within which economic life is conducted, and the adaptation of ideas and attitudes to these realities. People still like to think of themselves as 'producing goods', and doing 'a fair day's work for a fair day's pay' — even though the notions of entitlement implicit in such aphorisms have become major obstacles to solving the problems which society has generated for itself. The machine supervisors put in a claim for increased pay in line with increased 'productivity' — and get it. What happens to employment as a result?

The answer depends on how they choose to spend this extra money. If, as a result of rising incomes and an already high material standard of living, they choose to spend more on 'services', then employment rises. The machine supervisors gain a perceived increase in real income in the form of services, and the extra workers

174

drawn into employment in the service sector may then spend at least part of their extra income on the extra goods being produced by the machine sector. This difference in spending patterns between the already employed and the newly employed is attributable to their differing initial levels of consumption. There is in this case no conflict between the interests of those already in jobs, and those previously unemployed. Moreover, any income which the newly employed service workers themselves choose to spend on 'services' will create still more service employment, thus creating an 'employment multiplier' effect analogous to the Keynesian multiplier.

The limits to this multiplier effect are set by the additional demand for goods arising from service workers' spending, which cannot be allowed to exceed the increase in supply of goods. If it does, then the economy would tend to draw in extra imports and run into balance of payments difficulties, or to experience additional inflationary pressures. At least in the short run, the total real income of the economy is constrained by the supply of goods. This becomes even more evident if we envisage a situation where machine supervisors spend all their extra income on goods. There would then be no additional job generation resulting from this spending. Extra employment through increased public expenditure on services or infrastructure would be possible only to the extent that the machine supervisors' extra income would be transferred by taxation. Thus, in this case where machine supervisors want to buy more goods, the material interests of those in employment clearly conflict with the interests of those out of work and seeking jobs. Any attempt to avoid this conflict through allowing increases in total money incomes in the economy in excess of the original increase in production would run into the capacity constraints of the machine sector, and simply create inflationary pressure. This contrasts with the first scenario for machine supervisors' spending, in which the extra money income generated through extra expenditure was matched in real terms by the volume of services created.

It may ultimately be true, even in the machine economy, that people build the factories which produce the goods, and that the supply of goods can in principle be expanded by committing more effort to the goods sector. But this is no consolation to government economic advisers who need to know the limits to the generation of employment through demand-expansion today. The underlying problem is one that is very familiar to development economists, and is summed up in the economists' saying that 'one

175

cannot build today's factories with tomorrow's bricks'. The important thing about goods is that they embody past labour, and the more highly developed the machine economy, the more remote is this labour input from immediate production. In the machine sector, extra labour would contribute via construction to the production of tomorrow's goods, while the workers taking away their wage packets from the building site consume today's goods. In the context of demand-management to increase employment, it is therefore entirely misleading to regard the demand for goods simply as an indirect demand for the labour they embody. The constraints on demand-expansion tend to be set by existing productive capacity, and not by the size of the pool of unemployed labour. This is why the argument that 'spending creates jobs' — which has an obvious appeal within the trade union movement — never contains more than a partial truth. Only if the production of goods involved simple craft activities with a very short production period, would 'goods' and 'services' expenditures be approximately equivalent in their employment-generating effects.

In practice, 'goods' and 'services' are not sharply demarcated as in the 'dual' economy we have imagined. Service activities are never 'pure' labour services, but always require at least some goods as inputs, and are also subject to capacity constraints such as office or shop space. Some services like telecommunications are moreover highly automated. On the other hand, the production of goods always involves some direct labour, and the volume of output does influence the number of jobs. Nevertheless, the nearer we approach the dual economy with its automated industries, the more nearly it is true that extra demand for goods does not create employment, while the expenditure of existing employees competes for the goods which the potentially employed might otherwise consume.

To simplify radically, the dilemma is this: the production industries provide goods, but a diminishing number of jobs; whereas the provision of services creates jobs, but not the commodities on which its employees primarily spend their money. Therefore, the extent of growth of employment is dependent on the 'redistribution' of goods — from the industries that produce them into consumption by the people brought into employment in activities other than the production of goods. That is, the economic surplus arising from the automation of goods production must be transferred to the community as a whole. The *material* consumption of those already in employment would have to be constrained. The problem is how to induce people and firms to allow a larger part of the benefit from productivity increase to accrue in the form of either better social provision and more services, or a rapid reduction in hours worked — or both.

Distribution and technological change

The fundamental question is: what prevents our own society enjoying the benefits of technological change, without this change leading to heightened inequalities and to the irrationality and injustice which unemployment represents?

This question can be addressed at several levels, but there are three major aspects which concern us here:

1. New labour saving technology is not introduced to make workers better off, nor to shorten the working week for the same rate of real wages, nor to generate employment, nor to make possible a better provision of social services. It is introduced to ensure, at minimum, organizational survival through making profits. If the benefits were shared out by paying workers as much as before for a shorter week, or if the gain were simply taxed away to use the money to re-employ the others in the public sector, then the very thing which induces firms to invest in the new technology in the first place — profit — would be liable to disappear.
2. Those in employment do not in general press to receive their share of benefits from productivity increases in the form of a shorter working week or year. Their primary aim is to secure increased real income, mainly in the form of goods. Provided that the number employed in production shrinks fast enough, the management can concede some increase in pay to those remaining, while still cutting the total wage bill per unit of output, and securing profit from the new technology. However, this leaves a growing number 'out in the cold', excluded from the benefits of the technology which has rendered them redundant.
3. The 40-hour week remains central to attitudes about what constitutes a 'job', among the unemployed as well as the employed. This tends to reinforce the rigid division between being in employment and out of work. The unemployed want a 40-hour week job. There is no strong popular pressure for more flexible approaches to the working week, and still less for more radical concepts of work and income sharing (as we have seen in Chapter 7).

These distributional obstacles to employment thus involve the in-built conflict between capital and labour (between profits on one hand and wages and salaries on the other), and the conflict between the immediate interest of those in employment and the unemployed. Employers collectively always seek a solution to their own problems of profitability by holding down wage rates; but they can also each seek to cut their wage bill by employing fewer workers at higher productivity, enabling them to meet higher wage rates and still make a profit. When profitable techniques employ little labour, those in jobs can continue to gain (or at least hold their own) even in depression, while the overwhelming share of the cost of the failures of the economic system is borne by those excluded from jobs. The unemployment problem is inextricably linked with this problem of distribution. Future prospects for jobs depend crucially on how these conflicts are resolved — or not resolved.

Notes and references

1. McNay, Marie and Pond, Chris (1980) *Low Pay and Family Poverty*, Study Commission on the Family, London. This report, financed by the Leverhulme Trust, found that present economic pressures in the UK make it difficult for many families to achieve a 'generally accepted standard of living' where only one parent is working, and many families avoid hardship only through the joint contribution of two breadwinners. The generally strong correlation between level of household income and number of earners in the household is evident in the UK Family Expenditure Survey (CSO Annual).

2. Gregory, T E (1930) Rationalisation and technological unemployment. In Smith, R L (Ed) (1964) *Essays in the Economics of Socialism and Capitalism*, p327, Gerald Duckworth, London.

3. Beveridge, W H (1936) *Planning under Socialism*, pp73–4, Longman, London.

4. The need for translating productivity increase into shorter working time, and the obstacles to achieving this, have not gone unrecognized in the trade union movement. In 1982, the Secretary of the Post Office section of the Civil and Public Services Association stated: 'There are only two options when the efficiency of capital increases dramatically and the demand for labour falls. One is to produce more and more goods, and compete to the point of saturation to stimulate demand for the producable — the way to the society of total materialism and inevitable decay. The alternative is to use the benefits of new technology to offer full employment by a drastic reduction in hours of those in work. Remaining as we are is not one of the alternatives.' Recognizing that the initiative would not come from the employer, the author was appealing for the impetus to come from government, and concluded that 'we must consider legislation banning overtime, reducing hours and maintaining real levels of income' (*Tribune*, 3 September 1982). However, it also has to be recognized that reducing hours is unlikely to lead to a proportional increase in numbers of people required, even if the costs to employers did not increase. A report by the Policy Studies Institute, 'Case Studies of Shorter Working Time', October 1981, found 'little or no evidence that firms which had already reduced working time had been recruiting more workers. The implication was that output could be maintained without increasing employment' (*Financial Times*, 24 November 1981, p19). Another report, by PA Management Consultants, indicated that a 10 per cent reduction in working time might increase employment by 3 per cent, with a 7 to 8 per cent increase in productivity (*Financial Times*, 27 January 1982, p14).

CHAPTER 11

Costs and Incomes

In a society which had developed equitable systems of distribution of both employment and income, new techniques to reduce the amount of work involved in producing a given quantity of goods would not be considered a 'threat'. Such a society might choose both to invest more in and commit greater organizational efforts to the production of goods and to increase the employment of people to improve all kinds of public services and amenities. It might choose to harness technical innovation in order to shorten the working week for everyone, while enjoying as high a material income as before. 'Unemployment', in the sense of people being thrown out of work, would in no sense be a technological inevitability.

Technological unemployment is a consequence of the particular way the present system of production and distribution operates. This can be illustrated by imagining for a moment a future economy in which the basis for the distribution of income is entirely different from that of contemporary West European and North American societies. In a wage-labour economy such as ours, 'work' means engaging in formal employment in factories, warehouses, transport, shops or offices. There are, of course, many other activities involving time and effort which are unpaid and hence not regarded as 'work', many of which are wholly essential to society — most notably bringing up children and running the household.[1] On the other hand, there are formal jobs which may not be arduous and (if only because of the variable and unpredictable nature of the demands for the service supplied) there is considerable 'slack' time where the paper or magazine can be read or last night's soccer match re-lived. The distinction between 'work' and everything else has little to do with how essential the activity is nor with how demanding it is. It is simply a question of whether or not a wage or salary is paid. If people were not paid to work in 'jobs', then almost no one would do so, and if they were not paid to work, there would be hardly any purchasing power in the hands of consumers. The system itself could not then function — quite apart from the fact that people would be liable to starve!

In the envisaged future economy, a basic principle is distribution according to need. People are of course expected to contribute positively to the economic life of society, in accordance with their own circumstances and abilities. But this contribution is understood in a very broad sense, and many activities which would not command a wage in today's economy are highly valued by the society. Financial provision is accordingly made for those who undertake these activities, which include child rearing and, in addition, a much wider range of craft skills and individually creative activities than was able to survive within the wage-labour economy. With technologically sophisticated and highly automated industries for the production of everyday goods, only a small complement of managerial and supervisory staff is required in the factories, which have no need for 'blue collar' workers. The notion of a payment for work that is related to the output of the factory is recognized as an anachronism, and only remnants of that old way of thinking carry over into actual payment systems. People receive a basic income regardless of the kind of activity they undertake, and this ensures a reasonable standard of living. Beyond this, there are differentials related to occupation and to hours, which in a sense represent distribution 'according to work'. But there is in general no relationship between the level of these payments to individuals, and the amounts which enterprises have to enter in their books as 'labour costs'. In this sense, it is not a wage-labour economy.

Firms in this economy may still incur 'employment costs', but these need not bear any close relationship to the personal incomes of the individuals whom the enterprise happens to employ. The two things are worked out on entirely separate principles: personal incomes according to principles of distributive justice and personal incentive; employment costs according to the calculus of efficient resource allocation and inducements to firms to innovate. The state acts as an intermediary to 'balance the books', so that there is no reason why, at the level of the individual enterprise, incomes received and business charges incurred have to coincide. It also regulates the overall level of investment in the economy, either through direct forms of economic planning, or indirectly through regulating the disposal of funds. The balance between 'wages' and 'profits' therefore does not determine the distribution between consumption and investment. Given these conditions, a number of the vital functions which the wage rate fulfils in today's economy would be met in ways which are unrelated to the 'price of labour' to enterprises. To learn from our 'future economy', we therefore have to go back to first principles to establish whether labour use needs to be reckoned as a cost at all in the accounts of an enterprise, and, if so, on what basis it should be calculated. It is by no means self-evident that labour use would have to feature prominently in cost accounting in an economy which dealt with distribution in other ways. There are, after all, plenty of other things which the enterprise could be charged for, such as its demand for energy, the depletion of material resources, its use of land, its discharges to the sewage system — all of which could add up to a rational basis for the accounting of costs, the pricing of products, and the calculation of 'profits' as a measure of enterprise performance. The question about the rational price for the use of labour can only be answered by asking what functions the price of labour needs to fulfil within the system — beyond the distributional functions which it performs in the wage-economy.

The price of labour

In Chapter 2 we rejected the simplistic notion of workers 'pricing themselves into jobs', yet there remains a strong intuitive appeal in the proposition that if the price of something falls sufficiently low, it will almost always be possible to sell a greater quantity of what is available. If employing people did not constitute a cost to business enterprise or other organizations, how could unemployment exist? This line of thinking is impossible to pursue so long as there remains a rigid connection between personal incomes and business costs, but if the nature of this link were to be radically altered through imaginative reforms, then the 'neoclassical' role of price as a mechanism for balancing supply and demand might after all have a place. People are unemployed because it is unprofitable for businesses to employ them; yet there is not a shortage of potentially useful tasks to perform. It is therefore necessary to enquire into the basis of profits or, to turn the question round, to establish the nature of costs.

Financial costs and social costs

To firms, labour is a 'cost' simply because it stands in the way of profits, on which the survival of the firm is dependent. Labour

181

is indeed not simply one cost among many; even for manufacturing firms it underlies the whole structure of production costs. The prices of the raw materials, components and semi-finished products purchased by firms as inputs are in turn dependent on the labour costs incurred at all previous stages of production, including the manufacturing of the machinery and construction of the buildings used to produce these inputs. Viewing the market sector as a whole, what is not wages and salaries is profit — or very nearly so.[2]

However, a 'cost' need not just mean a financial outlay. Cost can be measured in real terms (in equivalent physical quantities of resources, commodities or assets) and it may be defined also as 'something which is sacrificed' or 'opportunities foregone'. This in turn implies scarcity; there would otherwise be no need to give anything up when pursuing a particular option. For a nation, 'production opportunity costs' are the output of other goods and services which could have been produced by some other branch of the economy, if the resources involved had not been committed to the particular enterprise under consideration. If the resources used are not limited in supply, no production opportunity cost is involved for the nation. However, it is likely to be misleading simply to treat as zero the real economic costs of employing an otherwise underutilized resource. For a firm, any task undertaken by management involves a 'management opportunity cost': if they are doing one thing, this generally precludes another. Even the decision to expand the management team involves in the short term the exclusion from attention of other possible opportunities, as well as permanent additional costs which must be met from turnover. Thus it would not cost 'nothing' for a firm to take on 'free' labour, and if this labour were not trained for the task in hand, it would not prove attractive even under this extreme theoretical model.

For society at large there is a different aspect to creating employment, because it will have implications for the distribution of income which can usefully be described as 'distributional costs'.[3] Again distributional costs do not represent any loss of potential output to the economy as a whole, but they do constitute a loss of potential income to some other group in society. Those persons drawn into employment will have more, and others — employees or investors — will have less. This contrast between opportunity costs and distributional costs leads to the centre of the contemporary employment problem. Viewed in terms of production opportunity costs alone, unemployment could be seen as the outcome of a divergence between financial costs to firms and real economic costs to society. Employing people appears to firms as a cost, despite the fact that labour is not a scarce resource, whereas the positive social benefits of additional employment do not appear in the accounts of firms. Although this serves to highlight an obvious irrationality in the system, it also glosses over a basic dilemma concerning the distribution of benefits from technical innovation and the distributional costs of maintaining employment. This dilemma may be illustrated by considering the problem of the profitability of a manufacturing establishment.

The 'unprofitable' factory

Consider a situation in which a factory producing consumer goods is found to be unprofitable because value added (the difference between total sales and purchases from other establishments of raw materials, components, fuel, etc) does not cover the wage and salary bill. Despite a continuing market for the goods being produced, the factory would be closed down if the state did not intervene. Suppose there is already an extremely high level of unemployment in the area, so that closure would mean adding to this unutilized resource, rather than the transfer of labour to more productive alternative activities. The factory already exists, so the investment cost lies in the past, and therefore makes no claim on current investment. If the factory closes, then the total volume of goods and services produced by the economy will be lower, incomes in the area will be reduced, and both the financial and social costs arising from unemployment will be increased. In what conceivable sense can keeping the factory open represent a real economic cost? Expressed in another way, what reason could there be for imputing a 'cost' to the employment of labour in these circumstances? Should not the factory be kept open, despite its accounting losses? Does not its threatened closure on the grounds of unprofitability merely illustrate the great divergence between financial costs to firms and real costs to society?

Unfortunately, the problem is not quite so simple. Let us assume that the reason the factory has become unprofitable is that other more modern plants have introduced technological changes which have substantially raised their level of labour productivity, and that the older plant inevitably lags behind in this respect. Let us further assume that, with regard to other operating characteristics, such as energy efficiency and materials use, the two plants are similar. For the economy as a whole, the widespread introduction of productivity-increasing technological change is precisely what has enabled the wage rates to rise, and this higher wage rate now renders the old plant unprofitable because it is 'technologically backward'. Let us further imagine (in order to simplify the analysis) that there are no income tax or National Insurance contributions, so that workers' take-home pay is the same as the cost to the firm of employing labour, and further that workers spend all their income. Workers' consumption in this case would be equal in value to the gross wage paid by the firms. The failure of the firm to cover its financial costs would therefore indicate that the consumption of the workers employed in the factory exceeded the value of consumer goods output from the factory. This difference would have to be made up from elsewhere in the economy.

The implications of making this transfer can be explored by considering, first, a hypothetical situation in which there are no unemployment benefits or other transfers to those who are unemployed and, second, the more realistic situation in which there is a potential saving of costs of unemployment to the state as a result of increasing the numbers in employment.

Case 1
To meet the factory's accounting losses by paying a state subsidy involves a net addition to tax requirements equivalent to the total financial deficit that has to be made good. If this is done by taxing existing wage and salary earners, the result will be a lower level of consumption on the part of workers in the newer, high-productivity factories, than they might otherwise have attained. The cost of keeping the factory open thus appears in the market economy as a redistribution of income towards workers in the factory and the neighbouring community, even though the total national income is likely to be higher if it continues to operate. Keeping the factory open brings a net benefit in terms of total national product and in social welfare, measured by indicators such as the level of employment and reduction of poverty — provided that it can be shown that an equivalent subsidy would not be more effective in achieving these goals if used elsewhere. The financial subsidy is nevertheless liable to lower the personal incomes of those who are already benefiting most from the fruits of technical change. Thus, although labour is not a scarce resource in the local economy and its use therefore involves no 'production opportunity cost', the scarcity of the *goods* which employees buy means that there is still a *distributional* cost involved.

Case 2

The saving of unemployment and other benefits, plus the tax revenue from the incomes of those employed in the factory, off-sets the apparent cost of the subsidy to the factory.[4] Provided the output of the factory equals or exceeds the *additional* consumption of the employees, compared with their consumption when unemployed, then there is no distribution cost involved in keeping the factory open. Since there is also no production opportunity cost, a rational assessment of labour costs from a social standpoint would involve deducting at least the savings of unemployment-related costs from the gross wage costs.

Why is the apparently straightforward principle illustrated by Case 2 so difficult to translate into actual cost accounting and real decision making? Part of the answer to this lies in the realities of political and economic power, and whose interests are uppermost in the whole process of decision making. Unemployment is not in practice counter to the interests of the businesses which survive depression, particularly as it tends to weaken the positions of trade unions and workers. Moreover, keeping open a branch factory can be presented as a threat to jobs elsewhere since it competes for funds with other plants using more modern technology and offering better prospects for the future. In these circumstances central management will be disinclined to incur the management opportunity cost of keeping the factory open.

The obstacles to change do not only lie directly in the political and management spheres, but also involve an extremely fundamental economic problem — the crux of which is that the price of labour fills a multiplicity of functions. On one hand, as the wage rate it has a set of distributive functions: the channelling of purchasing power into the economy via households, a strong influence on the division of the national product between consumption and investment, and the determination of relative incomes of different groups among wage and salary earners. On the other hand, there is a set of functions concerned with the regulation of production, which involve not just the allocation of labour as a current resource, but also the choice of technique associated with investment decisions and the orientation of research and development effort. We finish up with a list of at least half a dozen functions and it is somehow expected that a single price — 'the wage rate' will fulfil all these functions simultaneously with acceptable outcomes on all accounts. It is rather like having a set of six equations with

185

one unknown. Except by a remotely improbable chance such a set of equations will be inconsistent. Neoclassical economics represents an elaborate but unconvincing attempt to assert the consistency of the set of equations we are considering by treating the volume and intensity of capital investment and the quantity of labour supplied as variables whose levels are determined simultaneously with the wage rate.[5]

Our starting point is the opposite of the neoclassical assumption: we take it that there is no reason to expect that 'a' wage rate — constituting at the same time the cost to the employer and the personal income of the wage-earner — can yield all the desired results of distribution of income and regulation of production. There has always been a latent conflict between these functions, and it immediately surfaces in times of crisis and mass unemployment. As technology develops further along the path of automation and high capital intensity, the conflicts become more and more evident. An appreciation of the reasons for these conflicts may be gained by considering in more detail some of the roles of the price of labour.

Resource allocation

The first function of prices is simply to 'ration' scarce inputs — that is, things which in the short run are limited in supply in relation to the demands placed upon them at a point in time. If this were the only function of price, then it would be possible to prescribe a set of prices which would bring about fuller utilization of available labour and capacity, on the assumption that firms seek to maximize margins over costs. The cost incurred by an enterprise when it employs someone would simply need to be set low enough to minimize unemployment. This 'rationing price', for those employees whose skills were not in demand, generally would be far below the actual incomes of employees in conditions of high unemployment. At least this much can be drawn from neoclassical thinking.

The need to avoid the wasteful use of people's time in uncreative and unrewarding activities is a further reason for attaching a 'price-tag' to labour use. We have no desire to see a return to arduous or dangerous work practices which are more appropriately executed by machines. Indeed, there are still many such tasks to be eliminated and labour costs must remain at a level which would encourage this. However, this is not the same thing as allowing the motive of labour-saving to result in forced redundancies and dole queues. The provision of employment opportunities should be treated, not as a cost, but as a benefit, the ideal being an equitable distribution of both the opportunities for employment and the benefits of technological change, which would include reductions in working time. An important consideration here is that financial costs are not the only inducement to innovation. Even within the existing economic framework, scarcities of particular types of labour can prove a far more powerful inducement to innovation than wage rates.[6] A return to full employment would reinforce this incentive.

Investment and technological change

If the effective allocation and use of labour time were the only considerations in specifying a rational structure for labour and other costs, it would not be difficult on paper to construct an accounting formula for achieving the desired ends. However, in a rapidly changing technological environment, the use of existing resources in association with a given capital stock is almost a side issue. The main question for production economics is what kind of equipment to instal next. Historically, the price of labour has played an enormously important role here, acting as a driving force behind the introduction of new techniques.[7] Indeed, the belief of economists has usually been that without the relentless pressure of wage costs, economic growth would be slowed down by the emergence of labour scarcity. The pattern of incentives affects not just the next generation of investment, based on the existing state of knowledge, but also the type of inventions which enterprises seek to make in their research and development programmes. Although it is true that a high price-tag on labour time will tend to reinforce the effort directed to reducing labour input, motives other than cost savings are clearly involved. These include the consistency and reliability of production processes, and (within the existing structure of business enterprise) the strengthening of managerial control. The question, therefore, is not whether further increases in labour productivity are desirable, but whether the dominant role of cost reduction within much of present manufacturing industry should be allowed to stifle other possible sources of employment, whether in manufacturing or services, now that labour supply has ceased to be the constraint on how much can be produced in the goods economy.

Concepts of cost and ways of accommodating technological

innovation need to change as a matter of urgency if a further polarization of society is to be avoided.[8] The prevailing market pressures have been driving the economy towards a situation in which only the most highly productive plants operating at the technological 'frontier' can survive financially. The others, less well placed to adopt the new techniques, have gone out of business and their employees put out of work. This may have suited the interests of the surviving firms because it has meant a more rapid elimination of their competitors. It has equally suited the diminishing number of industrial workers, who have found themselves enjoying higher gross incomes than ever before — even if a sea of industrial dereliction surrounds their islands of prosperity. It is, however, totally unacceptable as a social outcome. To avoid this outcome, prominence needs to be given to altering the balance of labour costs in relation to income so as to allow more than just high technology ventures to survive and flourish.

The benefits which could stem from a reduction in the cost to enterprises of employing people are many, provided the incomes of wage and salary earners' households were maintained at the same time. It could enable undertakings to survive that would otherwise be found 'unprofitable'. It could allow a wide range of new ventures, in both manufacturing and services, to be commercially viable. It could also underpin community businesses by helping to overcome the problems associated with a lower output per person than is achieved with highly capital-intensive production lines. It could make room within manufacturing for a much greater component of design, quality control, and monitoring, while shifting the balance in favour of maintenance and repair rather than premature replacement. In the services sector it would allow many otherwise unattractively expensive activities to achieve commercial viability. However, a change in priorities of this kind remains impossible so long as the income of employees is at the same time the basis of costs to employers; the existing economic relationships which govern the market economy make it impossible for firms to adopt the necessary changes.

Among the most important obstacles is the dual role of the price of labour, as a cost to firms on one hand and a means of distributing income on the other. At the stage of development now reached in the industrially advanced countries, the compatibility of these two functions is increasingly in doubt and the contradictions become more and more evident. Their resolution requires both a shift away from wages as the underlying basis of operating costs, and a shift away from payment for work as the sole basis of income for most households. The measures outlined in the next chapter may be seen as steps in that direction.

Notes and references

1. A UK insurance group, Legal and General, estimated in 1981 that the work undertaken by a housewife was worth an average of £10,600 per year, on the basis of the wage and salary rates that would have to be paid for the equivalent tasks in the formal economy: 'the average housewife does a 90 hour week encompassing the tasks and responsibilities of a cook, waitress, dishwasher, driver, cleaner, laundress, cost clerk, childminder, seamstress, nurse, gardener and window cleaner'. The insurance company's purpose was to highlight the problem facing a widower with a family. The estimated value of domestic services would, it was reckoned, have put a housewife on a par with a primary school headmistress or a fire service chief.

2. Government taxes and subsidies, foreign trade, and interest and rents paid to financial institutions or individuals modify the relationship between wages and profits; but the link between the two remains so strong that, as a first approximation, the one can be treated as the reverse of the other.

3. This has been emphasized in debates by economists on the employment problems of developing countries at an early stage of industrialization. For example, A K Sen (replying to those who have stressed that labour in developing countries frequently has a zero production opportunity cost) insists that consumption represents a sacrifice of possible capital accumulation and therefore always constitutes a cost: 'Even if the alternative social product is nil, the cost of labour will be positive, given by the increase in consumption due to extra employment'. Sen, A K (1957) Some notes on the choice of capital intensity in development planning, *Quarterly Journal of Economics*. (Reprinted in Livingstone, I (Ed) (1981) *Development Economics and Policy Readings*, p216, George Allen and Unwin, London.)

4. The UK Treasury estimated the cost of an increase in unemployment of 100 thousand in 1981 to be £340 million, or £65 per week per extra person unemployed, and the Manpower Services Commission's estimate was 30 per cent higher than this (*Financial Times*, 10 November 1981, p9). On this basis, the cost was between 50 per cent and 70 per cent of the average earnings of those in jobs. However, attempts to estimate what the earnings of those currently unemployed would actually be if they were in employment (the 'replacement ratio') are fraught with difficulties, some of which are discussed in Trinder, C (1983) Income in work and when unemployed: some problems in calculating replacement ratios, *National Institute Economic Review*, 103, February. In the UK in 1982, the possible benefit entitlements, including supplementary benefit and rent allowances, would reach £40.05 per week for a single householder and £80.55 for a married couple with two children. However, Trinder estimated the average claimed by those unemployed and receiving benefit to be only £36.78 in 1982–83, and the inclusion of those receiving no benefit brought this figure down to no more than £32.50, which contrasts with figures in the range of £44.67 per week that had been used by other authors in estimating 'replacement ratios'.

189

Estimating the probable average earnings levels of those drawn into employment is even more difficult.

5. There are a few economists, who, although adopting a strongly neoclassical approach, reject this consistency and emphasize the importance of separating the distributional and production-regulating aspects of price. James Meade exemplifies this approach; see, for example, Meade, James (1964) *Efficiency, Equality and the Ownership of Property*, George Allen and Unwin, London.

6. For example, in the case of the introduction in Britain during the late 1960s and 1970s of one-man operated buses in place of the driver-and-conductor system, it was found that 'in many cases the cost-savings have been small' and 'its introduction has been largely in response to problems (at that time) of labour shortage and declining revenue'. Thomas, Barry and Eaton, David (1977) *Labour Shortage and Economic Analysis: A Study of Occupational Labour Markets*, Blackwell, Oxford.

7. Including the 'indirect' labour input embodied in intermediate goods and in capital goods. We have avoided the term 'labour-saving', which is given a specific technical meaning by economists in models of the process of capital accumulation and growth. Technical change does not have to be 'capital-biased' for there to be an employment problem, if the rate of technical change exceeds the realized rate of growth of output.

8. The principle that labour is the underlying basis of value is often thought of as a timeless truth in Marxist economic theory, but it was precisely the conflict between the system of distribution on one hand, and the production relationships of a technologically advanced society on the other hand, which Marx believed would ultimately necessitate a different kind of economy with a different value-system: 'As soon as labour, in its direct form, has ceased to be the main source of wealth, then labour time ceases and must cease, to be its standard of measurement.' (McLellan, D (1973) *Marx's Grundrisse*, p165, Paladin.) Marx went on to argue that 'an altered means of distribution will derive from an altered basis of production emerging from the historical process' (ibid., p175).

CHAPTER 12

Incentives to Employment

Policy objectives

If employment is to increase, then a greater proportion of the benefits from technological change will need to accrue in forms other than increases in material incomes for those already in jobs. The possibilities include:

1. People taking the benefits in shorter working time rather than increased income;
2. The encouragement of demand for certain types of activity which have a higher 'service' component and hence generate employment;
3. The acceptance of such taxation levels as would be necessary to re-employ those people whom industry no longer requires, in improving the provision of public services and amenities.

These possibilities have in common the requirement that extra *goods* associated with productivity increases in production industries become available for consumption by those newly entering or re-entering employment. This can be consistent with increases in living standards for those now in jobs, especially if this increase is perceived, at least in part, in terms of less stress, more leisure, or better service provision, either through the market or through the public purse. The underlying purpose of the kinds of policies outlined in this chapter is to begin to provide a framework of incentives which can encourage this.

The policies examined are:
  (a) Taxation and corporate incentives.
  (b) Taxation, social benefits and personal incentives.
  (c) Incentives to self-employment.

The objectives are:
1. The effects of the tax system should reduce, rather than increase, the cost to firms of providing employment.
2. The take-home pay of individuals should demonstrate a clear advantage from undertaking work, even if only for a few hours per week.
3. The resulting incentive structures should favour the employment of those

at or below the average in terms of their earning potential, rather than the absorption of more of the total wage and salary bill in paying people with above-average earnings.

4. Incentives to firms should encourage 'work-sharing' in a broad sense, involving reductions in hours with the retention of the same number of people on the pay-roll, an avoidance of overtime by carrying a sufficient staff complement, and improved opportunities for part-time employees.

5. Greater recognition by society of the contributions of those not seeking full-time paid employment, which particularly includes women in families with children and those who contribute through voluntary activities. The observed increase in part-time employment in recent years[1] should be regarded not simply as a negative consequence of depression, but as a social trend which may have positive and enduring features.

6. Improved opportunities for self-employment (some of which are at present confined to the 'black economy' and need to be legitimized).

In pursuing these employment objectives, a number of complementary aims can also be incorporated. These include a strengthening of the system of company taxation and incentive-based anti-inflationary measures, which are discussed in relation to the specific proposals for a turnover tax. Although the policies will be discussed in a UK context it is hoped that others will see how they might be modified to fit into their own circumstances. Indeed, it would have obvious advantages if a larger group of nations — such as the EEC — were to embark on a concerted employment expansion programme. The reflationary elements would then be less likely to lead to balance of payments problems for individual countries, and there would be less room for objections that the tax changes would adversely affect the international competitiveness of certain kinds of firm. The policies are thus seen as providing a framework rather than a set of blueprints.

Taxation, wages and employment

Real labour costs can be greatly in excess of the net amount received by the employee because of taxes levied on the employer and the impact of direct taxation on employee incomes. In the UK, labour costs normally exceed take-home pay by 50 to 60 per cent. Furthermore, the personal tax and benefits system is notorious for the earnings plateau which it produces, so that over a certain income range an increase in wages gives the wage earner effectively the same disposable income as before — despite the extra cost to the employer. There may thus be a disincentive for the employer to pay more and a disincentive for the worker to accept more work. This type of decoupling of the relationship between employers' wage costs and employee net income is to no one's advantage, and would certainly be judged by neoclassical economists to reduce the efficiency of the employment market.

The link between labour costs and employment levels should be considered an important positive aspect of employment policy which needs to go beyond merely removing some of the gross anomalies of the present tax system. In Chapter 11, while rejecting the cruder arguments about workers 'pricing themselves into jobs' which are often derived from neoclassical propositions about the labour market, we indicated that the effects of the cost structures facing firms and organizations need to be taken very seriously as a factor governing their decisions. Lowering the cost of employing people is a potentially important element in an employment strategy, and incorporating this element depends on three crucial points that are often absent from neoclassical debates:

1. A change in the cost to firms of employing labour must be distinguished from any change in net disposable incomes of wage-earner households.
2. Employing more *people* must be distinguished from employing more *labour*, in the sense of total work-hours.
3. The positive reasons for encouraging the employment of people need to be distinguished from the mechanistic notions of 'capital-labour substitution' which dominate so many economic models.

These distinctions are fundamental to the policy proposals we make.

The distinction between labour cost and household income has two basic aspects:

1. the way the tax system affects the relationship between take-home pay and employment costs;
2. the way that the benefits system affects the relationship between 'earnings' and income.

It is clear that from both points of view the existing UK tax-benefit system is perverse. A major share of the burden of taxation falls on labour, in the sense that it increases the costs of employing labour relative to the wage or salary earners' actual incomes. In terms of the impact on firms, the tax incidence could be shifted to fall more on output, on profits, on capital costs, or material and energy inputs, or in incomes paid out to those above the average wage salary level in the form of unearned income. Employment incentives would have the aim of *reducing* the basic costs of employment, and locating the incidence of taxation elsewhere, while benefits should complement lower earned incomes so that household incomes exceed the amount received as 'earnings'. These problems therefore need to be tackled both from the company taxation and the personal benefits side.

The distinction between the amount of employment generated and the actual number of work-hours is important for two reasons: first, in providing incentives it is by no means desirable to encourage less efficient use of peoples' time; organizations which increase hourly productivity must still be able to gain under any new system. Second, although we have argued that increasing the level of employment depends on restraining the increase in material incomes of those in jobs, nevertheless the acceptance of a wider distribution of employment opportunities through shorter working time will be dependent on higher *hourly* earnings, or an increase in household income from some other source — or both. Thus it is critical to ensure that hourly rates are high enough to enable an element of 'work sharing' through shorter working time or part-time employment to be a realistic proposition for a significant number of households. In direct contrast to the 'workers pricing themselves into jobs' argument, the aim would be to make *higher* hourly rates combined with shorter working hours (rather than increases in weekly earnings) a more attractive proposition both for employers and employees.

It is not the present purpose to rewrite tax laws but rather to show that the present system could be modified in ways which would be expected to increase employment. A start on such changes can moreover be made at reasonable cost and without a total recasting of present tax systems. In this way it is hoped to avoid the objections encountered by proposals for immediate radical reform,[2] which are often seen as hopelessly costly and liable to disrupt the workings of the economy. To illustrate the principles involved, a number of specific proposals for revision of the UK tax system will be described. The key features are to reduce the cost to companies of employing people at average and below-average incomes, and to ensure an incentive for those who are encouraged to take on these jobs. The net effect would be a substantial reduction in the gap between take-home pay and cost to the employer, with the aim of increasing the number of employment opportunities within the market sector.

A company turnover tax with employment allowances

The present company tax system raises revenue in three main ways: corporation tax levied on profits, employers' National Insurance contribution (ENIC), and value added tax (VAT). ENIC and VAT are unavoidable taxes, paid whether a company makes a profit or not. Corporation tax (being levied on profits) is to a considerable extent avoidable by claiming allowances which can be offset against tax liability.[3] To meet the aims outlined at the beginning of the chapter, a shift from taxation of employment to taxation of the value of output is proposed. ENIC would be replaced by a corporation turnover tax (CTT) coupled with a tax allowance based on the number of people on the pay-roll. This employment allowance, which parallels capital investment allowances currently available to companies for plant, machinery and building projects, would give the system the necessary flexibility to encourage both efficient use of employee time and more flexible arrangements with respect to working time. The taxable turnover would be approximately equivalent to value added, but the way in which the tax would operate is totally different from present VAT, and is more appropriately compared with the existing corporation tax.

The employment allowance would be set against CTT, thus reducing a firm's tax liability in accordance with the number of jobs it provided, whether these jobs were part time or full time. The employment allowance would be computed on a week-by-week basis, at a flat rate per person-week for all employees paid above a certain threshold level of pay. Below this threshold, the amount claimable would be a proportion of the actual pay of the employee concerned.[4]

Let us consider a firm with a computed turnover of £1 million of which £500 thousand is pay-roll, and let us assume the national average income to be £10,000. Then if the flat rate employment allowance was set at £10,000, the threshold set at £5000, and the turnover tax at 10 per cent, we can compute the resulting tax levels as shown in Table 12.1, and compare these with present ones under ENIC, as operated in 1984–85 and 1985–86.[5] These last two columns differ as a result of the changes to ENIC made in the March 1985 budget, which removed the previous ceiling of £13,000 above which ENIC was constant and applied lower rates to earnings below £6750 per year. These changes indeed indicate an increasing awareness that employment considerations need to be brought into the structure of taxes and benefits,

No of employees	Average pay £	Taxed turnover £	Tax liability £	ENIC 1984–85 £	ENIC 1985–86 £
0	—	1 000 000	100 000	Nil	Nil
10	50 000	900 000	90 000	13 585	52 250
20	25 000	800 000	80 000	27 170	52 250
50	10 000	500 000	50 000	52 250	52 250
80	6 250	200 000	20 000	52 250	45 000
100	5 000	Nil	Nil	52 250	45 000
125	4 000[a]	Nil	Nil	52 250	28 000

a For pay below the threshold the employment allowance would be 200 per cent, which at a turnover tax rate of 10 per cent is equivalent to an employment subsidy of 20 per cent.[4]

Table 12.1 *Sample taxation levels with combined corporation turnover tax and employment allowance, for a firm with £1 million annual turnover*

but do not do enough to provide positive employment incentives.

In Table 12.1 it has been assumed that the average pay is the actual pay of each employee but divergence from this could affect the calculations. (For instance, if the firm with 100 employees had 90 of these on £4000 pa and 10 on an average of £14,000 pa it would then have a tax liability of £18,000). The value to the employer of the employment allowance is the amount of tax saved, ie in this example, the saving is effectively £1000 per person employed above the threshold. The purpose of the threshold is to prevent an open-ended subsidy to low-paid employment, while in the range between the threshold level and the average wage, the value of the employment allowance as a percentage of the wage bill is higher than with above-average earnings. The justification for this is twofold. On one hand, it may enable the inclusion of part-time employees at the full rate of allowance, thus encouraging various forms of 'employment sharing'. At the same time, a majority of the unemployed would, on re-entering employment, be likely to get jobs somewhere within this band (since they are generally not well placed to command above-average rates). In this sense, the incentives would tend to have their effect where they are most needed.

In the UK, the system could in due course replace the existing corporation tax, because the scheme proposed in effect represents a modified profits tax. It differs from a conventional profits tax in that in calculating taxable income, the sum deducted for 'labour' is not the actual wage bill, but a standard allowance per worker.

Thus the 'extra' pay to above-average wage and salary earners is for the purposes of computing taxation, treated as if it were distributed profits.

A major advantage of introducing employment subsidies through tax allowances is that the scheme as a whole can be self-financing. 'Revenue neutral' changes in the size of the effective subsidy can be made by simultaneously altering the turnover tax rate and the employment allowance. (Further examples are discussed in Appendix 5.)

No explicit distinction between *full*-time and *part*-time employees need be made; the only criterion would be total earnings. However, employees would be required to identify for tax purposes their principal employment within any given period, and only this one employer would be able to claim the corresponding employment allowance.[6] This would encourage employers to take on persons who had no other job and thus encourage the spread of available work over as many people as possible. Equally, it would act as a barrier to the person with a full-time job from competing for additional part-time employment, and could (if desired) be used to discourage the employment of persons over retirement age.

From Table 12.1 it can be seen that the main advantages of a combined scheme for a company turnover tax and employment allowances are:

1. For any given total wage and salary bill and any given structure of hourly rates, employers would benefit from seeking to maximize the number on the pay-roll. In tax terms, they would gain by avoiding overtime above the threshold and by reorganizing shifts rather than reducing the number on the pay-roll. They would have a stronger incentive to attempt to negotiate with trade unions for a shorter working week with higher hourly rates, in lieu of increases in weekly earnings. Wherever a 'full-time' job was paid above the threshold, it would be in a firm's interest to encourage work-sharing arrangements.
2. Because the full wage and salary expenditure would contribute to value added, and hence to gross tax liability, the fraction of any employee's earnings which was above the threshold would result in the firm paying extra tax. The scheme would thus mean a progressively increasing effective tax rate on above-threshold wage and salary payments.
3. While discriminating against high weekly rates, the proposals would in no way penalize the payment of higher *hourly* rates, if accompanied by reduced working hours. Thus, although the scheme is implicitly an incentive-based incomes policy aimed at putting a brake on average earnings, it does not side with employers who aim to hold down the rate of pay for a given amount of work.
4. The scheme would offer a tax-based 'incomes policy'. Increases in earnings for the very low paid would in effect be subsidized by an amount

dependent on the turnover tax rate and the percentage tax allowance at below-threshold earnings. Meanwhile, pay rises for those already above the threshold would automatically bear the full rate of turnover tax if the increase exceeded the annual adjustment of the threshold to allow for inflation.

It must be recognized that there would be opposition from employees whose income was reduced by loss of overtime, and from unions who found that in place of an expected offer of an across-the-board pay increase they were offered a reduction in working hours for the same total earnings. The argument is that from society's point of view this is better than giving all the benefits from productivity increases to a smaller group of people and only unemployment benefit or social security benefit to the rest.

Obviously the taxation scheme outlined above would be resisted by highly capital-intensive firms and others, such as computer software houses, which employ only a few highly paid employees in relation to the total value added. Under the turnover tax and employment allowance system, they would have to bear a substantially bigger share of the total tax burden. Indeed, if the corporation turnover tax were extended to include the amount otherwise raised by the existing corporation tax (profits tax) then the prices of capital-intensive and other goods would need to rise, to allow the tax liability to be paid while still leaving a post-tax profit. Conversely, the relative price of more labour-intensive goods and services would be expected to fall. This could bring some further positive impact on employment through longer run demand adjustments. In this event, transitional arrangements would certainly be needed to allow highly capital-intensive sectors like petrochemicals to adjust, and the need to avoid any negative effects on the rate of innovation could be one of the factors which would set an upper limit on the acceptable rate of corporation turnover tax.[7]

Other proposals have been made for somewhat similar company taxation systems, of which Layard's[8] is the best known in Britain. The objective, however, has usually been to tax increases in pay essentially as an anti-inflation device. This immediately poses the problem of defining a change in the rate of pay, and raises the question of the formula to be used in calculating a firm's total tax liability. The possibility that the use of the total wage bill (divided by the number of employees) would lead to firms 'diluting' the pay-roll with part-time employees has been raised as an objection to Layard's proposals. While this may be a drawback if one is attempting to tax pay increases as such, it ceases to be a problem (and may even be an advantage) if the scheme is formulated primarily with a view to promoting employment rather than controlling inflation. In the turnover tax/employment allowance scheme, no attempt is made to define full-time jobs or to define a single rate of pay increase. Indeed, pay increases at the bottom of the scale are intentionally encouraged.

Employment incentives within public bodies

It is important that public employment should operate in a similar climate, with inducements to maximize the employment opportunities generated by any given level of expenditure. This could be done by establishing similar guiding principles to those encapsulated in the combination of corporation turnover tax and employment allowance. One possible mechanism would be to specify for public bodies — including local authorities, health boards, and universities — a 'reserve' element in the total amount allocated, against which total they would be granted an employment allowance on the same basis as private firms. Organizations meeting or exceeding a target ratio of employment to total expenditure would keep all of their allocation of funds, including the reserve, and might be eligible for an additional payment. Meanwhile, other organizations could lose all or part of their 'reserve' funding. In the UK, it would be possible for central government to establish such a system through a revised form of rate support grant. The government would not underwrite unlimited expenditure on employment creation by local authorities and other public bodies, but would offer some inducement to use the available funds to provide as many employment opportunities as possible. For example, if a local authority avoided the need for a senior level post at £20,000 per year, but employed three people at £6000 or £7000 per year, it would gain under the system proposed.

A personal benefit

Just as the cost of labour is important to the employing firm, so is the take-home pay to the individual worker. The worker must see a clear advantage in extra effort, and there must be a reasonably consistent relationship between extra work and extra income, particularly at lower levels of pay. It is unrealistic to expect an unemployed person to be willing to take a job at a wage which is so low that, after deduction of necessary expenses for travelling, clothes, and meals at work, the net take-home pay is little higher than the income available from unemployment or social security benefit. The existence of the present 'poverty trap' has predictably led to right-wing pressure to cut benefits, not only to cut expenditure but also in the hope of driving people to take low-paid jobs. But when jobs are in very short supply the notion of tackling the problem through increasingly repressive social policies is not only morally indefensible, but also generally ineffective. In contrast a system geared to encouraging work requires a recognition that it ought to become possible for a person's income to be derived from a number of sources, including an element from unemployment or social security benefits.

The proposal outlined below is for a weekly payment — a personal benefit — available as of right and non-taxable. This is then the minimum support that any individual can receive no matter how they organize their life, and would not be subject to any conflicts with the authorities over regulations concerning the payment of other benefits. The personal benefit would be paid to all adults — men and women, rich or poor, low-income or high-income earners. It would provide a non-working spouse with an income in his or her own right and lead to separate taxation for all wives.[9] All income would be taxed and the National Insurance contribution would be incorporated in the payment so that there would be no threshold levels causing sudden imposition of contributions — and hence creating poverty traps which result in take-home pay falling as the result of a rise in pay.

For those receiving pensions, other social security benefits, or student grants, the personal benefit would replace the equivalent part of their entitlement. The payment has been called the 'personal benefit' because, far from being revolutionary, it would, in the UK, be a direct descendant of the child benefit. In order to bring in this benefit without incurring excessive budget costs, it is proposed to introduce it at a level equivalent to *the value to those in employment of the existing single-person's tax allowance*, which it would replace (see Appendix 6). In contrast, tax allowances are in effect benefits given by the state — but only to those individuals in jobs. The personal benefit would simply extend the benefit to everyone, by giving them a payment totalling £600 pa in place of a tax allowance of £2005 to be set against income — which would otherwise be taxed at 30 per cent (1984–85 values). The personal benefit could be paid in a number of ways, eg through the Post Office or direct into a bank or building society account.

The personal benefit could be expected to influence employment in several ways:

1. It would be payable to *all* adults, including those not in employment, irrespective of the employment status of any other member of the household. This might induce some people — for instance, those with spouses who have a regular wage or salary — to choose not to seek full-time paid employment but, for example, to undertake voluntary work — or, with the additional incentives outlined later in this chapter, to enter into self-employment.
2. It could help to facilitate activities that would be socially useful, but cannot at present support well-paid full-time employment. These activities include those that community businesses might undertake and which would become more viable for some groups, particularly the young, at the lower end of the earnings scale.
3. It would extend the principle of an entitlement to *some* income not related to 'work' as formally defined by the economic system. This entitlement would automatically provide an income for child rearing, home maintenance, and related everyday activities which society currently acknowledges as 'work' only when someone *else* is paid to do them!
4. It could encourage staying on in the educational system whether at school or by transfer to further education, provided the necessary places were provided.

There have been many such proposals made over a long period of time: 'negative income tax', 'tax credits', 'benefit credits', 'social dividend' and 'national dividend'.[10] The present proposal has something in common with these earlier ideas, and has three main aims:

1. To ensure that an adequate total income is provided for those who have only low earnings from their work.
2. To ensure smoothly increasing net income for all increases in earnings. (This elementary, common sense requirement is not even provided by the present UK system.)
3. To offer a system that can be introduced at a cost in keeping with the existing UK tax system and thus can avoid the charge of being unrealistic. The proposed personal benefit would be largely financed by recasting the present personal tax allowance system and the cost would be containable within the cost of normal income tax adjustments in annual budgets over a two- or three-year period. The cost would be borne mainly by those with above-average incomes (see Appendix 6).

The salient details of the personal benefit tax system as shown in Table 12.2 are:

1. Very low net incomes would exceed the total income before the addition of personal benefit.
2. Net incomes are increased up to about £7300 for a single person, £9600 for a married couple where the wife does not work and £4900 for a married

| Total income before tax and benefit £ | Single person | | Married couple | | | |
| | 1984–85 TAX+NIC system £ | Personal benefit system £ | One spouse working[a] | | Both working[a] | |
			1984–85 Tax+NIC system £	Personal benefit system £	1984–85 Tax+NIC system £	Personal benefit system £
1 000	1 000	1 400	1 000	2 000	1 000	2 000
1 750	1 750	1 850	1 750	2 450	1 750	2 600
1 800	1 638	1 880	1 638	2 480	1 638	2 640
3 200	2 554	2 720	2 912	3 320	3 200	3 520
5 500	3 957	4 100	4 302	4 700	4 903	4 900
11 000	7 312	7 310	7 657	7 910	8 258	8 200
15 700	10 422	9 989	10 767	10 589	11 125	10 882
23 600	15 162	14 450	15 680	15 050	16 267	15 397

a   For the UK income tax system, the 'one spouse' must be the husband and 'both' includes the case where only the wife works.

Table 12.2 *Comparison of net annual incomes: 1984–85 tax system and proposed personal benefit system*

Source: Table A6.3 in Appendix 6.

couple, both working or the wife only working. The income tax system has given larger allowances to married couples who both work and thus any change to separate taxation for husbands and wives is bound to increase their taxation. However, in the example given the increase is still only £58 pa at £8258 pa.

3. As indexation of tax allowances in line with inflation would have increased net incomes for all persons, the levels at which falls in real income would be perceived would be somewhat lower than those indicated in 2. (See Appendix 6 for further comment.)

4. The NIC 'trap' is shown by the £112 drop in net income for a single person between total incomes of £1750 and £1800, in contrast to the graded increase of £30 for the personal benefit system.[11,12] (An example involving this problem is given in Appendix 6.)

In the short run it might appear that the additional taxation involved in financing the personal benefit could be used more directly as public expenditure to create jobs in, for example, public services. However, if it is accepted that society needs to view work and income in new ways, and that the 'job creation' approach alone is insufficient, then the personal benefit is justified not only because of its role in altering the incidence of taxation, but also because it may be expected to encourage further changes in attitudes and policies.

Incentives for self-employment

An employment allowance scheme ought to be paralleled by tax benefits available to the self-employed, with a subsidy operating below a certain threshold. The budgetary and social costs of unemployment would thus be recognized. This appears to be accepted in principle in the UK government's Enterprise Allowance scheme, which offers £40 a week for a period of one year to someone starting up in business as a self-employed person instead of drawing unemployment benefit. The trouble is that this scheme is seen as temporary, whereas what is required is that such schemes become permanent. It ought to be made possible for a person to make a reasonable income from the personal benefit, self-employment and some unemployment benefit. To be attractive, the 'rate of pay' for the self-employed needs to exceed the loss in benefit, and a system in which a person loses a pound of benefit for every pound earned is no way to encourage self-employment — it only leads to work being undertaken in the black economy.

In this scheme someone previously unemployed who became self-employed would lose only a proportion, say 50p, of each pound of unemployment and supplementary benefit for every pound of self-employment income earned. This could continue to apply up to the level where the benefit disappeared under this formula, and the person would, of course, still receive the personal benefit. A person who was already self-employed, whose total income fell below a prescribed level, would be entitled to draw a proportion of the benefit for which he or she would be eligible if wholly unemployed. Unlike the government's present self-employment support scheme, these provisions would not be viewed as temporary measures, but as a permanent complement to the incentives embodied in the business taxation scheme.

The gap between labour cost and take-home pay

We have pointed to the need to reduce the gap between labour cost of the employer and the take-home pay of employees at average pay and below. The combination of the corporation turnover tax, employment allowance and personal benefit schemes would produce such an effect. An illustration of the possible change which could result is given in Table 12.3.

The new systems would allow very low-paid employees to have a 'home income' — ie take-home pay plus personal benefit — which exceeded the labour cost to the employer. It would reduce the gap for other wages and salaries below and around the mean, and would increase the gap for gross earnings substantially above the average

Gross wage or salary £	Labour cost 1984–85[d] £	Take-home pay 1984–85 £	Differ-ence 1984–85 £	Labour cost with CTT-EA[a] £	Home income with PB[b] £	Differ-ence with CTT-EA and PB £
1 750	1 750	1 750	0	1 750	1 850	− 100
1 800	1 988	1 638	350	1 800	1 880	− 80
3 200	3 534	2 554	980	3 200	2 720	480
7 900	8 725	5 421	3 304	8 487	5 540	2 947
11 000	12 150	7 312	4 838	12 212	7 310	4 902
23 600	24 959[c]	15 162	9 797	27 320	14 450	12 870

a   Corporation turnover tax — employment allowance.
b   Personal benefit.
c   The 1985 budget will increase this to £26,066.
d   The actual labour cost would be larger than this in most cases because of employer's pension contribution and liability to sickness payments.

Table 12.3 *Difference between labour cost and take-home pay gaps (single person)*

Source: Tables 12.1 and 12.2.

(the average gross earnings, for full-time and part-time work, in the UK in 1984–85 was approximately £7300 pa).

The limits of incentive policies

The proposals made in this chapter are intended as a call for permanent major reforms in incentives. They must emphatically not be regarded as advocating temporary employment subsidies and income support which would be phased out as full employment returned. The measures advocated here are indeed modest compared with the magnitude of the task. This is because they are intended to be capable of implementation by any government, almost irrespective of its general political stance, that is seriously concerned to make tax and benefit systems work in favour of, rather than against, employment. The proposals are not put forward as policies that are in themselves capable of overcoming the unemployment problem, but any government that is not prepared even to act on this level cannot claim to have taken seriously the distributional problems of 'full' employment.

A temptation facing any advocate of incentive schemes is, however, to claim too much for their favoured policies. The possible impact of incentive policies alone is necessarily severely circumscribed. In the face of unemployment on the scale of the capitalist economies today, mere changes in tax structures can offer but modest benefits. In the context of the problems of areas of high local unemployment, where the whole base of the local economy has been undermined and where unemployment is 25 per cent or more, such reforms may have little relevance. The fundamental issues of planning to meet the needs of such communities, and establishing the right to work as a basic principal of society, reach far beyond the bounds of company tax law and fiscal reforms. But incentive policies should at least point in the right direction, and in so doing help to encourage attitudes and decisions which are conducive to the more basic changes that are needed. Above all, they must not make matters worse. The present UK tax system fails to meet even these minimum requirements. Tax allowances have been concerned with investment, not employment, on the assumption (no longer acceptable) that if investment were encouraged the jobs would follow. There are no incentives to distribute employment opportunities more widely, nor to achieve a more equitable distribution of income from employment. It is time that tax systems were made to work in favour of employment, rather than against it.

Notes and references

1. See Robinson, O and Wallace, J (1984) Growth and utilisation of part-time labour in Great Britain, *Department of Employment Gazette*, 92.9, September, pp391–7. This study found that, with one exception, part-time labour was not engaged as a substitute for full-time labour and that part-time employment grew from 15 per cent to 21 per cent of total employment in Great Britain between 1971 and 1981.
2. For example, Roberts, Keith (1983) *Automation, Unemployment and the Distribution of Income* (2nd edn), European Centre for Work and Society, Maastricht.
3. A study of taxation in the UK in the late 1970s revealed that only five of the 20 leading industrial companies paid any corporation tax in 1977, and the authors suggested that tax allowances had resulted in a situation where 'for the "average" industrial company corporation tax has effectively been abolished'. Kay, J A and King, M A (1978) *The British Tax System*, p198, University Press, Oxford.
4. For a threshold T and flat rate employment allowance E, then the proportion P would be given by $P = E/T$. The employment allowance for a salary, S, where $S < T$ would be PS, whereas for $S > T$, the employment allowance would be the flat rate of E.
5. The rates of ENIC are:

Earnings £ pa	Employers National Insurance contributions rate on all earnings %	
	1984–85	1985–86[a]
Below 1 768	Nil	Nil
1 768 to 13 000	10.45	See values below
1 846–2 860	10.45	5
2 861–4 680	10.45	7
4 681–6 760	10.45	9
6 761–13 000	10.45	10.45
13 000 and over	Flat rate[b]	10.45

a From 6 October 1985.
b Calculated on £13,000, ie £1358.50.

6. The employment allowance would be specifically identified against individual National Insurance numbers, and would be checkable against PAYE records for purposes of detecting fraud.

7. We do not believe that taxation policy has a dominant role to play in inducing the establishment of the new technology system which we regard as the precondition of an extended period of growth. The risks inherent in establishing new ventures, and perhaps especially those in new technology, far outweigh any likely taxation regime and are balanced by the enormous opportunities for capital gains. The UK's new Unlisted Securities Market shows the risk-opportunity span quite dramatically. In just under a 12-month period £100 invested in the 'best performer' would have grown to £470, and in the 'worst performer' shrunk to only £16 (see *Financial Times*, 29 December 1984). As Fred Hirsch's concept of social limits to growth shows, making money is by no means a sufficient reason for entrepreneurship. The excitement of involvement in the new technology will be for many a prime motivation, and the ability to obtain capital to support what is, after all, a risky venture, may be more important than the size of the fortune which may result from the venture. Indeed, those who wish to lend such venture capital (and who do wish to make large fortunes) have to contend with the technological entrepreneur's desire to keep personal control of the firm.

8. Layard, Richard (1982) Is incomes policy the answer to unemployment?, *Economica*, 49, pp219–39. Previous versions include Wallich, A and Weintraub, S (1971) A tax-based incomes policy, *Journal of Economic Issues*, 5, pp1–19; and Kotowitz, V and Portes, R (1974) A tax on wage increases, *Journal of Public Economics*, 3, pp113–32.

9. Of course, those who wished would be free to decline to accept payment!

10. A recent proposal in this vein was Cooper, A G B (1983) Negative income tax and unemployment, *Journal of the Operational Research Society*, **34**, 9, pp876–84. Although the idea of social dividend as a remedy for unemployment is often opposed by economists, Joan Robinson suggested that the reason was 'not an economic objection' but simply that it threatened to undermine the power of the monetary authorities (Robinson, Joan (1969) *Introduction to the Theory of Employment*, pp73–4, Macmillan, London).

11. For a review of the problems of the impact of the UK tax structure and

welfare system see Parker, Hermoine (1982) The moral hazard of social benefits, *Research Monograph*, 37, The Institute of Economic Affairs. The problem of the employee's National Insurance contribution is dealt with in Appendix 6.

12. In line with the changes made in the March 1985 budget to the employer's NIC, the rates for employee's NIC have also been reduced for lower paid workers — although not imposed on those above the ceiling. From October 1985, persons earning less than £35.50 per week (£1846 pa) will pay nothing; £35.50 to £55 per week (£2869 pa), 5 per cent; £55 to £90 per week (£4690 pa), 7 per cent; and £90 to £265 per week (£13,780), 9 per cent. This will help the very lowest paid by reducing the trap from the 1984–85 level of £3.06 at £34 per week to £1.77 at £35.50. However, because the step in the NIC rate applies to all income and not that above an allowance the single 'trap' at £34 per week has been replaced by three traps, one each at £35.50, £55 and £90 per week. Thus, the revised system will mean that a person earning £89.50 per week will pay NIC of £6.26, but should the income rise to £90.00 per week, NIC will be £8.10. Further, the scheme remains in a form which will discourage certain forms of flexible working. Thus a part-time job based on 18 weeks in a year at £100 per week would involve the payment of £162 in NIC, whereas one of 52 weeks at £34.90 would not require any payment of NIC.

CHAPTER 13

The Will to Change

Summary

The opportunity to participate constructively in the economic life of the community must be regarded as one of the basic requirements of any civilised society. Our society is manifestly failing to meet this requirement. The loss of confidence that the employment problem can be solved has now become one of the biggest obstacles to change. The ability of technology to increase productivity faster than production has resulted in a downward trend in industrial employment from its historic high point, which occurred in Western industrial nations in the 1960s and 1970s, and it is now widely accepted that a solution to unemployment will not be found in manufacturing jobs. It is further apparent that employment in private services has so far had very little to offer as an alternative source of jobs, and only employment generated by public expenditure has shown a substantial increase. Given these realities, the failure to break out of conventional ways of thinking has led to a mood of pessimism that 'we will never get back to full employment'.

The role of economic growth has been seen as problematic. As an outcome of technological change, involving the establishment of concomitant social structures, it cannot be started to order by governments. A new period of growth based on information technology could create a climate more favourable to the adoption of policies to expand employment, but its direct impact in industry will be merely to stem job losses. To reduce unemployment, the fruits of growth must be distributed both as income and employment to the whole of the available labour-force. To meet the above challenges a shift in perspective in economic theory is essential and policies need to change with respect to the corporate and personal taxation systems. Given the political will to make major adjustments to these systems, so as to secure the separation of labour costs from personal income, a serious start could be made on reducing the present unacceptably high levels of unemployment. The introduction of policies of higher public expenditure and taxation reform, provided economic growth persisted, could lead to a steady reduction of unemployment throughout the 1990s. Such a future would require that people owning, managing and working in the growing industries should share the increase in GDP with the rest of their fellow citizens. This would be assisted through the reformed tax systems.

If a new phase of economic growth fails to materialize, a steady increase of unemployment and a slide into the 'depression scenario' must be expected. This would present a far more difficult challenge because in these circumstances the redistribution of work and income required to reduce unemployment would demand from those already in work, at best, a standstill in their standard of living — if not a decline. The role which new employment policies will need to play depends partly on whether a sustainable new growth curve becomes established. Growth or no growth, a start on radical new policies to combat unemployment is needed now: with growth their extension can be slower; without growth they will have had the status of pilot projects.

Unemployment is not an inevitable consequence of technical innovation and structural change in the economy, but it will undoubtedly endure if there continues to be a refusal to recognize the true dimensions of the problem. The first step towards a solution is to relinquish the hope that old recipes for stimulating growth are in themselves capable of overcoming mass unemployment. The second step is accepting that the obstacles to achieving full employment are primarily related to the distribution of income, both corporate and personal, and therefore go much deeper than the mere mismanagement of fiscal or monetary policies by governments. The belief in growth as a panacea has always been convenient, because it makes it possible to evade awkward issues concerning the distribution of benefits from technical change. However, this belief no longer accords with contemporary social and technological realities, and the distributional issues must therefore be faced squarely.

The scale of change

Even if we look on the bright side, and assume that economic growth will be available to lubricate the necessary employment-centred policy changes, then these changes must not be seen as an end in themselves but merely the precursor of further change. Even if we are not hurled into a vortex of change by the trauma of the depression scenario, the early part of the twenty-first century must be expected to see the renewal of decline of industrial employment and, if history repeats itself, the search for yet another 'new' technology, to take over from information technology. Of course, this may prove to be available in the guise of biotechnology — but the re-establishment of the creative-destruction process would then further reduce industrial employment in advanced nations. But this time-scale is only a decade beyond the end of the scenarios of Chapter 9 and, while a week may be a long time in the fortunes of politicians and their parties, ten years is a brief moment in the development of political values and in the shifting of social and cultural attitudes. Our policy proposals are intended to contribute to securing the necessary changes in attitude as well as to provide signposts for immediate action. Indeed, what we seek is acceptance that change must be secured rather than the exact form of that change.

One means of redistributing the benefits of increasing productivity in the production industries is through increased public expenditure, and we see this as having a vital role in helping to reduce unemployment. Certainly the policies on public expenditure and taxation incentives must not be viewed as short-term palliatives, to be set aside as soon as unemployment starts to decline, but rather as precursors of futher more radical change. The later their introduction, the greater the pressure for early radical action. Introduced soon, the measures outlined in Chapter 12 could not only secure alleviation of unemployment in the 1980s but act as catalysts encouraging a shift in the economic and political climate within which future policy would be formulated. The terms of political debate on employment must be upgraded — it must be seen as requiring separate policies and not be regarded as a by-product of economic growth. Debate between political parties requires to centre on measures to promote desired technological innovations,[1] the recasting of personal and company taxation to secure a more equitable distribution of jobs and new attitudes to work, and on how to achieve public acceptance of expanded public service employment. There are in fact many currents discernible within industrial societies today which are conducive to change, provided a way can be found to bridge the gap between general goals and specific strategies. These currents involve attitudes to work, peoples' rights both within and outside formal employment, the wider impact of economic activity and the costs imposed on society. We must be especially aware of the central role of young people — not only in regard to the heavy burden which they bear from unemployment but also of the flexibility of attitude of which they are capable. The young do not necessarily see jobs, careers and working lives in the same way that previous generations saw them.

Work and income

Just as a general consensus has developed that extreme disparities of income (as in the nineteenth century) are unjust, it must be established that the gross inequalities of work opportunity that currently exist are equally immoral. Up until now work has been so self-legitimating that the more a man had (eg in overtime) the more prestige he earned: he could rarely do too much work, especially if he had no family commitments. These are very strong attitudes which need to change — private ambition must be moderated by a collective conscience.

Among the attitudes which require reappraisal are those concerning the work-income relationships. Like too many aspects of life, present attitudes are inconsistent. A person on social benefit is always in danger of being viewed as a 'scrounger' who is not entitled to visit a football match, hairdresser, or public house because he or she did not earn the money. (Indeed, they are in danger of losing part of their income if an official investigator finds a transgression of the labyrinthine rule book which controls the award of benefits.) Yet it is interesting to observe that a person living quietly on the interest payments from inherited wealth is not subject to the same harassment — our social structures legitimate the notion that such a person is entitled to income independent of work. In some respects the barriers are already breaking down — we have long accepted that a retired person has income independent of his or her present work; and, with the growth of early retirement, the age at which this happens has for some individuals already come down from 60–65 to 50–55. For a growing minority this means that the work-income link will only apply for about 30 years between education and retirement. At all other periods of their life, income will be at least partially divorced from formal work.

This process needs to go much further. The seminal importance of the personal benefit lies in its dissociation of an element of income from work — for all persons throughout their whole lives. Books, articles in newspapers, and speeches in Parliament all help persuade, but they reach only a short way into the consciousness of the population at large. The possession of a personal benefit book for weekly encashment at a Post Office, or the receipt of regular monthly payments into an individual's bank or building society account, would convey the message of changed attitudes to literally everyone. It must be expected that the passsage into law of such a system would provoke controversy and that this would help raise awareness of the reasons for the change. But whether the reasons are understood or not, the personal benefit would be a major breach in a system whose roots predate the poor laws. In a poor agrarian economy, virtually all have to work or they and their families will starve. This is not the problem of industrializ-ed Western societies — we are not going to let anyone starve. The question is whether we recognize the vast change in employment circumstances and accept that, while all cannot be 'rich', all are entitled to a measure of income independent of their contemporary personal work input, and all are equally entitled to a fair share of regular employment throughout their adult working lives. The system has to be flexible enough for a person's income to be made up from a number of sources including transfer payments from the state, and the personal benefit could be raised to the level at which it would absorb most other social security benefits.

Flexible attitudes to working lives need to be encouraged. For instance, it needs to be easier to take sabbatical years, especially if these are unpaid. In the past, the possibility of doing this has been restricted to very few occupations, such as university sab-baticals to allow people to write books or undertake research in other institutions. These opportunities have increasingly come under attack as an unjustified privilege not shared by anyone else, but a more positive response would be to argue for the extension of opportunities for 'leave of absence' to other occupations. An example of the kind of activity which could then be undertaken is the formation of a co-operative by people with skills in various building trades (bricklaying, plumbing, electrical fitting, etc), to build each other's houses. Some ventures of this kind have work-ed successfully without any provision being made by employers — and the scope would be much wider if the 'job-release' idea were promoted.

At present, employers too often treat such suggestions with suspicion, but young people especially should be encouraged to undertake these kinds of initiative. The essential support that is needed is the employer's guarantee of job security when the person returns. Employees occupying graded posts within career structures would also need some indication that future promotion prospects would not thereby be unreasonably impaired. Such changes would act as models which can spark-off other ideas. In some other occupations (and certainly, for instance, in higher education) it ought to be made possible to switch to part-time contracts for fixed periods. There should not need to be any specific reason for such a move but it could provide the opportunity for other activities. A scientist, engineer, marketing, or other specialist who wished to start up in business could then do so while still retaining long-term job security, with the right to return to full-time employment at the end of a specified period. This flies in the face of the conventional wisdom — that anyone who wishes to start up in business on their own account should leave their job and commit themselves totally. As this involves risking everything it is only going to happen in exceptional cases — most people will only get involved if they do so from a position of personal and family security.

A related problem is the need to distinguish income from 'welfare' in the widest sense — including the collective benefits derived from formal and voluntary social services as well as material benefits. Traditionally most people have gained income from activities for which they have received a wage or a payment for goods or services which they have provided. In turn the results of that work, whether goods or services, have contributed to the welfare of those who have been the recipients. But because of the need for 'a living wage', it is only those aspects of welfare which are viable in the market place and for which full payment is made which receive full recognition. Other 'unprofitable' activities, which contribute to welfare in the wider sense, receive only such attention as those with spare time choose to give in a voluntary capacity. To take full advantage of the potential for these activities it will be necessary to increase male participation in them and so enhance their role in male eyes.

It is to be hoped that, by reducing the costs of employing people and, eventually, by challenging current orthodoxies about work and income, many desirable welfare tasks would move into the category of 'profitable' and that others would benefit from the availability of more spare time through generally lower working hours. In theory, it might be thought that those who are at present wholly unemployed could do more voluntary work; in practice many are demoralized to the point at which life becomes a burden. An individual who is well motivated, but not dominated by the lack of a job, is more likely to be persuaded of the need to give time for the provision of welfare.

These functions of income, work and welfare have been diverging in advanced industrial countries and, as the contradictions arising from their close ties become more and more evident, it becomes necessary to decouple them to lessen the dominance of wages as the underlying basis of production costs, to demote payment for work from pre-eminence as the basis of distribution, and to encourage the perception that welfare provision is its own justification.

The society envisaged

Although the policies advocated are no more than tentative first steps, the society we envisage is seen as incorporating certain definite features. The most important of these is the absence of long-term unemployment, and with it the disappearance of the current growing section of the population that is dependent on whatever survival payments the political system bequeaths. It is intended that anyone who wishes should be able to participate in the formal economy, as a result of the more equitable distribution of employment opportunities. It is emphatically not intended that any reduction in economic activity rates should come about through women being relegated to domestic work. Rather, the emphasis would be on breaking down the presently rigid attitudes about the distinction of being 'economically active' — which for men still seems to be 40 hours a week for life but excludes much else including tasks in the home. At the same time formal employment for women (where the availability and status of jobs which 'match' with domestic responsibilities are often severely restricted) as well as political and social activity, need to be expanded so that all women who wish to may participate.

One of the preconditions for this greater flexibility of roles is that a higher proportion of the gains from technological change be taken in the form of reduced working time rather than increased consumption. At the same time, the establishment on a much wider scale of publically funded community projects could offer great scope for greater participation of women; not only through employment directly but also through training, including instruction in traditionally 'male' skills. The assurance of an opportunity for everyone to participate in economic activity is therefore not to be taken to mean everyone having 'full-time jobs' as presently conceived.

Other pressures for change could come more directly from what happens in the business of production. The increasing involvement of trade unions in issues of health and safety at work indicates that there is a demand not only for 'the right to work', but also for the kinds of work suitable for people, as opposed to machines. The replacement of people by machines in tasks which are dangerous, injurious to health, repetitive or monotonous could be welcomed as a release from much of the drudgery that has dogged industrial societies, if people's livelihoods were not threatened as a result. Whether from liberal or socialist traditions, some of the profounder economic thinkers, including John Stuart Mill and Karl Marx, have regarded a reduction in the length of the working day and working week as a basic condition for social progress, and have reflected on the irony that all the 'labour-saving' inventions that men have devised have done so little to reduce drudgery and toil.[2] In the age of robots and computer-controlled automation, we find now the fulfilment of the prophecies of these nineteenth century writers concerning the impact of technology, and it becomes more and more absurd that we should fail to put this technology to the liberating purpose of a drastic reduction in working time. The aim would be to free people for work in which their human qualities were at a premium, such as in personal and community services, or in the use of design skills and the improved management of resources. Related to the hazards arising from industrial and extractive processes are the environmental impacts and resource costs involved, and a change in the balance of costs facing firms could give expression to the widespread concerns on these issues. The current dominance of employment costs in shaping profitability could give way to the inclusion of a wide range of social and environmental costs which are at present not adequately reflected in the profit and loss accounts of businesses.

Motivation for change thus comes from many quarters, and there is a potentially powerful alliance of interests which could be brought together behind an economic programme aimed at modifying the decision-making environment in which firms operate. One of the obstacles is that the advocates of change often appear to be appealing for some new economic morality, without translating these concerns into specific economic measures which are capable of implementation. We have suggested that an important clue to

215

breaking through this barrier lies in a re-examination of the link between costs and incomes. We envisage a society in which, on the one hand, labour time ceases to be so dominant in production costs while, on the other hand, wages and salaries may cease to be the sole form of income for most households.

In Chapter 12 we illustrated, by reference to the UK tax and benefit system, some possible first steps in these directions. These would not only challenge several hallowed economic precepts, but would also involve fundamental shifts in social attitudes — within business, among trade unions and governments, as well as for individuals. The precise directions in which things might then evolve cannot be foreseen. Some would argue for an extension of the personal benefit to encompass all social security payments, in order to overcome the massive complexities, anomalies, and intrusions into the personal affairs of individuals with which social security systems are usually associated. Others would emphasize the importance of shifting the incidence of firms' costs away from employment, on to other resources (including energy and raw materials) and on to the 'hidden' costs imposed on society (including, for instance, industrial pollution and heavy lorries). At the same time, those concerned particularly with the encouragement of more flexible arrangements for working time will stress the need for legislation supporting an individual's right to work less than full-time, and seek to ensure that they are not discriminated against as a result of exercising this right. We have offered no blueprint for the future, but only pointers to the kinds of innovation in economic thinking and policy which appear to be needed.

In concrete terms, the adjustments which would need to be brought about to facilitate the universal opportunity of employment are not impossibly large. Consider the income aspect: as we have shown in Chapter 9 the 'redistribution' associated with bringing three to four million extra people into employment is likely to be only of the order of 4 per cent of GNP. Alternatively, viewing the 'redistribution' in terms of numbers of jobs (and making some allowance for projected increases in public and market sector jobs as a result of growth), the challenge might be seen as equivalent to allowing 100 people to do the projected work of 90. In neither respect is the magnitude of adjustment extraordinarily large; yet the in-built obstacles of the economic system and society's norms make the task appear formidable. There seems no reason why changes of such a magnitude should not be contained within cultural shifts no larger than those experienced between, say, the heyday of late nineteenth century industrial society and the relative emancipation following World War I. Those who would oppose change must face the likelihood that doing too little now will lead to more radical change in the long run.

Changing attitudes

It is obvious that if attitudes among those in key positions do not shift then all is in vain. It is thus mildly encouraging to find an EEC commissioner advocating that trade unions need to be told:

> 'It is possible to at least maintain, and possibly to increase, jobs by a reduction in hours, though this will almost certainly mean some loss in wages. But of course the price that you will probably have to pay is to agree with the employers to adopt more realistic and efficient work practices'.[3]

It is discouraging to find that there was an immediate negative reaction from an engineering employer's representative who relied on appeals for a 'vigorous business life' which would 'thus improve employment prospects'.[4] In other words, if growth is alright then employment will follow.

Obviously, if those in control of industry and other business, and the financial institutions which back their operations, are more worried by ideas to reform the taxation system and increase public expenditure than they are by the social and economic inequality resulting from unemployment, then they will inevitably obstruct the changes which we have argued are vital. Equally, if trade unionists regard it as their duty solely to represent the interests of their present members they will not potently challenge the climate of *laissez-faire*, because under it the income of those in work — their members — rises faster than the rate of inflation. (Or, rather, the income of those of their members who will have a job *next year* will be so raised.)

As yet, as we have clearly shown in Chapter 7, even the best intentioned actions are in danger of running into sands of cultural incomprehension in the areas of the Western industrial nations which, like Cauldmoss, have suffered most from the destruction of industrial jobs. But those whose jobs have been destroyed must also change their attitudes. There can be no half-heartedness here — the nature of technology-based economies precludes, at least for the foreseeable future, the state of stasis. The present realities of Cauldmoss bind people into subservient roles and, in a host of apparently minor ways, deny them access even to such possibilities as are available. However, just as a personal benefit-type tax system can alter attitudes to the relationship of income, work, welfare, and wages, so the establishing of successful community-based ventures, to expand both do-it-yourself activities in the home and at least partially commercial schemes, might act as exemplars. The 'good worker' image might be transferred from the role of wage earner in a factory or mine to participant in a community enterprise. The hope must be that the youth of Cauldmoss will cease to expect work to have the inherently unenjoyable nature which has been the experience of their parents. Initiative and responsibility might take the place of stoic self-discipline and the self-confidence so created could then spill over and lead to expansion of self-employment and creation of small businesses. Although this is by no means a solution in itself, it could both assist with reducing unemployment and overcoming the problems, which we have noted, of lack of entrepreneurial and management skills in the communities concerned. Indeed, to assume that working-class culture is unable to respond is unrealistic. As Gans has pointed out, the holistic quality of cultural analysis always emphasizes the obstacles to change,[5] but it is obvious that all cultural ideas develop in response to a situation and in the long run cannot persist.

For all these reasons it is essential to expose the forces which are at work and to secure a better understanding of the mechanics of the processes involved. The part played by technology in generating economic growth and reducing the volume of low-skill industrial employment, the limited direct contribution of economic growth to employment, the problematic nature of its re-establishment let alone duration once established, and the limitations of present economic orthodoxies, all require to be clearly seen and understood. In emphasizing the limits to orthodox prescriptions, we are by no means denying the significance for employment of established issues like the level of public expenditure or the balance between market forces and economic planning, as instruments of change. At the same time, it should be impossible for leaders of society — politicians, academics, trade unionists, employers, civil servants and financiers — to shelter behind the ready cliché, whether of right, left or centre, about 'freedom to grow', 'centralized planning' or 'industrial democracy'. The debate on 'future employment' must be joined on the issue of new policies which could allow the necessary changes to take place. Those who still put their faith in the old economic orthodoxies must be challenged to show the reasons why they should be believed. At the same time, of those who would uphold a 'new economic morality', it must be demanded that they tell what it is that they would do *now*. There can be no room in policy making for either the complacency of the established nor the imprecise generalities of the utopian reformer. A future of employment for all who wish it is within our grasp if we all have the insight and will to make the necessary changes of policy and attitude.

Notes and references

1. This book has not been concerned with the issues of social control of technology and we have, for the purpose of our argument, not disputed the view that IT is a non-controversial technology in its societal impacts. Indeed, the need for economic growth is such that we must be thankful that it is not nuclear power technology which is seen as the focus of new economic growth.
2. Marx quoted J S Mill: 'It is questionable if all the mechanical inventions yet made have lightened the toil of any human being' (*Capital*, Vol 1 (English edn), 1909, p366, William Glaisher Ltd, London); and he observed that 'free time — which includes leisure time as well as time for higher activities — naturally transforms anyone who enjoys it into a different person' (*Grundrisse* (English edn), 1953, p599).
3. Report of a speech by Ivor Richards to the Confederation of British Industry Annual Conference, Europe 84, December, p14, Commission of the EEC.
4. Europe 84, December, p15.
5. Gans, Herbert (1970) Poverty & culture: some basic questions about methods of studying life-styles of the poor. In Townsend, Peter (Ed) *The Concept of Poverty*, Heinemann, London.

Appendices

Capital Investment, Output and Employment

The outcome of investment in manufacturing industry can be viewed in terms of both its output-generating and employment effects. The combination of the output and the labour-saving effects of a set of investments might be termed the 'productivity of capital investment' (remembering that this is not the same thing as profitability, because of relative price changes — indeed, there is some tendency to transfer to consumers the benefits of exceptional rapid productivity increases for particular goods, through lower real prices). If there were no other resource use, environmental, or social considerations, then this 'productivity of capital investment' might be regarded as the economic gain to society from the investment, and as such it may be taken as an indicator of the potential of technology as it becomes embodied in the means of production. However, the balance between output-generating and employment effects is clearly of crucial importance.

The declining output/physical capital ratio[1] in manufacturing industries in traditionally advanced countries has been pointed out by a number of commentators[2] and is also evident in aggregate estimates of changes in capital stock, employment, and output in Table A1.1. Since it could imply a continually increasing share of output needing to be 'earmarked' for replacement investment, it might appear to pose a serious problem and place pressures on net profitability.[3] However, physical measures of capital are of limited usefulness in making comparisons over time, because rising productivity in the capital goods industries themselves may reduce both the financial outlays and real resource requirements associated with any given volume of capital goods. Moreover, the meaning of the 'value of capital' is a complex question, and the official statistical estimates do not coincide with any agreed theoretical concept. The incremental output/capital ratios in Table A1.1 are therefore based on comparisons of the change in value of output divided by the value of capital invested (both at the prices

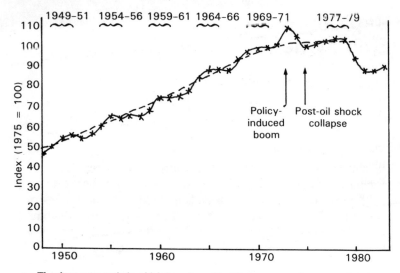

a   The three-year periods which have been identified represent the crests of each
successive cycle (excluding the exceptional 1972–73 boom, and subsequent post-
oil shock collapse). These crests of the cycles form the periods for the
comparison of output and employment in Table A1.1.

Figure A1.1 *Index of manufacturing industry output (UK), 1948–83*[a]

then prevailing) over successive periods. From this is deducted
the net change in labour input (valued at prevailing wage rates)
involved in producing that output, to give the 'productivity of
capital investment'. The three-year periods chosen correspond to
the successive 'peaks' in the production cycle (see Figure A1.1),
to avoid the problem of isolating the 'trend' factor from the cyclical
disturbances. Table A1.1 highlights the way in which the outcome
of investment has shifted more and more towards labour-reduction,
whereas in the 1950s there was a simultaneous increase in output
and employment. At the same time, the productivity of capital investment has tended to fall from the peak reached in the early
1960s. The output data of table A1.1 (i) are shown graphically
in Figure A1.2. This tendency for manufacturing investment to
become more employment-reducing than output-increasing is once
again not a phenomenon that is unique to the UK, but is reflected
in trends observable in other industrialized countries. The case
of West Germany is shown in Table A1.1 (ii), and although the
falling-off in the rate of increase in output in the 1970s is less marked, and the productivity of capital investment appears to have been
maintained at a higher level, the falling output/capital ratio

(i) UK manufacturing industry 1949–51 to 1977–79

	Change in output £ billion (1975 prices)	Change in employment, million employees	Incremental output/capital ratio[a]	Estimated 'productivity of capital investment' ratio[a]
1949/51– 1959/61	5.39	0.98	0.23	0.15
1959/61– 1964/66	4.38	0.19	0.28	0.26
1964/66– 1969/71	3.59	−0.28	0.20	0.24
1969/71– 1977/79	1.72	−1.01	0.05	0.14

(ii) West German manufacturing industry 1955–57

	Change in output, billion DM employees	Change in employment, million employees	Incremental output/capital ratio[a]	Estimated 'productivity of capital investment' ratio[a]
1955–64	140.3	2.06	0.53	0.39
1965–69	79.1	0.33	0.34	0.30
1970–77	70.1	−1.32	0.19	0.33

a   Owing to the different bases used in national statistics, these ratios should not be regarded as comparable between countries, but indicate only the trends within each country.

Table A1.1 *Changes in output and employment*

Sources: *UK:* CSO National Income and Expenditure (annual). Economic Trends, February 1976, November 1977, December 1980 (Employment estimates). *West Germany:* OECD National Accounts Statistics, 1953–69 and 1964–81; OECD Manpower Statistics, 1954–64; OECD Labour Force Statistics, 1959–70 and 1969–80.

and relative shift towards employment reduction is clearly observable. Thus, although the problems faced in the UK may be worse than in some other countries, they need to be seen not as a specifically British problem but as an outcome of processes which have affected industrially advanced capitalist countries in general over the period since the mid-1960s.

Both the crisis of profitability and the increasing capital intensity of investment tend in some quarters to be attributed to the effects of wage-bargaining pressure: a version of the 'workers pricing themselves out of jobs' argument. The theoretical arguments apart, which are discussed in Chapters 10 and 11, there is no clear

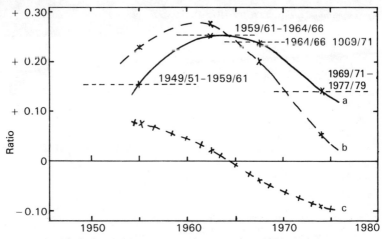

a   'Productivity' of capital investment as the economic surplus/cumulative
    investment ratio.
b   Incremental output/capital ratio.
c   Incremental employment/capital ratio.

Figure A1.2 *Relationship between capital investment, output and
employment UK manufacturing industry 1949–51 to 1977–79*

evidence that 'wage pressure' in the UK was greater since the
mid-1960s, when manufacturing employment began to decline,
than before.[4] Table A1.2 shows the estimated rates of increase of
productivity and average earnings respectively in UK manufacturing since 1949–51.

A much more convincing interpretation of the changing outcome of investment since the mid-1960s, as shown in Table A1.1,
lies in there being two phases of development for the industries
which provided the basis of the post-1945 economic boom. In the
'first generation' phase of investment in the mass production of
cars and other consumer goods, this investment created jobs as
markets expanded and growth consisted of adding to the existing
type of production capacity. However, the 'second generation'
phase of investment, when maturity had been reached in the
development of the industry, tended not to replicate the past pattern of expansion but to consist in the refinement of the technologies
and the search for ways of doing more cheaply, and with improved design, what was already being done. In this second phase investment did tend to be labour-reducing, and this tendency can
scarcely be resisted without undermining the capability of the industry to keep its markets. We discuss the implications of this view
of growth in Chapter 8.

Period	Average rate of increase in productivity (output per person employed) % per annum	Average rate of increase in real earnings % per annum[a]
1949/51–1964/66	2.55	1.49
1964/66–1977/79	2.80	1.52

a Average weekly earnings for full-time males/retail price index.

Table A1.2 *Rates of increase in productivity and earnings in UK manufacturing industry, 1949–51 to 1966–79*

Notes and references

1. More usually expressed by economists as its reciprocal: the capital/output ratio.
2. Heathfield, D (1979) Capital utilisation and input substitution, in Patterson, K D and Schott, K *The Measurement of Capital; Theory and Practice*, Macmillan, London.
3. This is a very familiar issue for economists, because it underlies Marx's theory of the falling rate of profit.
4. Using statistics for whole economies (for which productivity estimates pose even greater difficulties than for manufacturing alone), there is some evidence of a rising real wage share contributing to a 'profits squeeze' in the industrially advanced capitalist countries; this is discussed by Armstrong, P, Glyn, A and Harrison, J (1984) *Capitalism Since World War II*, p 259, Fontana, London. However, the authors also point out that 'in the period of rapid growth in real wages prior to 1973 there was no substantial increase in unemployment' and conclude that 'it was by no means the central factor behind rising unemployment in the seventies and early eighties' (pp 334–5).

APPENDIX 2

Modelling of Employment in UK IOP Industries

(Adapted from Leach, Donald (1985) Production, productivity and employment, *Journal of Interdisciplinary Economics*, **1**, 1, pp29–42, by kind permission of A B Academic Publishers.)

In 1975 the UK Department of Employment revised their estimates of employment in the Index of Production (IOP) industries and provided these on a continuous basis for the period from 1959; subsequent figures on the same basis have been available from the *Monthly Abstract of Statistics*. Three series of IOP figures are available for base years of 1958, 1970 and 1975, and can be converted to a continuous series by use of multiplicative factors. The Index of Production per employee (IOP/E) for each year has been obtained by dividing the latter figures by the former and rescaling to 100 for a base year of 1975. The series for IOP and IOP/E may then have curves fitted to them by standard least squares techniques. The choice of curve is obviously of considerable importance and discussion about economic growth often has implicit within it a model of exponential increase; in contrast many social activities seem to result in periods of rapid growth giving way to a gradual slowing down as forces of restraint become larger than those of expansion. Population growth is one example and such behaviour is consistent with an S-shaped, or sigmoid, curve as shown in Figure A2.1. Sigmoids have the advantage that by using parts of them it is possible to model growth trends subject to widely differing degrees of restraint; the lower part of the sigmoid is near exponential but if the point of inflection is included then a saturation level may be approached. The question of behaviour when the saturation level is attained is often seen as problematic but, for the purposes of examining changes in growth of production and productivity over the period 1959 to 1972, saturation is not closely approached. Moreover, renewed growth can be modelled by a break to a new sigmoid.[1]

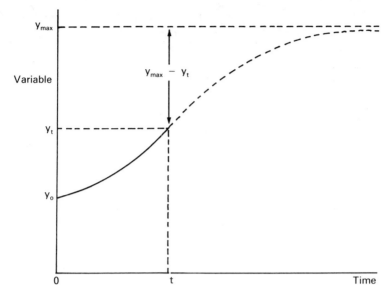

Figure A2.1 *Constrained growth on a sigmoid curve*

The sigmoid shown in Figure A2.1 is of the particular form known as the logistic curve. The logistic curve has a growth rate parameter 'c' which is used in fractional form and can be regarded as the 'initial growth rate' — actual growth rates are less than c at all points on the curve and decrease towards the limiting value of zero as the upper saturation level is approached. The logistic curve has the form:

$y_t = y_{max}/(1 + (y_{max}/y_o - 1)\exp(-ct))$, where y_t is the value after t years from the starting value y_o, y_{max} is the saturation level and c is the growth rate.

The fitted curves are:
Production (IOP) for period 1959 to 1972

$y_{max} = 121.8$, $y_o = 70.53$, $c = 0.1058$ (y_o in 1959)

Productivity (IOP/E) for period 1959 to 1969

$y_{max} = 1664$, $y_o = 61.37$, $c = 0.03699$ (y_o in 1959)

Notes and references

1. The use of sigmoids was reviewed by Stone, Richard (1979) in *Sigmoids*, Royal Statistical Society Conference, Oxford; and an example of the use of escalated logistic curves is contained in Leach, Donald (1981)

Appendix 2

Re-evaluation of the logistic curve for human populations, *Journal of the Royal Statistical Society*, A, **144**, 1, pp94-103.

Analysis of Employment by 'Goods' and 'Service' Sectors

The years included in the analysis are those for which input-output tables have been compiled by the Central Statistical Office (CSO). Input-output tables are used to allocate the employment in the individual service industries listed in Table A3.1 to five categories of expenditure (intermediate demand by production industries other than construction; consumer demand; sales of services to public authorities; intermediate services associated with Gross Domestic Capital Formation; 'invisible' exports).

	Employment (millions)			
Service sector[a]	1963	1968	1974	1979
Distribution and repairs, hotels and catering	3.75	3.74	3.66	3.66
Transport	1.33	1.22	1.08	1.07
Post and telecommunications	0.43	0.45	0.50	0.48
Insurance, banking and finance		0.86	1.12	1.24
Other[b] (excluding public employment)	(3.45)[c]	2.86	3.33	3.15
Total	8.96	9.13	9.69	9.60

a Including estimate for employers and self-employed.
b Consists mainly of professional and scientific services not included directly within the public sector, and miscellaneous consumer services.
c Including insurance, banking and finance.

Table A3.1 *Employment in market sector services by industry, UK 1963–79*

Source: Figures for the total indirect public employment are based on the estimates published in *Economic Trends*, November 1979 and November 1980. The totals given for education, health and social services differ from those based on the Standard Industrial Classification, since some educational and health services are outside the public sector.

The detailed distribution of the requirements from individual market service industries by category of final demand for 1979 are shown in Table A3.2. The allocation of service employment in Table A3.3 is based on this and corresponding tables for the three earlier years.

Table A3.4 shows the data on total expenditure by category of final demand on which column A of Table 4.5 (Chapter 4) is based.

Service sector	Intermediate services supplied to production industries	Consumer services (households)	Public authorities	Construction and other GDCF[a]	Export	Total
Distribution and repairs	90	10	—	—	—	100
Hotels and catering	3	77	7	1	12	100
Post and telecommunications	18	43	16	17	6	100
Insurance, banking and finance	10	32	16	18	24	100
Transport and other	49	28	10	1	12	100

a Gross domestic capital formation.

Table A3.2 *Estimated distribution of market sector services by category of expenditure, 1979 (proportions %)*

Method and sources

1. Estimates of total employment and numbers in public employment in the service sector are from *Economic Trends*, November 1979 and November 1980 (articles on employment by sector and industry).
2. Numbers in employment in the production industries and construction for 1974 and 1979 are also from *Economic Trends*, loc. cit. For 1963 and 1968, the estimates of employees from the same source are adjusted to allow for self-employment on the basis of the 1971 ratio for self-employed to employees.
3. The estimated total employment in all other services is derived by difference using the above estimates. The breakdown

Employment (employees and self-employed) millions			

A **Goods**	*1963*	*1968*	*1974*	*1979*
Production industries	10.33[b]	9.70	9.01	8.60
Transport and distribution of goods plus 'other intermediate services'[a]	4.60[b]	4.49	4.85	4.91
Total 'goods economy'	14.93[b]	14.19	13.86	13.51
B Services				
(i) *Consumers (households)*				
Public transport	0.31	0.27	0.20	0.18
Postal and telephone services	0.18	0.18	0.21	0.21
Financial services[c]			0.56	0.40
Catering and hotels	2.43	2.22	0.43	0.40
Other services			1.42	1.19
Total consumer services	2.92	2.77	2.72	2.38
(ii) *Public authorities*				
Education[d] (local authorities)	0.87	1.13	1.50	1.59
Health and social services	0.80	0.96	1.24	1.59
Public administration and other public services	1.83	1.96	1.95	2.02
Total in public employment[e]	3.50	4.05	4.69	5.15
Intermediate services[f]	0.49	0.61	0.61	0.64
Total public services	3.99	4.66	5.30	5.79
C Other employment				
Construction[g]	1.95	1.97	1.73	1.68
Investment-related services and export of services	0.95	1.26	1.51	1.67
Total 'other' employment	2.90	3.23	3.24	3.35
Total in employment	24.74	24.85	25.12	25.03
Registered unemployed		0.55	0.55	1.30

a Services supplied to industries producing and distributing goods.
b The allocation of this employment between 'production industries' and other employment is not strictly comparable with later years.
c Insurance, banking, etc.
d Excludes institutions directly funded by central government, eg universities.
e Excludes public employees in the production industries and construction.
f Private sector services supplied to public authorities.
g The IOP industry figures used in Chapter 2 include construction but are less than the total obtained here by function, thus indicating the extent of services to industry. However, the fall from 11.67 million in 1968 to 10.28 million in 1979 for the total sum of production and construction given here is similar to that from 10.11 million to 9.18 million for those directly employed in the IOP industries.

Table A3.3 *Employment in the UK economy by 'goods' and 'services' sectors, 1963–79*

233

of this total between transport, communications, distributive trades and (from 1974) insurance, banking and finance, catering and hotels, and 'other' is based on the figures for employees in employment published annually in the *CSO Annual Abstract of Statistics*, adjusted for the estimated proportions of self-employed.

4.   The allocation of these services between the 'goods economy', consumer services, and public authorities is based on the CSO input-output tables for the respective years, using the industry × industry flows and industry analysis of final demand. The allocation of employment according to final use is based on the requirements by end use for each service industry's output. Demand by the production industries and construction is treated as 'final' in this context, ie the destinations of services are considered to be the production industries, construction and GDCF, consumers, public authorities, and export.

| Category of final demand | Expenditure (£ billions, 1975 prices) | | | |
	1968	1979	Increase	% of total increase
Consumers' expenditure	56.03	71.60	+ 15.57	69
Government consumption (public authorities' expenditure on current goods and services)	19.19	23.87	+ 4.68	21
Investment (gross domestic fixed capital formation)	18.88	21.04	+ 2.16	10
Total	94.10	116.51	+ 22.41	100

Table A3.4 *UK domestic expenditure by category of final demand, 1968 and 1979*

Source: *CSO National Income and Expenditure*; 1963–73 and 1981 editions.

Employment Projections, 1984-96

The projections of employment for the UK economy (Chapter 9) are disaggregated into the following categories: IOP industries; agriculture; transport and communications; public services; distribution; hotel and catering; banking, finance and insurance; other services; and self-employment. It is assumed that the Armed Services remain constant in size at 0.33 million. The trends since 1971 are shown in Table A4.1 and these values have been used in Figures 9.2 and 9.3. Public services comprises public administration, education, medical and other health, and veterinary services. All categories are defined according to the Standard Industrial Classification, 1980. Projections shown in Figures 9.2 and 9.3 and used in Table 9.1, for 1990 and 1996, are mostly by linear extrapolations from the trends of the values in Table A4.1.

Decreasing employment (Figure 9.2)

IOP industries:
As discussed in Chapters 3 and 9.

Agriculture:
(i)   New growth — no further decline below 1984 level.
(ii) Low growth — extrapolation of 1971–84 trend.

Transport and communications:
(i)   New growth — recovery to extrapolation of 1976–80 trend.
(ii) Low growth — extrapolation of 1971–75 and 1982–84 trend.

Increasing employment (Figure 9.3)

Public services:
Assumed constant at 1984 level, rounded to 4.85 million.

Distribution:
(i)   New growth — extrapolation of 1971–84 trend.

Year	Agriculture[a]	Distribution	Transport and communications	Hotel and catering	Banking, finance and insurance	Public services	Other services	Self-employed	IOP industries
1971	0.432	2.990	1.550	0.688	1.335	4.082	0.953	1.909	10.090
1972	0.427		1.543	0.722		4.231		1.899	9.814
1973	0.421		1.524	0.784		4.380		1.947	9.917
1974	0.404		1.506	0.805		4.503		1.925	9.897
1975	0.397	3.132	1.499	0.840	1.489	4.703	1.138	1.994	9.507
1976	0.393	3.100	1.456	0.864	1.494	4.782	1.193	1.949	9.254
1977	0.388	3.145	1.449	0.877	1.518	4.775	1.204	1.904	9.260
1978	0.382	3.188	1.463	0.898	1.571	4.814	1.245	1.904	9.215
1979	0.368	3.302	1.473	0.950	1.663	4.877	1.291	1.903	9.234
1980	0.361	3.338	1.484	0.979	1.714	4.856	1.323	2.011	8.918
1981	0.352	3.217	1.423	0.950	1.740	4.798	1.325	2.118	8.064
1982	0.354	3.194	1.373	0.992	1.783	4.790	1.337	2.190	7.657
1983	0.349	3.233	1.332	0.975	1.837	4.828	1.336	2.260	7.320
1984	0.340	3.342	1.320	1.021	1.901	4.837	1.401	2.331	7.230

a Including forestry and fishing.

Table A4.1 *Employment by category 1971–1984 (millions)*

Source: Various *Monthly Digests of Statistics, Annual Abstracts of Statistics* and *Social Trends*, 15.

(ii) Low growth — extrapolation of 1979–84 trend.

Self-employment:
(i) New growth — extrapolation of 1971–75 and 1981–84 trend.
(ii) Low growth — as new growth extrapolation rounding out after 1990 as happened between 1975 and 1980.

Banking, finance and insurance:
(i) New growth — extrapolation of 1971–84 trend.
(ii) Low growth — as new growth extrapolation but rounding out after 1990 as productivity increases from new technology exceed sector growth rate.

Other services:
(i) New growth — extrapolation of 1971–84 trend.
(ii) Low growth — extrapolation of 1980–84 trend.

Hotel and catering:
(i) New growth — extrapolation of 1973–84 trend.
(ii) Low growth — extrapolation of 1980–84 trend.

The 'Warwick' IER scenario

The Institute for Employment Research (IER) 'has grown out of the former Manpower Research Group which was established in 1975 with a major programme grant from the Manpower Services Commission'. Its views are, of course, its own responsibility and not those of the MSC. The 'Warwick' projections use a different disaggregation than the one employed in this book and, in particular, allocate the self-employed to the various employing activities. The IER use 1982 as the base year to project the change to 1990, as shown in Table A4.2. The IER figures have been compared with the Department of Employment figures to allow the self-employed total to be checked and its growth rate to be estimated. Then, by applying the IER rates of change (Table A4.2) to the 1984 Department of Employment 'base' figures used in Chapter 9, the revised projections shown in Table A4.3 have been obtained.

The most significant difference from the original 'Warwick' projection is the reduction in IOP industry employment because of the actual fall from 7657 to 7216 thousand between the two base years of 1982 and 1984. However, this is more than compensated for by larger than predicted rises in other categories so that the total for 1990 is now projected as 24,161 thousand, 62

237

Employing activity	IER 1982	Change 1982–90 % pa	IER 1990	Department of Employment employees 1982	Self-employed 1982
Mining	332	+ 0.1	334	329	3
Manufacturing	5 905	− 0.2	5 806	5 912	—
Construction	1 498	+ 1.4	1 672	1 059	439
Public utilities	336	− 1.4	300	356	—
IOP industries	8 071	+ 0.06	8 112	7 657	—
Agriculture	653	− 1.7	568	354	299
Transport and communications	1 496	− 0.4	1 443	1 374	122
Distribution	3 141	− 0.4	3 049	3 194	—
Professional services	2 014	1.0	2 182	1 783[a]	231
Miscellaneous services	2 961	+ 1.3	3 282	2 319[b]	642
Social services	3 495	− 0.1	3 458	3 092[c]	403
Public administration	1 870	+ 0.9	2 005	1 872	—
Total	23 701		24 099	21 645	2 139[d]

Table A4.2 *IER employment projections, 1982–1990 (thousands)*

a Taken as banking, finance and insurance.
b Taken as other services, and hotel and catering.
c Taken as education, medical and other health services, veterinary services plus 174 thousand for private domestic service.
d Department of Employment estimates is 2190 for June 1982.

Sources: *Review of the Economy and Employment,* summer 1983, and *Monthly Digests of Statistics.*

Employment category	Department of Employment employees 1984 thousands	Rate of change % pa	Revised Projection 1990 thousands
Agriculture	340	− 1.7	307
Transport and communications	1 320	− 0.4	1 289
IOP industries	7 216	+ 0.06	7 242
Hotel and catering	1 021	+ 1.3	1 104
Other services	1 401	+ 1.3	1 515
Banking, finance and insurance	1 901	+ 1.0	2 019
Self-employment	2 331	+ 0.75[a]	2 438
Distribution	3 342	− 0.4	3 263
Public service	4 837	+ 0.5[b]	4 984
Total	23 709	—	24 161

a   The average of the rates of change of employment weighted in proportion to the elements of the self-employed 1982 column of Table A4.2.
b   The weighted average of the rates of change of employment for public administration and social services as in Table A4.2.

Table A4.3 *Revision of projections shown in Table A4.3*

Source: *Monthly Digest of Statistics* and Table A4.2

thousand higher than the 24,099 thousand shown in Table A4.2. The projections of Table A4.3 are used in Table 9.1.

Corporation Turnover Tax and the Employment Allowance

Tax rate

If the tax rate is increased, then the opportunity to discriminate in favour of firms with larger numbers of employees on below average pay is increased. For a gross turnover of £1 million, a pay-roll of £500 thousand, the threshold at £6000, the employment allowance at £12,000, and a tax rate of 20 per cent, the tax liability changes to the levels given in Table A5.1.

No of employees	Average pay	Taxed turnover 10% rate[a]	Taxed turnover 20% rate[b]	Tax liability 10% rate[a]	Tax liability 20% rate[b]
	£	£	£	£	£
Firms with £1 million turnover					
10	50 000	900 000	880 000	90 000	176 000
20	25 000	800 000	760 000	80 000	152 000
50	10 000	500 000	400 000	50 000	80 000
80	6 250	200 000	40 000	20 000	8 000
100	5 000	Nil	Nil	Nil	Nil

a   Employment allowance £10,000, threshold £5000.
b   Employment allowance £12,000, threshold £6000.

Table A5.1 *Increased tax rate*

For an organization with more employees in relation to its turnover the effect is yet more pronounced, as shown in Table A5.2.

Allowances and tax rates

Our present concern is with reduction of unemployment but no major tax revision could be undertaken without certain other needs being taken into account. Rent and interest on external borrowings would require to be deductable from turnover and an allowance might also be needed on investment financed from own resources. On the other hand, certain expenditures such as advertising and sales promotion need not automatically be allowable as deductions in calculating taxable turnover.

No of employees	Average pay £	Total pay £	Turnover £	Total taxed 10% rate[a] £	Turnover 20% rate[b] £	Tax liability 10% rate[a] £	Tax liability 20% rate[b] £
(i) Firms with £750 thousand turnover							
10	25 000	250 000	750 000	650 000	630 000	65 000	126 000
20	12 500	250 000	750 000	550 000	510 000	55 000	102 000
(ii) Firms each with 50 employees; varying levels of turnover							
50	8 000	400 000	900 000	400 000	300 000	40 000	60 000
50	8 000	400 000	600 000	100 000	Nil	10 000	Nil
50	14 000	700 000	2 000 000	1 500 000	1 400 000	150 000	280 000

a, b As for Table A5.1.

Table A5.2 Effect of labour intensity relative to total turnover

241

A major advantage of embodying subsidies within tax allowances is that the scheme as a whole is by its nature self-financing. 'Revenue neutral' changes in the size of the effective subsidy can be made by altering simultaneously the turnover tax rate and the employment allowance. To achieve any substantial impact, decisive benefits must be created for firms adopting different approaches to work organization. However, at some point, barriers to raising the levels of allowances and tax rates might be encountered if the changes were seen as liable to affect adversely the more innovative firm, and thus become counterproductive. It is not possible to predict precisely the level of incentives which may be feasible in the longer run.

Cost of the self-employment allowance

The self-employment scheme would not be self-financing. Although there would be 'limited liability' in the case of people now unemployed who became self-employed, there would be a net increase in expenditure in respect of those currently self-employed who earn little more than benefits to which they would be entitled if unemployed. The possible extent of such expenditure would be one of the considerations determining how steeply the benefits might need to decline with the level of income, but the important step is obtaining acceptance of the principle of a partial retention of benefits.

The Personal Benefit System Applied to the UK

For any proposed change to the tax system to appear realistic it must not require an unduly large initial increase in taxation and should be able to be formulated as a continuing development of the present system. This not only minimizes administrative problems, but also side-effects of the changes which result in unintended reductions of the relative advantage of particular groups of the population. The proposed replacement of basic personal allowances — single person, married man and wife's earned income — by a flat-rate benefit paid to all adults independently of the tax system meets these requirements.

This payment has been named the 'personal benefit' because, far from being revolutionary, it is a direct descendent of the change made between 1977 and 1979 in the UK to the tax allowances and social benefits systems for children. The peculiar property of all tax allowances is that they are worth twice as much to those paying the highest rate of income tax relative to those paying the lowest. For a taxable income of over £38,000 pa the top rate of tax of 60 per cent applies and a £1000 allowance saves £600 tax, whereas the same allowance for a taxable income of less than £15,400 pa (that is for most people) is worth only £300.

Those who have no income receive no benefit from tax allowances and up to 1977 this applied to tax allowances given to parents (and guardians) for all dependent children, but at the same time there was a cash family allowance paid weekly through the Post Office for second and subsequent children. This combination of tax allowance and social security benefit was rationalized into a single cash benefit, the child benefit, paid through the Post Office for all children including the first. Its 1984–85 value was £6.85 per week. It exemplifies two vital achievements: a successful rationalization of the tax and social security systems and the acceptance that support from the state should be at a flat rate, independent of income level.

243

It is proposed that over a two- or three-year period the precedent of the child benefit be repeated, and the tax allowance system for individuals and couples be replaced by a personal benefit paid to all as of right. It would replace part of all other state benefits — pensions, student grants, unemployment and social security benefits, etc — but it would be a non-taxable element. The single person's tax allowance in 1984–85 was £2005 and converted at the standard rate of tax it is equivalent to a £600 pa, £12 per week, personal benefit. This would be paid to all, whether working or not, and there would be no single person's, married man's nor wife's earned income allowance to set against tax. With a married couple, the wife would have her own personal benefit.

To gain the greatest advantage from introducing the personal benefit, it should be operated so as to overcome as many as possible of the 'traps' which arise from the working of the present tax and social security systems. One trap is that arising from the operation of the employee's National Insurance contribution (NIC) which, in 1984–85, did not apply to incomes below a floor of £1768 pa and then applied at a rate of 9 per cent up to a ceiling of £13,000 pa.[1] The trap occurred because a gross income of £1768 would have had £159 pa deducted so that it was less than any nominally lower gross income down to £1609 pa. In 1984, when NIC was considered together with the tax system, the joint rates were 9 per cent between £1768 and at least £2005 (higher levels arise because of additional tax allowances) and then 39 per cent.[2] But above the ceiling the effective marginal tax rate fell from 39 per cent to 30 per cent, for a range of income dependent on the size of the individual's tax allowances, before rising again to 40 per cent, and then increasing in steps of 5 per cent up to a maximum of 60 per cent. It seems sensible that the introduction of the personal benefit should be combined with the removal of this anomaly by aligning the operation of NIC with the tax system.[3] (The further possibility of fully incorporating NIC into the tax system is not examined.)

In the 1985 budget the NIC anomaly was lessened by reducing the rate to 5 per cent between the new floor of £1846 pa and £2860 pa, then 7 per cent up to £4680 pa and 9 per cent up to £13,780 pa. Thus the trap has been reduced from £159 to £92 but it would be better to eliminate it entirely.

The following calculations have drawn extensively on data published by the UK Board of Inland Revenue for 1979–80,[4] adjusted for inflation. The tax rates for the personal benefit system to be outlined are given in Table A6.1. The initial band of £1000 at a joint rate of 20 per cent is necessary to give benefit to low-income earners who have no deductions, eg for superannuation, or mortgage for house purchase, and who will pay tax on all they earn. (In the light of the 1985 budget change to employee's NIC, an adjustment to the joint rate of 20 per cent would be required — perhaps to reduce it to 16 per cent.)

Taxable income bands	Income Tax rate %	NIC rate %	Joint rate %
1–1 000	11	9	20
1 001–8 000	31	9	40
8 001–13 000	34	9	43
13 001–23 000	43	0	43
23 001–30 000	50	0	50
30 001–38 000	55	0	55
over 38 000	60	0	60

Table A6.1 *Proposed NIC and tax rates for personal benefit system, based on 1984–85 incomes, UK*

Above £30,000 the rates are approximately the same as for the present system of tax rates which is given in Table A6.2.

Taxable income bands	Tax rates %
1–15 400	30
15 401–18 200	40
18 201–23 100	45
23 101–30 600	50
30 601–38 100	55
over 38 100	60

a Because income tax is levied only on income in excess of tax allowances, it is not possible to include NIC in this table.

Table A6.2 *Actual UK tax rates, 1984–85*[a]

In Table A6.3 the rates of Tables A6.1 and A6.2 are applied to total incomes[5] to give a comparison of net incomes from the two systems. These values are to be used to estimate the cost of introducing the personal benefit system and must be treated with caution concerning their implications for individual tax circumstances. The table takes no account of mortgage interest payments, the income figures are net of superannuation payments, and different balances of earnings between a wife and husband from those assumed for the table will also affect personal tax positions.

Table A6.4 shows that the estimated 1984–85 cost of replacing

Total Before tax/benefit £	Single person		One spouse working [a,b]		Married couple Both working [a,b]	
	1984–85 Tax + NIC system £	Personal benefit system £	1984–85 Tax + NIC system £	Personal benefit system £	1984–85 Tax + NIC system £	Personal benefit system £
1	1	601	1	1 201	1	1 201
1 000	1 000	1 400	1 000	2 000	1 000	2 000
1 600	1 600	1 760	1 600	2 360	1 600	2 480
3 200	2 554	2 720	2 912	3 320	3 200	3 520
4 000	3 042	3 200	3 387	3 800	3 640	4 000
4 700	3 469	3 620	3 814	4 220	4 174	4 420
5 500	3 957	4 100	4 302	4 700	4 903	4 900
6 300	4 445	4 580	4 790	5 180	5 391	5 380
7 100	4 933	5 060	5 278	5 660	5 879	5 860
7 900	5 421	5 540	5 766	6 140	6 367	6 340
8 600	5 848	5 942	6 193	6 542	6 794	6 760
9 400	6 336	6 398	6 681	6 998	7 282	7 240
11 000	7 312	7 310	7 657	7 910	8 258	8 200
12 600	8 288	8 222	8 633	8 822	9 234	9 112
15 700	10 422	9 989	10 767	10 589	11 125	10 882
18 800	12 452	11 756	12 912	12 356	13 241	12 655
23 600	15 162	14 450	15 680	15 050	16 267	15 397
31 400	19 138	18 280	19 713	18 880	20 346	19 560
47 100	25 913	24 890	26 603	25 490	27 383	26 630

a For the income tax system, the 'one spouse' must be the husband and 'both' includes the case where only the wife works.

b Up to £3200 joint income no account has been taken of the balance of income between wife and husband, and at £4000 and £4700 they are taken as having equal incomes. From £5500 upwards the wife's income has been taken as the mean value cross-classified with the husband's income from Table 69 in *The Survey of Personal Incomes, 1979–80.*⁴ Hence, for a joint income of £5500 the wife's income is taken as £2200 and for £47,100 it is taken as £4700.

Table A6.3 *Comparison of net annual incomes, UK 1984–85 income tax system and proposed personal benefit system*

| Lower limit of income £[a] | Single person | | Married couple | | | | Number tax cases thousands | Total cost £ million[d] |
| | Cost pp £ | Number persons[b] thousands | One person earning[f] | | Both earning[f] | | | |
			Cost per couple £	Number couples[b] thousands	Cost per couple £	Number couples[b] thousands		
1	600	1 100	1 200	868	1 200	0[c]	1 968	1 269
1 600	160	1 709	760	183	880	110	2 002	452
3 200	167	1 011	409	123	320	92	1 226	246
4 000	159	1 082	414	191	360	122	1 395	283
4 700	152	1 067	407	284	246.5	157	1 508	291
5 500	144	884	399	315	−3	177	1 376	246
6 300	136	724	391	423	−11	253	1 400	255
7 100	128	594	383	535	−19	293	1 422	269
7 900	120	433	375	478	−27	377	1 288	208
8 600	95	306	350	356	−34	444	1 106	126
9 400	63	376	318	593	−42	1 073	2 042	127
11 000	−1	219	254	378	−58	1 052	1 649	−18
12 600	−65	175	190	415	−122	1 340	1 930	−285
15 700	−432	72	−177	169	−243	591	832	−347
18 800	−696	42	−556	126	−586	335	503	−348
23 600	−712	27	−629	87	−870	161	275	−218
31 400	−857	13	−832	47	−786	68	128	−110
47 100	−1 023	7	−1 113	19	−753	32	58	−52
Totals		9 841		5 590		6 677	22 108[e]	2 391

a The lower limits of £1600 and above have been derived from those in the tables in the source by allowing for 57 per cent inflation between 1979 and 1984.

b There was a total of 23 million taxpayers in 1979–80 and a further 2.3 million earners with records in the (PAYE) system but who were below the tax thresholds. The numbers given for each category of taxpayer and lower limit of income have been reduced by the number of persons over 65 with incomes below the age allowance upper limit. For the £1 lower limit this has been estimated from the trends for incomes of £1600 and above.

c All wives included in 868 thousand.

d Except for £47,100 the total cost at each lower limit level is the sum of the products of the members in each category — persons or couples — multiplied by the average of the cost at that lower limit and the one above.

e The 22.1 million 'tax cases' concern 34.4 million persons because of the joint taxation of husbands and wives.

f See note a of Table A6.3.

Table A6.4 *Estimate of cost of personal benefit*

Source: Board of Inland Revenue (1983) *The Survey of Personal Incomes, 1979–80*, HMSO, London; and Table A6.3.

personal allowances by a personal benefit as £2.4 billion. However, the figures in Table A6.4 do not allow for the effect of deductions, such as mortgage interest payments, which increases the number of incomes in the lower income ranges of Table A6.4. An adjustment for this may be made by using the numbers of 'total net incomes', ie the number after allowing for such deductions, and this raises the cost to £2.7 billion. This calculation includes all persons in receipt of incomes who pay tax, plus those who pay no tax but have tax records (and their spouses where relevant); but National Insurance pensioners over 65 have been excluded because part of all National Insurance pensions would be redesignated as personal benefit. For the over 65s it would be necessary to keep an age allowance so that their income was maintained at approximately its present level. The remaining group whom it would be desirable to include are the 16- to 18-year-olds. Those who are in work, or who receive social security payments, or who are on MSC-funded schemes, would not add to the cost but there are about 0.96 million who are at school or in further education. The additional cost above present child benefit for each of these would be £286 pa, and the total cost £275 million pa.

These groups include the entire adult population (over 16 years of age) of the UK; in 1980 an estimated population of 56.3 million could be broken down as in Table A6.5.

In tax system (excluding over 65s)	35.0
Over 65 (3.8 million in tax system)	8.4
Child benefit recipients	13.3
Total	56.7

Table A6.5 *Breakdown of UK population*

Source: Board of Inland Revenue (1983) *The Survey of Personal Incomes, 1979–80*, HMSO, London; and Central Statistical Office (1985) *Social Trends*, 15, HMSO, London.

In 1983 there were some 600 thousand students in receipt of student awards, 900 thousand on pensions other than retirement, 2.7 million on supplementary allowances and one million on unemployment benefit. Thus, while the total cost of the personal benefit for all persons over 16 has been identified as approximately £3 billion, this would be reduced by any part which was counted as replacing these payments. Phased over two or three budgets such a sum is well within the compass of even a very cautious Chancellor of the Exchequer — in the budgets of 1984 and 1985 income tax adjustments of £1750 and £1600 million respectively were made. A large proportion of these sums was used to provide an increase in tax allowances and tax bands to keep up with the effects of inflation. The tax bands and rates which are used in Table A6.1 require that the inflation adjustment be foregone for the period of two or three future budgets, and that this be redistributed as the personal benefit, which will be biased in favour of those on low incomes. At higher incomes it is proposed that there should be an increase in the absolute level of taxation. However, extract comparisons are difficult because it is also normal to increase NIC at each budget which, for many people around the average income, greatly reduces the benefit from the tax allowance changes. However, a Chancellor who did not support the degree of redistribution shown in Table A6.4 would require (again over the two or three budgets) to find an additional £1.6 billion over and above the £3 billion to adjust the tax bands so as to avoid any tax increases.

An example of the impact on individuals

The effect of the personal benefit is to encourage the search for a higher income by avoiding penalties on additional earnings. This can be seen from the example in Table A6.6 concerning trainee hairdressers, which has been adapted from one given by Hermione Parker.[6] The example has been left in the context of 1982 and, in consequence, the personal benefit reduced to £450, approximately 30 per cent of £1565 — the 1982–83 single person's allowance — and the limit of the first tax band reduced pro rata to £750. This example shows that the gap of £5.47 in favour of the person on supplementary benefit over the second-year trainee would have been reduced to £2.87 — less than the assumed £4 earnings. A further advantage is the removal of the NIC trap which reduced the net pay after income tax and NIC to £28.03, only 53p more than a first-year trainee on a basic wage of £27.50, for whom there would have been no deduction of income tax or NIC. The personal benefit would leave the second-year trainee with a clear differential over the first-year trainee. The first-year trainee would have received £27.50 plus £9.00 less £5.50 tax and £2.48 NIC, ie £28.52 against £30.63 for the second-year trainee — a differential of £2.11 per week for the latter, in place of the 53p actually experienced.

Although the introduction of the personal benefit would help in cases like that of the trainee, the level proposed would require

	Second-year trainee		Unemployed young person on supplementary benefit	
	Personal benefit	Tax allowance		
Wage	31.00	31.00	Supplementary benefit	9.60
Personal benefit (1982) rate	9.00		Personal benefit	9.00
Income	40.00	31.00		18.60
			Plus non-householder's housing addition	2.50
			Disregarded earning	4.00
Less				
Income tax	6.58	0.26		
NIC	2.79	2.71		
Net pay	31.63	28.03		
Fares to work	5.00	5.00		
College fees, etc	1.35	1.35		
Fares to college, etc	2.00	2.00		
Net weekly spending power	22.28	19.68		25.15

Table A6.6 *Spending power of trainee hairdresser compared with supplementary benefit (1982)*

to be considerably increased before it could make much difference to the total income of those dependent on social security for raising a family. The longer term aim of policy would be to increase its real value to a level at which the enhancement given by other benefits — eg unemployment and supplementary — would be sufficiently small so that their loss could be readily accepted by persons undertaking casual work. This would imply a deliberate expansion of the informal economy and would doubtless raise administrative problems for the collection of income tax and NIC. In the shorter term a target level could be £1000 (1984 values) per year but it seems inevitable that for the foreseeable future most forms of social security benefit would have to remain in existence, and only the balance between benefits-of-right and discretionary benefits would be altered. The rate of personal benefit would require annual review to take account of inflation in the same ways as present tax allowances and this would give an annual opportunity to move towards a better distribution of income.

Change begets change, and if there is to be a flat-rate personal benefit then it will necessarily raise the question of whether other benefits, such as relief on house purchase mortgages, should be a function of an individual's spending power or whether these should also become a flat-rate element added to the personal benefit. At its most basic level this would simply be the total currently allocated to mortgage tax relief divided by the total number of personal benefit recipients, ie about £170 per person per annum. This change could be adjusted for the overlap with assistance towards rent and rates currently provided to pensioners and others on low incomes — which would allow its value to be higher than £170. The principle would be that each individual should receive an identical allowance, and that this allowance should be divorced from the act of working and level of income.[7]

Notes and references

1. Married women can have a reduced rate of contribution.
2. Persons in approved superannuation schemes ('contracted out') pay a reduced rate of contribution.
3. Indeed, there are many inconsistencies from the point of view of the wage earner. In 1984–85 a wage of £1750 paid uniformly throughout the year would have incurred no NIC — a wage of £35 per week paid for a short period would have been liable to NIC even though the annual total was well below £1768.
4. Board of Inland Revenue (1983) *The Survey of Personal Incomes, 1979–80,* HMSO, London.
5. Ibid., p9. For most people the main deductions from gross earned income to get total income are superannuation and employment expenses. Further deductions, of which mortgage interest payments are the main item, gives total net income.
6. Parker, Hermione (1982) *The Moral Hazard of Social Benefits,* p93, Institute for Economic Affairs, London.
7. Based on 1979–80 figures, Board of Inland Revenue (1983) *The Survey of Personal Incomes, 1979–80,* HMSO, Table 30, £4857 million mortgage interest, taken as £7625 million at 1984 prices. Personal benefit recipients assumed to total 44 million.

Index